The Waterman's Tale

To Graham, By Sean Wood

Best wishes, pal,

Seán Wood FBNA

Foreword:

On 10th February 1980, Bleak House, a Grade 2 listed Reservoir Keepers House at Crowden in Longdendale became my home. For a young lad who loved the countryside, the move to the hills promised much, and over the twenty eight years of my tenure it certainly delivered, and as you will discover, much, much more than I ever could ever have imagined.

The Watermen of the Longdendale chain of reservoirs were highly regarded, the Waterman at Woodhead was legend. I was lucky enough to be the last in a long line of Watermen at Woodhead stretching back to the end of the 19th Century and this book, originally titled 'The Crowden Years, Volume 1, tells the tale of my first five years at Bleak House, Crowden, 1980-85, and there's another twenty three to go at.

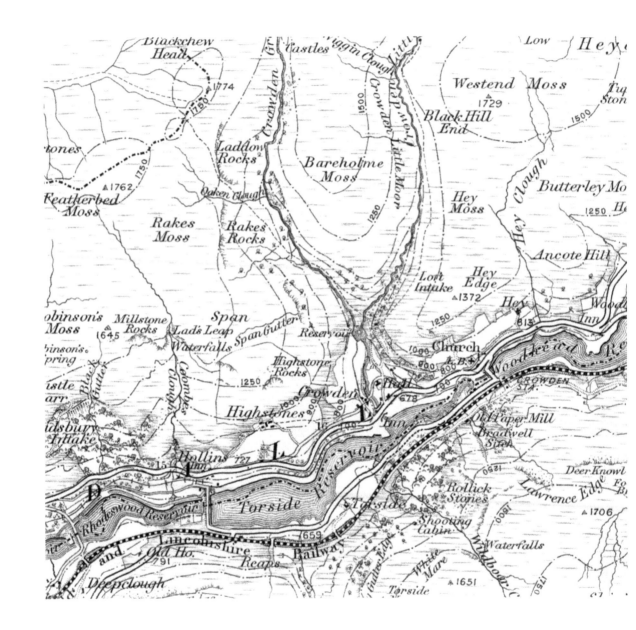

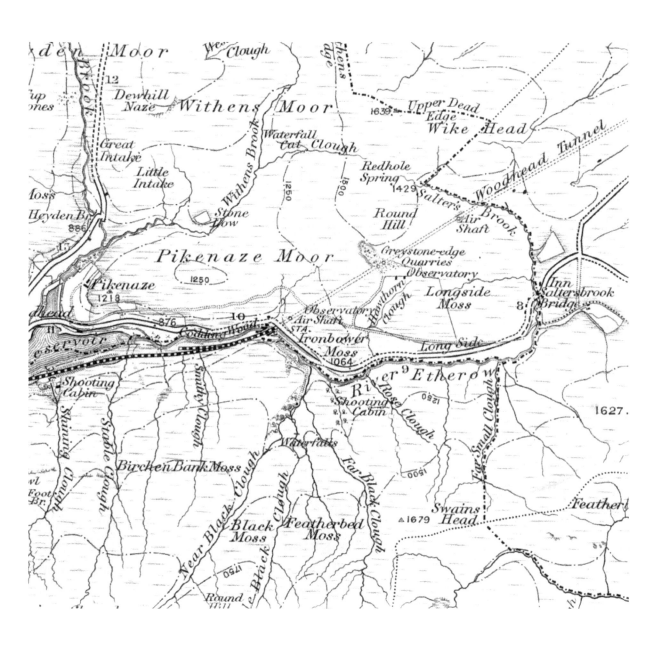

Acknowledgements:

In many ways 2017 was a year to forget for me, I lost my Mum, one of my best friends, Oaf, and my wife left the building. Somehow, in amongst the grief good things happened, including this book, and I also completed and performed my first play with songs, The Angel On O'Connell Street. Let it be known that I could not possibly have done it without the wonderful tacit support of my beautiful and very talented daughter Niamh. Special mention also to my twin Sons, Oisin and Culain, and just the very thought of my amazing granddaughter Orlaith Edna kept a smile on my face, and now as I write the beautiful, Erin Mary, born to Chloe and Culain in May 2018. Of course and quite rightly, a big hand is due to the best of friends from all my worlds but, in particular Glossop Rugby Club, Rob, Nolene, Martin, Bev, Sash, Moz, Oaf RIP and the rest of crew, and as for my many compardres in the music world, put your hands together for Paul 'Spiggy' Higham, India and Sean, Mulligan, Paul Newland, Gordon Trunkfield, Steve Massey and Amy Griffiths. Let's also not forget the regulars in my Laughing Badger Gallery and Cellar Bar; for you I kept my best face on and carried on, and that includes you Chellie Carroll, oh lovely one, and indeed Robin Barker and Ten Coats. Hats off and hot poitins to my bestest Kinvara buddies who all wrapped me up in their blankets and sent kind words across from the west, stand up and be counted Mooney, Huban, Johnny 'cute as a button' O'Dea, Forks and the Sexton's. And last but not least my patient readers and editors, Berrie Broderick, Moira Shelton, Alan Walmsley, Val Hardaker, Chris Revell, Pete Jones and of course to my main Editors, Glynis Greenman and the quite wonderful Dame Vivienne Westwood who loved the book so much and has written the Introduction. I should be so lucky.

**For Me Mam, A bright light indeed. And of course she knew.
Claire:**

Silence fills the home, A bright light Passes over

Shorn inside to roam I cried.

Hovered a long-tail away, whose song broke the day

But it's nothing like the way you showed me.

Moonlight Fills the yard. A child would knock me over

No man's land a life held in my hand

I've been a father a beau the wrong man to know

But I have nothing more to show for you loved me. **Lee Bardsley**

Dedication:

In the darkest moments of 2017, while on tour with my play in Ireland, I wrote Low Ebb - Little Critter and promised myself at that moment I would never be so low again, and to be truthful, I came very close but never touched that nadir.

Hello little critter in the fast flowing river, to the sea from the lake and back again.
How deep can you dive?
Not as deep as me I fear, sitting here as I do between the Devil and the blue.
How deep can you dive?
Is that all dishevelled shallow fellow, to the first rock and back, and you with the caddis supper and me with my last.
How deep do you dive?
One fathom from the beach bonfire, first love and the Claddagh band bathed in gold across the strand.
How deep you can dive?
Not as deep as me little critter but, you made me smile on a dark day, threw me a line and I will come back as sure as the tide turns and sends you home beneath the two way bridge.

I had managed to hoist myself up by the skin of my teeth, but then the magic happened, and on St Patrick's Day 2018, of all days, my Joanie Lucy Edge completed the job and lifted me into the light. In no particular order she is, a beauty, wise beyond her years, an amazing Mum to Niamh, Bria and Aoife, kind, considerate and most importantly she showed me real affection when most needed and gave me everything expecting nothing in return, least of all this dedication. I owe Joanie more than she will ever know.

My song 'One Last Feather' is for Joanie. It is a celebration. The raven had just one feather left and was in danger of falling from the sky. But the girl wrapped him up in her arms and stopped the feather spinning to the ground. Very soon the raven's wings were complete again and once more he soared above the valley and let the world know that he was back, he was safe and he was sound.

Introduction by Dame Vivienne Westwood:

Dear Sean, I will talk about me so as to link with you and your world during the Crowden Years. I'm near a generation older than you. Go back in Time – perhaps link to your walkers from earlier lives.

Go back in time.

Vivienne Isabelle Swire: I was born in 1941 during the war at 6 Millbrook between two villages. My father Gordon came from Hollingworth, my mother Dora from Tintwistle - cousins and their families in both villages. Crowden is 4 miles up from Tintwistle. I was the oldest of three children, my mother's side of the family were Irish and came to work in the cotton mills, my father's side came from the Bronte area in Yorkshire and were shoemakers and cobblers.

Dora was a weaver in the mill from the age of fourteen until she married, she was clever and a reader. She read to her children; we sat by the fire playing whilst she nursed our baby brother. Dora made our clothes on a treadle sewing machine by the window – also costumes for the church Christmas pantomime. I sat in the window bottom with my book; the walls were nearly two feet thick. In a storm the heavens opened, the rain shot down like arrows attacking the flags and bounced back up, amidst a wash of bubbles. But best was when the flocks of snow came whirling down ever faster, and when I looked up into the sky the window went up like a lift to the land of the Snow Queen.

My father Gordon was very entrepreneurial, at Christmas the kitchen was filled with holly and evergreen and we all helped him to make wreaths – and we often had puppies for sale. He was very good with his hands, during the war he made aircraft and therefore didn't have to go to fight. Bombs went over us to Manchester 12 miles away. During the time of rationing he worked at Walls Ice-cream in the engine room and there he made us sledges, a go-kart and the best whips and tops.

I'm glad I was born then and wasn't inundated with fuchsia and yellow plastic toys. My ambition was to own a peacock feather.

Our long backyard was communal, every house had its washing line, and neighbours chatted at the back doors. Even as a toddler, my mother lifted me over the wall to play in a bluebell wood at the bottom of a quarry. The beech trees, which grew on the earth path leading up the quarry wall, had massive cavities under the roots. I dreamed of living there on my own in my own little underground house. I remember one morning in May, climbing up this path into the morning sun of Cooper's meadow and sitting in the grass as the dew rose up, skylarks high in the sky and the scent of hawthorn in the hedges. I said to myself "I am happy." My sister Olga loved us to make moss gardens between tree roots – with a bit of mirror for a pond, twigs for trees and miniature plants.

Aged 3 I did my mother's shopping in Hollingworth in the boot of my tricycle and I stopped to play with the village children. I miss the seasons with its traditional games. Recently I looked out of the window in Clapham and said out loud "Oh what a lovely day!" My husband Andreas, who comes from the Tyrol, was astonished: it was grey with a fine drizzle. It was so lovely to me because it reminded me of walking to school in the autumn. I loved school and my home - weather is great when you have a cosy home to go to.

The reason we were safe to roam was that cars were few and far between and any stranger would have stood out. We lived on the main Manchester to Sheffield road. My brother Gordon used to sit on the doorstep with the boys of the local farm copying down number plates. In winter time we used to pull our sledges up to Tintwistle to meet our friends where the best hill for sledging was. We set off from Stocks Brow across this main road and down Bonkie - Bank Lane – right down to bridge over the river Etherow. There was no danger from cars or lorries because the road was covered with snow.

I remember at Easter and in the early afternoon after Sunday school, walking over the hills in white dresses and straw hats with our families. Up Arnfield, through Swallow's Wood and down to Devil's Bridge – our favourite walk where we sat down for a picnic and played in the water; then back "over the top" where peewits cried – and once in winter we saw a lamb born in the snow.

We lived in the Longdendale Valley amongst the hills, Tintwistle was at the bottom of the last reservoir. In geography, the first map we drew was of all five reservoirs, Tintwistle was then in Cheshire. The map of Cheshire looked like a teapot, the Wirral Peninsula was the spout and Tintwistle was in the small handle. From my home I could immediately walk into any of three directions; the woods of Cheshire, the green hills of Derbyshire and the moorland territory that headed into Yorkshire. My mother allowed me to roam all day alone and I knew exactly where to look for the flowers and I was waiting for them. Families walked the hills. We walked everywhere.

At the stile in Arnfield there was a very big boulder, maybe it came from when they built Arnfield reservoir. I told my teacher that this stone was the one that was rolled over Jesus' grave. This was the whole world for me, the crucible where I grew up.

Sean, you've been living life to the full and you have now enlarged my crucible for me because I am so connected to what you tell.

Aristotle said: The acorn is happy to become an oak. He was obsessed by the fact that form is always becoming something else, and he defines happiness as fulfilling your potential, like the acorn - become who you are.

Your character is your bag of tools, use it to discover the world! You will always behave "in character" and the secret is that by following your deep interests you will forget yourself and Get a Life! "You get out what you put in" - that's our maxim.

The Tao says the same thing. You have lived your life according to the Tao. Tao means Way, it's a spiritual system because it's a metaphor for the cosmos, a path, a process. It's the cosmos folding and unfolding. It makes no claims except to common sense, boils everything down to rock bottom fact.

The 10.000 things that exist – call that Presence!

When they don't exist call that Absence!

Nobody knows where life comes from, things just happen - there is no god needed! Occurrence appearing of itself, the direct translation from the Chinese word is "Self Ablaze".

Heaven goes on forever.

Earth endures forever.

There is a reason heaven and earth go on enduring forever:

their life is not their own,

so they go on living forever.

Hence the sage by putting himself last

puts himself first,

by giving himself up

he protects himself.

If you are not free of yourself,

how will you ever become yourself?

It's really comforting to me to know that my life is not my own, that I'm just tapping into it. What this means is you should do what comes naturally, you shouldn't step out of yourself and push yourself forward by false ambition, but rely on your natural talents.

Whatever we believe, it is a fact of experience that we are spiritual creatures. Our belonging to earth's natural processes within the cosmos has always been the primary source of spiritual affirmation.

No time to think about that now! In my 70's I am an activist trying to save the planet and its lifeforms. The human race has never before faced mass extinction. How can we help each other? Every minute counts.

Vivienne Westwood

Chapter One:
They First Awoke...Early Days At Bleak House

November 1979 would prove an eventful month both for myself and the World:

Vivienne Westwood, of this Parish, was doing her damnedest to put '...a spoke in the system in some way', Iranian students had just overrun the American Embassy in Tehran on the 4th taking ninety hostages, an action publicly supported by the Ayatollah Khomeini when he took over the country two days later, Pink Floyd had launched their best selling album 'The Wall', and I had the chance for a job of a lifetime.

Tom Quayle, North West Water's, Manager, in Longdendale, was sitting opposite me during the Interview at their Tintwistle Depot, and although I had no idea what being a Reservoir Keeper at Woodhead entailed, I knew I wanted the job. The place was buzzing with all manner of workers, from painters and blacksmiths, to drystone-wallers and Engineers, and although many 'gangs' of men had already left the yard several hours earlier in a convoy of minibuses, cabins and Land Rovers, there was still as much activity as an average sized village going about its business.

At the desk, it was just me and him. We shook hands and he stared at me with his piercing blue eyes and the first thing he did was throw me a curved ball, "You're too well qualified for this job lad, why do you want it?" Truth is, I cannot remember how I answered the question but, I must have said something coherent, perhaps, "Well I don't know about that but, I'd really like to get the job because I love the countryside". "Yes, but have you any experience in the Water

Industry, are you used to operating machinery?" he countered, and obviously the answer was no, unless you count flushing a toilet, turning a tap on and drinking the water.

"I see you were a Teacher, and in Toxteth, Toxteth, of all places, it's a bit dangerous around those streets isn't it, you need an armed guard I've been told", he said laughing to himself. He was referring to the simmering civil unrest in Liverpool in the late 1970's, and although I had nothing to do with any anarchy, I am fairly sure that some of my students at St Martin's Catholic Secondary Modern Boys School on Park Road could well have been involved, and if not them, certainly some of their parents, as it had been on the cards for years. The area was very run down, and it all boiled over into full blown riots a year later on a muggy evening in July 1981, when police intercepted a motorcyclist in Selbourne Street.

A crowd gathered, name-calling grew into jostling and within minutes there was a full-scale fracas that saw three police officers hurt and a young local man, Leroy Cooper, arrested on assault charges.

It did not stop there. Police mounted extra patrols in the area and early the following evening, July 4th, they came under attack from a crowd armed with bricks and petrol bombs. The fuse had been lit on nine days of disorder that saw hundreds of police and public injured, one man dead, 500 arrested, 70 buildings destroyed and damage estimated at £11m.

Most of the damage took place in the so-called Granby Triangle, bounded by Upper Parliament Street, Lodge Lane and Sefton Park Road, and Princes Road and Croxteth Road. St Martin was bang in the middle.

Bob Nolan, the larger than life, Deputy Head Teacher, often used to say of the unrest, "I wish they'd bring back the Foreign Legion, they would sort them out", and I never thought to ask what he meant, just assuming that he was referring to the Legion's legendary status as trouble-shooters in the war-torn regions of the World. Forty years later I discover that, in 1940 the Free French

13th Demi Brigade of the Legion had been stationed in Toxteth before setting off to fight the Vichy, at the Battle of Libreville in French Equatorial Africa, and Bob Nolan would have remembered this. Bob would have made a good Legionnaire himself, six-foot-three in his bare feet, drank beer by the gallon and was as hard as nails. He was also the go-to-guy if there was any trouble in the school, with a fearsome reputation for calling a spade a spade. I witnessed his unique approach to Home-School liaison one afternoon after he had come into my room to see how I was getting on.

As he was taking in the delights of my wall decorations, in particular the 'Bumper Book of Animal Shit', as he put it, I preferred, 'Field Guide to the droppings and scats of British Wildlife', an irate parent burst into the room to give me a piece of his mind, shouting, "Aye you, ya big boned bastard...'. Before he finished his sentence Bob interceded with, "Say that again and I'll punch your lights out". With the utmost stupidity, and a school-boy error of epic proportions the mad Dad, continued his rant, and as promised, Bob Nolan put out his lights with a left hook reminiscent of Henry Cooper's fabled 'hammer'. The said, 'Hammer' had once sat Cassius Clay on his backside.

The previous day I had taken a double-decker bus full of St Martin's Boys on a trip to Chester Zoo, and the son of my assailant had managed to kidnap an Adelie Penguin from its enclosure and secrete the poor creature in his duffle bag for the bus journey home. We should have realised something was amiss when the rowdiest boy on the way to the zoo, was the quietest on the return leg. The Keepers at the Zoo must have been tipped off, because after a hasty headcount they were on the phone to the School to request the return of their penguin, who was apparently named Zac. Unfortunately the boys had all gone home but, we didn't need Sherlock Holmes to detect our culprit. As the family had no telephone it fell to myself and Joe Burns to visit the boy's house and ask if he had the bird. The Father, who had been a docker before being made redundant was not in the mood for visitors but, he did as we asked and went to question his Son.

The boy had Zac in the bath and was attempting to feed him a tin of sardines in tomato sauce. Although I wanted to smile and praise the boy for his resourcefulness, Joe Burns gave him a dressing down, for show really, because on our drive of shame back to the Zoo he kept bursting out laughing, although he didn't find it so funny when St Martin's became the only school ever to be banned from Chester Zoo.

Next day the miscreant was given a detention for his sins, which is why the Father had come in to 'sort me out', as his Son had a job immediately after school and the detention would have made him late.

St Martin's was a 'helmet and battle-dress' kind of school but, with my long curly hair strung up on top of my head like a giant plume, Physical Education was a breeze, as the pupils could not believe what they were seeing and all thoughts of misbehaving was forgotten. "Come on we've got Woody, he's mad!" in a broad Liverpudlian accent could be heard along the corridors, much to the annoyance of some of the more mature and dyed-in-the-wool old-school Teachers who, to a man, despised change of any sort. Some of these men were brutal and they used to watch with glee as certain boys were caned outside the Head's Office, and I'm talking like six of the best on the hands, as thankfully caning on the backside was all but done in 1975, although, even I administered a couple of slippers to a rear end but, my efforts were more 'show', than cruelty. Boy oh boy, did some of the St Martin's Staff enjoy watching the kids suffer. I would be having a cup of coffee and a biscuit at break-time and they would be sniggering as they peeked through the crack of the half opened Staff Room door. "Did you see O'Toole, Fred gave it to him good style, and wait until I have him this afternoon so I can remind him that he was crying in front of his mates", was one remark I recall. Sad to say, it was the done thing, and to be fair to the Teachers, most of them were very good at teaching, and getting on with children, and surprise, surprise, the pupils thought caning was de rigueur as well. It was never a deterrent.

I think the secret of my early success at the school, had been to arrive on my first morning wearing a cardboard box on my head, with a handy letterbox-size hole cut out for my eyes. It had been pouring with rain and, I thought understandably, I didn't want to get my hair wet. It played Hell with my curls. I certainly cut a dash bouncing along Lime Street at 8am.

I loved the St Martin's Boys, they had a great sense of humour, and my three years there stood me in good stead for the future, it was a full-on life-class, and I had gained more from the first three months in Toxteth, than I did during my three years at Christ's College in Liverpool, where I had completed my Teacher Training. In the early Summer of 1975, our Head of PE, Gerry Quinn, said to me, "Wood, there is only one School in Liverpool that will take you for your final Teaching Practice with hair like that!" Three weeks later it was me who was laughing, as I got offered a job straight away, and was on the payroll over the Summer Holidays. The joys of seeing that first monthly pay-slip in June 1975, £135.50p, I was loaded.

Tom Quayle relaxed somewhat and removed the bristles from up his 'jacksie' during our conversation about Liverpool. I found out subsequently he was born in the City, and it was then that he handed me down a couple more lifelines, firstly, "And what's this about you working with nutters in Scotland?" he asked. He was referring to my year, 1971/72, working in the wilds of Argyll, as a Volunteer at Achnamara Residential School, which catered for challenging teenagers from schools all over Glasgow, in those days they were called, 'maladjusted', whereas, in modern-day politically correct parlance, the kids would be classified as 'disaffected'; in reality they were normal, and although some had a few issues, they were just kids, and once they alighted from the bus in this most idyllic of settings their faces lit up, and so did they at every chance. My lifelong affinity with these children was long ago put down to the fact I had been just like them when I was at school, ditto for Toxteth. The children were obviously not 'nutters', as Quayle so eloquently put it, and I am sure he was just trying me out with a couple of controversial comments.

It was easy to enthuse about my times in Argyll, I was 18 years old, a full blown but, sporty hippie with spiralling ringlets, purple loons and an Oxfam bought three quarter-length musquash fur coat, and not forgetting my orange javelin, a must-have accessory for the reigning Leicestershire County Champion spear-chucker.

The School had originally been the 19th Century hunting lodge of the Coates Thread Family, and was situated amidst the wonders of Knapdale Forest on a low prominence above Loch Sween, a five-fingered sea loch with amazing views westward to the Paps of Jura. The area was packed to the brim with wildcats, pine martens, golden eagles and otters, I was quite literally, in Heaven. And to cap it all, the two women that ran the place, the late Audrey Stone and Scottish Artist Edna Whyte have been my touchstones in life ever since. Edna still lives on the tiny Inner Hebridean Island of Luing and at something like 86 years old, she'll scold me if I'm wrong, still painting for exhibitions a year and more from now.

This gave Quayle an inroad to my experience, and my next life-line was,"So that's where you became interested in wildlife?" he asked. "And I believe that you began writing about animals while still teaching in Toxteth, I like writing myself". Tom is still writing at the age of 92, and now lives in Scotland with his wife.

"Yes", I replied, "For the, Liverpool Weekly News, and the Runcorn & Widnes Weekly News, and my first ever column, concerned the kestrels which were nesting in the Anglican Cathedral. You could see the Cathedral from the school, and in June, 1976, the article appeared with the headline, 'A Kestrel Kills In Liverpool', long before the 'urban wildlife' trend which began a number of years later with the likes of Chris Baines and David MacDonald. Two million words and several thousand weekly columns published since, and I still get as much pleasure out of writing, and then seeing my work in print a few days later. I wasted no time in introducing Natural History to the timetable at St Martin's, reasoning that the so-called, 'Gash Periods', where literally nothing was taught and the teachers read the, Sporting Life, would be better filled with something interesting and the kids loved it, but, I once again attracted the ire of some of the older teachers. Ironically, and probably because of my manner and my size, no one ever criticised me to my face, and to be honest it never entered my head that there would be opposition to what I was trying to do. I will always be grateful to the Headteacher, Joe Burns, as he could see there was some mileage in my efforts and he encouraged me, not least I feel because there was no trouble in any of my lessons. Natural History was now officially on the School Curriculum, and the story attracted some interest from the Press, in particular the Liverpool Echo and the National Catholic Newspaper, The Universe, and Joe Burns enjoyed this. I was his fledgling with something to say, he also gave me a very good reference, and I could see that Tom Quayle had this in front of him, so I made a point of mentioning it and took the opportunity to introduce my Inquisitor, to Joe Burns favourite Natural History story from my classroom, which was affectionately known as the 'bared room' by the pupils. That's the best I can do phonetically with a Toxteth accent, and I do apologise to any of my friends from the 'Pool'.

The boys had been asked to name and draw three birds of prey for their homework, and one piece of work stood out above the rest with three beautifully rendered drawings of a Golden Eagle, a Kestrel and a 'Shite Hawk'. When questioned about the latter the boy told me that his Father had insisted that this rare species was often seen around the Docks in Liverpool. To be fair, Tom Quayle laughed heartily at this, as did most of the Staff at St Martin's and the drawing stayed on the Staff Room notice board for over a year.

Joe Burns, looking at the larger picture for his charges, and although he loved the Shite Hawk, he was more impressed with the fact that there were no absences when the Boys had Natural History. The way I tackled the subject also threw up elements of local history that no one had noticed, or thought of before, probably because it was right in front of them. The school had access to football pitches at a place called Otterspool, right on the edge of the Mersey, and the link to otters was immediately obvious to me, although it was many a year since this particular mammal had hunted fish in the area. Otterspool was a small offshoot from the River Mersey which was used by fishermen for centuries. Many species of fish were caught, including an abundance of salmon which once ventured into the small inland creek. Unfortunately the Industrial Revolution put paid to the salmon, and the Mersey became one of the most polluted rivers in the U.K. Thankfully in 2017, I can report that the water quality has improved tremendously and salmon have been been seen leaping the weir on the river at Woolston, near Warrington, and the Agency often receives calls from members of the public who have spotted the fish, which need good quality water to thrive.

Tom Quayle seemed impressed with my sojourns in Liverpool and Scotland, and continued with, "And I believe you have a permit for birdwatching on our land?" with the first discernible hint of a kind of Big Brother tone, as in 'Our' land, which I had detected a number of times on my walks through the so-called Reservoir Enclosures and Catchment Areas, when men, as it turned out other Reservoir Keepers of the 'Old School', would appear out of nowhere to challenge your presence.

"Yes that is correct, and I have just handed in my first yearly report of sightings," "I know", said Quayle, "I have it here, and it makes very interesting reading, especially the bit where you tell 'Us' how to do 'Our' job?" as he snatched the rug from under my feet, just as I thought the interview was swinging my way.

He was referring to my observations about the cutting down of dead trees in the woods above Rhodeswood Reservoir, number three, the middle one, in the Longdendale Chain of five. I maintained that the trees, mostly birch, were ideal nesting and feeding trees for great spotted woodpeckers, and to cut them down would deprive this beautiful bird of a place to live and eat, especially as the tree felling seemed to be ad-hoc, and previously when I had asked a North West Water Forestry Operative why he was cutting them down, he had said, 'Because they are dead, and also we are not bothered about birch as it is a self-seeder, they're a weed really'.

"We decide what we do on 'Our' land", said Quayle, "And besides, the trees may have been diseased, and that is why they had died and we cannot risk leaving the dead trees in amongst the healthy specimens". "They are still on the ground though", I replied cheekily, "And they were cut down at least six months ago". To be fair to Tom Quayle, I don't think he was used to an Employee or indeed, a prospective employee arguing with him, and he seemed momentarily rattled, and at this stage I thought any hope of me becoming the new Reservoir Keeper for Woodhead Reservoir was pie in the sky, and all thoughts of myself and my first wife, Moira, taking up residence at the aptly named Bleak House at Crowden had as much life as one of the dead silver birch I had mentioned in my report.

I remember my heart sinking at that point, not least because the house was, for me, a massive incentive to get the job. A large grit-stone eyrie at 800 feet above sea level, built to withstand the cruel North East Winds which whipped down the Valley, crowned with twenty feet high chimneys, erected to counter the downdrafts but, fail miserably, and crazily steep roofs, by all accounts modelled on Alpine architecture, although in Switzerland the tiles were mostly made of wooden shingles, whereas Bleak House was hung with slates the size of gravestones. The very notion that Bleak House would be free of rent was enough but, this decision had been made because a number of successive couples had lived at the house but, only for a short time before, because for one reason or another they left or requested a transfer, although I believe one guy was asked to leave after using a North West Water Land Rover for a day trip to Blackpool. As for the others whose tenure was short-lived, their varied rationales for 'flitting' were, too expensive, too cold, or even too far from civilisation, this was particularly true for the wives, especially if they could not drive, and although Tintwistle at four miles, Hadfield and Glossop at five and six miles respectively were within striking distance, they may as well have been on the Moon. Factor in the prevailing winter weather, cost of a taxi cab, and lack of public transport, and you may understand why some wives felt isolated from their friends and the shops, and maybe the world. Longdendale was, and still is one of the most sparsely populated places in the United Kingdom; in 1980, there were around forty people scattered along the eight miles between the outskirts of Tintwistle and Saltersbrook on the Yorkshire border, and barely thirty hardy souls in the four miles between Austin Hawksworth, Farmer and Organist at the Quiet Shepherd, to Nutty Nora who lived in the 'new-build at the Woodhead Tunnel.

Tom Quayle went on to ask more questions but, it was more like a lecture as he wasn't expecting any answers, about rainfall, the acidic qualities of Valley Water, and even Millowners. I remember he seemed very interested in the Millowners, and he waxed lyrical about the Victorian Engineer, La Trobe Bateman, who had designed the Reservoir Construction in the 1850's and 60's. Quayle subsequently authored two books, 'The Reservoirs In The Hills', and 'The Cotton Industry in Longdendale & Glossopdale'.

With the end in sight, or so I thought, Quayle came in with a blow way below the belt when he asked, "Is it true that you were a witness for the Prosecution in a murder trial in Inverness, and the man in the Dock was one of your best friends?"

Fortunately for me there was a knock at the door before Quayle could continue, and it was one of the workers, an Electrician, who had been given the task of showing me around Bleak House. To my shame I cannot remember his name now but, he was a likeable sort and was keen to hear how I had got on with Tom Quayle, and it soon transpired that he was a tough Boss but, a well respected man, and that was probably a fair enough summation.

Perhaps foolishly in the event that I didn't get the job, I had already visited the house and could hardly bear to think about living there, it literally would be, a dream come true, and any other corny hyperbole one can think of.

Moira and I were married in December 1977, and bought a new three-bedroomed semi-detached at the top of Brosscroft in Hadfield, just above Bottoms Reservoir, while Bleak House, was at the other end of the Valley on the side of Woodhead Reservoir. Across the road from 77 Brosscroft was the Victoria Inn, better known as the 'Vic', and it was in the bar that I met Tommy Gunner, a North West Water worker, and it was Tommy who told me about the job at Woodhead. Thanks Tommy, without you I would not have written this.

Once inside the property the desire to live there multiplied tenfold, mullion windows all round, with a fantastic view from one hundred panes a glass, and although upstairs was greatly affected by the steeply sloping roof, and only one of the three bedrooms was of a decent size, the ground floor made up for it, with a large kitchen and two similar sized reception rooms. Outside was even better than I had remembered, with a cobbled courtyard and several outbuildings. Originally, the Under Reservoir Keeper, or Waterman, would de-camp to the larger of the outbuildings in the mornings, along with the workers who were dropped off with him before setting off around the top end of the Valley to complete any jobs that needed doing but, first they had the all important brew, and depending on the weather this could take until lunchtime. By 1979, those early morning get-togethers were a thing of the past, and the Reservoir Keepers worked very much alone, and as mentioned earlier, it was the Depot at Tintwistle which disgorged the men to all points from 8am, and the famous 'brews' were carried in flasks. I was later to discover though, that the little cabins, which were conveniently parked up, near to the various jobs, and also, almost always situated at a contrived angle and elevation to enable the men to see any of the Bosses coming, were well stocked with camping stoves and kettles, and all manner of life's little comforts. I was beginning to understand why jobs with the 'Corp', or

Manchester Corporation to give the company its original title, were greatly sought after and, in many cases, was a family affair, Brothers, Uncles, Fathers and Sons, and in some cases, Aunties but, asked my guide for the day, "Everyone is wondering how the kid from the 'Chron', got an interview?" He was referring to my writing occasional wildlife articles for the local newspaper the Glossop Chronicle but, more importantly, to the fact that, traditionally no one from the 'outside' ever got a job in the Valley. I still write for the Chronicle today and my column is called 'The Valley And Beyond'.

"Your guess is as good as mine", I replied, "But the way that interview has just gone, you can tell them all they can sleep tonight". He then told me something fairly cryptic, "Funny thing is, everyone thought it was earmarked for someone else, but no one else has been given an interview but you".

"Anyway, have a look outside, I've just got to wire up a few electric fires and make sure they are safe."

He was finishing off little 'bits', that needed doing before the new Reservoir Keeper moved in. The freshly installed heating system was knocking out the heat, and although empty of any furniture, the place felt like home but, I couldn't let myself think about getting the job, and besides, the possibility of me being the only candidate was too far fetched, after the chat with Tom Quayle, I could have been the token outsider.

Bleak House, although only twenty feet from the infamous A628 which traverses the Woodhead Pass, was in those days almost a country lane, and besides there was back garden to die for. Climb over the wall and the next road was Saddleworth Moor seven miles distant, via Blackhill or Laddow Rocks and Chew Reservoir. Not a garden in the traditional sense, as the building was surrounded by a steep sided amphitheatre of rock, rough grasses and heather, and only the dry-stone wall prevented it from being part of the moor. The wall was Grade 2 Listed, as was the house, not least because of the way it had been built but also because of the way it hugs the contours of the slopes, at times ten feet high and at others five, with coping stones as level as level can be. A Masterpiece in dry-stone walling. Beyond the wall, rolling hills, disused quarries, small woodlands and brooks, wonderful meandering streams and gullies, or 'groughs' to give them their correct name, and best of all it was packed with wildlife. In the fifteen minutes I was on my own, the Bleak House courtyard showed a small array of 'garden birds' quite unlike any other, and I was privy to red legged partridge and a cock red grouse on the wall, while closer in a grey wagtail seemed to pay no attention to my presence whatsoever, and neither did the common sandpiper which shot in and out the courtyard like a rocket, and then to cap it all, I first heard and then spotted, a peregrine falcon high in the sky.

The Electrician shouted out from an upstairs window, "I'll be done in a minute, and we can get off!".

The minute was more like ten and it gave me a chance to sit down and take in the ambience of the place; for a time I became apprehensive, and for no apparent reason I began to think along the lines of that, it might be better if we didn't move in, the odds were surely stacked against me anyway, with another operative probably already in place for a 'shoe-in' to the role. And besides, I didn't get chance to answer Quayle's parting shot about the murder trial at Inverness Crown Court where Menzies Campbell was the presiding Judge.

I had always been a self doubter, and some readers who know me may find this hard to believe but, I still am today, and although I would have to be fairly pleased with my current CV I always beat myself up, thinking that I could and should have done more with my time. At sixty four years old, I still have days where either side of a moment in time, with nothing altered, nothing different, I can be flush with enthusiasm, equipped with an unwavering belief in my ability, while on the other side of that moment, there is no good, I am tired, cannot face what is to come, and I question, question, question, what has gone before, and more importantly, what may be to come.

My sudden reticence back then was a classic example, and 'what if I get the job', was running around my head like a hamster in a cage-wheel on overdrive, 'I'll be better off working in a paint factory in an old Mill in Padfield', which is what I was doing after a couple of terms at the Comprehensive School in Glossop. The Head, wanted me carry on at the school after I was working in their Special Unit with some success, the kids, very similar to those from Glasgow, had been upgraded from 'Maladjusted', to 'Remedial' by 1978. At this stage however, I had decided to do one of my 'bail-outs', and left the building, which in hindsight was a stupid thing to do, as we had not long splashed out £9,000 on a Ryder & Dutton marketed property on Brosscroft. That was a lot of money in 1977. Fortunately my partner, Moira (Crean), of Dinting Vale, was running the Education side of Redcourt, the well known home for children and young adults with Downs Syndrome, so there was one decent wage coming into the house. Moira, whose Irish parents, John and Mary, had come over to England for work in the 1940's; Mary, in the Cotton Industry from Kilkenny, and John, from County Roscommon, as a miner and Bevan Boy. Mary, along with many other Irish girls was billeted in the building which would become the Redcourt School for young adults with Downs Syndrome. The couple had met through the Pen Pals page of the very popular 'Ireland's Own' magazine.

I am undoubtedly some ways down the road toward full blown bipolar disorder, described as a mental illness that brings severe high and low moods, hence the 'polar', and changes in sleep, energy, thinking, and behavior. However, I would describe the effect on me as 'severe' at times but variable, and most often, 'mild' to 'tough', and maybe more accurately diagnosed as Cyclothymia, or cyclothymic disorder, a mild mood disorder with symptoms similar to bipolar disorder. Both cyclothymia and bipolar disorder cause emotional ups and downs, from manic highs to depressive lows.

I have always managed, and importantly recognised the situation to a greater or lesser extent, and further have always believed that none of the symptoms have been helped by my dyslexia and dyscalculia. (Typing 'dyscalculia' I could not see what was wrong with my first attempt 'discalculia') Without going into too much detail to this day if I had to recite the Times Table to save my life, I would be a goner, and the same if I had to explain exactly where the 'I' comes before the 'E', and I can honestly say that, if I was given the job of scoring a darts match, I would go into meltdown. I can laugh about it now, with two million published words, a Masters Degree in Education, and invite to the Palace, the sandwiches were rubbish, and I am a Fellow of the British Naturalists Association, an honour I was handed by Sir David Attenborough. I had just begun a Phd at this stage, for the fun of it but, with MBA after my name I was satisfied I had proved my Teacher wrong and packed it in. Attenborough is, as one may expect an absolute Gent and as we were getting robed-up at Epping Forest School prior to a formal procession of Fellows through the grounds and into the School Chapel, I found myself getting dressed next to him. "Sean," he says, "These silk hoods are beggars to get on, can you give me some help please?" Okay I was starstruck, here was the voice of my life, and I thought, don't ask about hoods you are meant to be talking about gorillas. "No worries Sir David", I replied. "Just call me David", said Sir David. What a day that was.

In spite of these palpable achievements the difficulties I face are just not funny in reality and very difficult to explain. Firstly, I had to invent coping strategies, and secondly, by and large I avoided all avenues of possible revelation and embarrassment. I confess now to walking away from many opportunities, involving paid world travel, highly paid consultancy opportunities in Education which also meant International travel, and perhaps most unfathomable the chance to be a Presenter on shows like 'Countryfile'. For the record I do not regret missing out on any of these chances, it is part of who I am. It has to be said that, I became very good with the avoidance tactics, and many readers will possibly be scratching their heads now wondering if what I am saying is true because they see me as a person who can probably do anything because I am told that, I make things look easy and spin many plates at once.

As a classic and further example of how, for example, the dyslexia affects me and I'm talking 1st September 2017; I was writing an article about a trip to Ireland which included the words, Mediterranean and Fuchsia. I could not get either word correct and that loud, loud red-line appeared under each word no matter how many times I looked at them and tried again. In the end I googled them, great you would think but no, as I just done the search and went back to the document, the words had disappeared from my head in a nano-second and in the end I was forced to copy and paste the words into place, and me almost crying with frustration. Dyslexia has also, in my opinion, had a profound effect on other aspects of my life including, believe it or not, bird identification. I have always found it very difficult to process and retain certain, sometimes tiny, pieces of information, and quite often with the most common of birds. It's my 'i before the e' moment, where after over forty years of serious wildlife watching, I still have trouble sorting out various species and indeed bird song but, usually only when there is an audience, like when a Teacher asked me what 7 times 7 was in front of the class. I once pointed out five golden-eye ducks on Woodhead Reservoir, and actually said the name, before immediately correcting myself in my head as they were tufted ducks but, did not admit my mistake to the friend I was with, even when he argued with me about the ID. The mistake then worried me for the next two hours and I eventually blurted out, 'Yes they were tufted, I can't imagine why I said goldeneye, I've never seen one on Woodhead yet?' Contrary to popular misconception, Dyslexia is not only about literacy, although weaknesses in literacy are often the most visible sign. Dyslexia affects the way information is processed, stored and retrieved, with problems of memory, speed of processing, time perception, organisation and sequencing. Welcome to my world.

Back in 1980, I was not so skilled at the pretence, and I genuinely began to think that the job, the house, and indeed the Valley was a little bit more than I could chew at twenty six years old. At this stage, the Electrician had forgotten one more wiring job, and had called out of an upstairs window for me to come in from the cold but, after my year in the wilds of Argyll, my years of rough camping in the Scouts, and my time spent in the fields behind my Dad's Butchers Shop in Sutton Bonington, in Leicestershire, cold was something which didn't really bother me, and I preferred to sit outside, with my mood tipping back the other way at the thought of the parties and barbecues we could have in this wonderful place. In the time it took you to read the last paragraph, I was back to firing on all cylinders, and of course I wanted the job, and I was getting the job, fact.

From out of nowhere came the sense that my thoughts of success, were being corroborated from elsewhere, as though another person was agreeing with me and I was picking it up telepathically.

These thoughts were accompanied by a feeling that most readers will be familiar with but not perhaps in these circumstances, I had a chill up my neck like 'someone was walking over my grave', and I felt that someone was watching me. As I looked around the yard and before I could think much more of it, the Electrician called once more from the kitchen window this time, "Did you not hear the phone ringing, it's Tom Quayle for you, come on, quick he's waiting".

"Mr Wood," said Tom Quayle, "Against my better judgement, we have decided to offer you the job, will you accept the position? We need to know as soon as possible as there are others in line but, please go home and speak to your wife and get back to me today as a matter of urgency."

"Thank you very much, I accept, and I feel like the cat who has got the cream."

I may be rubbish at maths, and not able to cross my I's and my T's but, I have a photographic memory for things said and things seen, and my reference to the smiling cat was exactly what I said to Tom Quayle, and I also remember word for word what Moira said when I phoned the School to tell her the news, 'Wow, that's so exciting we're so lucky". This ability of total recall provides the perfect lexicon for the coming chapters, along with the notes I made in my North West Water Record Books. Not the Guinness-type of records but rather the daily records of wind, rain and reservoir levels, jobs done and jobs needed to be done, and of course all my little nuggets preserved for history including, the peregrine falcon hitting a racing pigeon with such force that, it was like an explosion in a mattress factory, twenty ring ouzels, or mountain blackbirds feeding on worms at Crowden Campsite and the poor stiff dead guy who had killed himself behind Bleak House, and who, while I nipped over the wall to make brews for the Emergency Services and the Police, was removed from his seated position and placed sitting on the back steps of the attending ambulance. Gallows humour at its best, how they laughed when I said, 'Jesus where is he..........ah.....very funny lads". It wasn't quite so hilarious when three handwritten letters were found on the back seat, each in an envelope with a stamp and address, one to his daughter, another to his wife and one to his girlfriend.

Mr Quayle was being a little disingenuous with his remarks, as there was no else in the frame, and it transpired that, the whole interview was verging on a farce, as it had been preordained by Quayle's Boss, the Regional Manager, Ronnie Clayton, that I should be given the job. Clayton was based at North West Water's Head Office, which at the time was in Great Sankey, and he lived in the circulation area of the Runcorn and Widnes Weekly News. When he saw the press cuttings included with my application, he realised he was already a reader of my columns, and made his mind up there and then that, I was the ideal person, and not least because I wanted the job, both for where the job was based, and what it entailed, as this was, "Obvious in your writing Sean, that you are the person for this job", he said. A few days later when I returned to sign the contract, I could sense Quayle getting uncomfortable as myself and Ronnie

Clayton, the Big Cheese, were chatting like old mates about my recent articles concerning a trip to Sweden and how big elk were. "I'm looking forward to reading about the wildlife of Longdendale in the coming months", he said, as he left the office, and then shouted back, "Oh, and Tom, will you tell the Forestry people not to cut down anymore dead trees please?"

I'm fairly sure that I left any smirks at Mr Quayle's obvious discomfort until later, I was just delighted to have the job, floated home to Brosscroft in Hadfield, and straight into the Vic' for a pint or five. All thoughts of my 'funny' inklings of someone watching me were shelved, as I shared the good news with all and sundry, and celebrated once again when Moira arrived home from work.

The next few months passed passed very quickly, and with Christmas '79, and New Year '80 out of the way, and our house sold for 18K, with a clear profit of 9K in only two years, we had a few quid in the bank and an exciting time ahead. Moira went to America for a month to visit her best friends, and I bought a red Triumph Dolomite, and successive nights were spent in the 'Vic'.

There was no television signal at Crowden, except for intermittent Welsh TV, and even in the summer Bleak House would prove to be cool but, in the winter, it was thoroughly Arctic and picture postcard freezing cold. No wonder it was given the name.

Before we had arrived, the Bosses in their wisdom had ensured that the place was 'modernised', and for 'modernised', please read, 'ruined', as the original doors were faced with hardboard, metal latches replaced with ancient brown bakelite models from the Stores, Victorian stone fireplaces were ripped out, bricked up and replaced with four-bar electric heaters, and to cap it all, the heating boiler only used Anthracite beans, the most expensive type of domestic fuel on earth; and to make matters worse, you could not fill the hopper as the downdrafts quickly caused the lot to ignite. The place was still an idyll to me, and I was like the proverbial pig in shit, although it has to be said that my wife was not over enamoured with the cow piss which found its way into the open water supply as it dog-legged down the hill from a spring. She wasn't that keen on the dessicated rat I found in the stone water tank either, nor hardly impressed with the occasional froglet extricating itself from the tap. Happy Days.

On the plus side, I am convinced that there, are and were, untold health benefits to all those little microbes, and to this day I never catch a cold, and you can count on one hand the amount of times that I have had anything resembling influenza.

My first few weeks were spent acquainting myself with the Valley, and for the purpose of this book, it may be helpful for readers who are not familiar with the area to listen carefully to the next public announcement.

The eastern part of the valley is in the non-metropolitan county of Derbyshire and includes the village of Tintwistle and, further east, part of the Peak District National Park, with the last half-mile or so falling into the Metropolitan Borough of Barnsley in South Yorkshire. The western part of the valley, including the villages of Broadbottom, Mottram in Longdendale and Hollingworth is part of Tameside in the metropolitan county of Greater Manchester. The whole of Longdendale forms the easternmost extension of the lands within the historic boundaries of Cheshire.

The River Etherow, a tributary of the River Mersey, rises south of Holmfirth and then flows through a chain of six reservoirs known as the Longdendale Chain: Woodhead Reservoir, Torside Reservoir, Rhodeswood Reservoir, Valehouse Reservoir, Bottoms Reservoir and Arnfield Reservoir. There was a seventh reservoir at Hollingworth, but it was abandoned in 1990 and now forms part of Swallows Wood Nature Reserve.

The lordship of Longdendale was an ancient feudal estate encompassing the medieval manors of Godley, Hattersley, Hollingworth, Matley, Mottram, Newton, Staley, Tintwistle and Werneth. The lordship was created by the Earl of Chester in the late twelfth century; William de Neville was the first lord of Longdendale, as appointed by the Earl of Chester. Buckton Castle, near

Carrbrook, was probably built by William de Neville in the late twelfth century and was also probably the centre of lordship of Longdendale as it is the only castle within the lordship. One of the privileges of the lordship was to carry out trial by combat. The lordship of Longdendale was passed from de Neville to his son in law, Thomas de Burgh, in 1211 on his death. The lordship reverted to the control of the crown in 1357, and remained under crown control until 1374. The lordship was given to Matilda Lovell and the Lovells controlled Longdendale until 1465 when control again reverted to the crown. The lordship was granted to Sir William Stanley in 1489, however the lordship once again reverted to the Crown when Stanley was executed in 1495 as a supporter of Perkin Warbeck. In 1554 the lordship was granted to Richard Wilbraham. The Tollemache family inherited lordship of Longdendale from the Wilbrahams in the 1690s, and Manchester Corporation purchased the land on which Bleak House sits from the family around 1843.

Longdendale was part of the Hundred of Macclesfield. An estate survey, or 'Extent' of the lordship for 1360 was published by the Record Society of Lancashire and Cheshire in July 2005.

A packhorse route called a Salt Way was maintained from the Middle Ages onwards for the purpose of allowing the export of salt from the Cheshire wiches of Nantwich, Northwich and Middlewich across the Pennines. The passing trade brought prosperity to settlements along the route. The importance of the salt trade along such saltways is shown by surviving place names; for example Salter's Brook (SK137999) is where the Salt Way forked, with one route leading to Wakefield and another to Barnsley. The stone Lady Shaw Bridge still exists at this point, as do the ruins of an old inn. The bridge is just wide enough for a packhorse, though it is suspected that the bridge may have originally been wider and was deliberately narrowed when the Saltersbrook turnpike was built, to prevent vehicles bypassing the toll barrier. The turnpike road from Manchester to

Saltersbrook connected to further turnpikes for Yorkshire destinations and was built in the mid-18th century, based on the older saltway route.

Over the years I have written hundreds of articles about Longdendale but, to a large degree I have kept quiet about my personal history, and my many experiences with what can only be described as the, 'other worldly', at Woodhead and Crowden. I did this for what I thought were obvious reasons, not least because I had children for all of the time we lived there, but also because, when I was younger I was probably concerned what people might think, whereas now, I couldn't care less. I have been quoted worldwide in print, and on screen, about the renowned Longdendale Lights but, the lights, are simply the lights, they were just there, nothing spooky, a fact of life at Crowden, and I will discuss them later in the book, as for the unusual neighbours I encountered, readers can make their own minds up. My daily contact with past residents of the Valley, were always a blessing, and only once frightening.

Not many people know this but, the whole adventure could have come to an abrupt halt thanks to one more element, literally, in the pantheon of Woodhead Weather Patterns. I remember the day very well, as it was a Sunday, and St Patrick's Day, March 17th, 1980, and the UK had been experiencing a blast of Siberian Weather, with Woodhead being no exception, and snow began to fall. At one stage in the day, the sky achieved a kind of clarity rarely seen, where every detail, across every blue, grey and white in the spectrum, was picked out with a kind of iridescent gold, silver or purple. You could tell a storm was on the way, there was a wonderful silence, and the air was calm. All this changed before the white stuff piled high, and a flash of lightning broke into the quiet, followed a short time later, like a the sound of a gun-shot, by a peal of thunder. Another bolt shot out of the sky and seemed to hit the ground near the old blacksmiths which stood out on a little promontory into the Reservoir opposite the Holmfirth turn off, and very close to the site of the long demolished, George & Dragon Public House. On my first day on the job with an old map in hand, I excitedly walked off in search of the G&D, thinking how handy it was for Bleak House, only be nearly in Yorkshire before I discovered it was no more. Best laid plans and all that.

With the storm a brewing and more lightning likely, I rushed into the house, grabbed my camera, an Olympus OM1 at the time, and climbed over the wall at the side of the house, and stood, at the ready, on a small parcel of land which at one time was the Bleak House vegetable garden. It was the perfect vantage point for a photograph of the maelstrom which was occurring.

School-Boy Error Number 1, don't try and take pictures of lightning on an exposed hillside. School-Boy Error 2, If you ignore Number 1, then don't wear steel toe-caps. School-Boy Error 3, always check your immediate surroundings.

Having paid scant attention to the first two errors, I went straight in with both feet and mindlessly discounted number three, which would soon prove to be my undoing. Perhaps 'one foot' would be a better description of my folly because, the next thing I knew I was thrown ten feet backwards as lightning struck my foot. I was alive but obviously shocked and sat on my arse as I quickly put one and two together. There was no warning, and even if there had been, I had had my camera to my eye and was weighing up when and where the next strike may occur and I had clicked on the auto-drive.

To explain, I was standing ten feet from the perimeter stone-wall of the house, this wall is of such character that it remains as part of the Grade 2 Listing of the property, and I was looking towards Woodhead. Originally the land was surrounded by metal railings but, these had fallen into disrepair, however, parts of the railing were, and probably still are, just below the surface and a massive lightning strike had hit a piece of this first, before ricocheting off in my direction, and blitzing into the metal toe-cap of the North West Water issue-boot on my right foot. This is sometimes known as a 'side flash' or 'splash'.

Although I was only thirty feet away from the primary-strike, there is little doubt that the subsequent dissipation of the lightning's power saved my life on that day. When my wife came home from work, I was able to point out the damage to the shoe, and over tea, if I recall correctly, we both laughed about it. My Dad, John, when I telephoned him was not laughing, and proceeded to admonish me in his inimitable fashion by reciting the three school-boy errors I have already told you about. "Yes Dad", I replied, "I know".

It has been recorded that there can be neuropsychiatric complications such as depression, anxiety, memory deficits, and post-traumatic stress disorder after a lightning strike, and Professor Mary Ann Cooper of the University of Chicago, says, 'Lightning strike can scramble each individual survivors unique internal circuitry'.

There is undoubted evidence to support Cooper's thesis, for example a Doctor, Tony Cicoria, of New York was struck by lightning in 1994 while using a public phone. He was lucky that a passerby was a trained Paramedic who managed to resuscitate Tony after his heart stopped.

Soon into his recovery he felt compelled to buy a piano after claiming he was hearing music in his head. He taught himself to play the piano and was composing what he heard within a matter of weeks. His first composition was, perhaps unsurprisingly, called 'The Lightning Sonata'. After a few months he largely dropped his career as an Orthopedic Surgeon and began a new career as a classical musician. There are other reported cases concerning similar incidents when people struck by lightning have gone on to become great artists, when they had never held a brush before, or even begun to speak a language they had never spoken. It is possible that there may be a link with the lightning strike and the stories I tell. Suffice to say, what came next was the beginning of, what might be called, the 'unnatural-history' of the Valley, although it very soon became the norm.

They first awoke, to me anyway, on Thursday March 20th, 1980, it was around midday and we had only been in the house a month and I was tidying the courtyard, still getting used to the idea that we were living in the Valley the proverbial 'kid in a sweet shop'. The air was cold and still but, with a large bonfire going, the first of many wonderful 'bonnys' at Bleak House, and a cheeky woodmouse taking scraps from my hand my face was aching from smiling. Just when I was thinking it doesn't get any better, a common buzzard passed overhead and Stan Arnfield, my immediate Boss, pulled into the drive and handed over my first wage packet in cash. Stan, was a proper nice bloke, old school, a true gentleman, and he always treated me with respect, probably because he could never fathom why I wanted the job in the first place, it had just never happened before that, an 'outsider' had become a Waterman, and Stan, like Tom Quayle, may have thought that I had a direct line to Ronnie Clayton. The little brown envelope contained, if I remember correctly around £70; not as much pay as the Teaching but, certainly more than the Paint Dispersion Company in the bowels of Rhodes Mill in Padfield where I worked for a short time after leaving my first stint at Glossop Comprehensive. Ironically a hundred metres from where I now live.

After Stan left I carried on with, not much really, apart from watching the 'bonny', before I set off on another Patrol along the reservoir banks. I clearly remember downing tools several times because I had that niggling sensation that there was someone watching me again, and ridiculous as it may sound now, whoever, it was, or may have been seemed very close. One second behind me, another in front of me, and then inexplicably not there at all, or at least that's what it felt like. I left the brush on the ground, and threw another pallet on the fire and poked the flames into life with a big stick, you need a good stick for sorting a fire out especially if there is no breeze to coax it into life. Famous last words, as they say, because out of nowhere a sudden rush of wind dashed between the house and the largest outbuilding, lifted the brush in the air along with a flurry of dead leaves and caused the fire to explode into life. The wind, which had come down from the North East, a wind I would become very familiar with in the next few years, was literally passing through, subsided in a matter of seconds, as in gale force to becalmed.

Wind is natural, what else did I expect so far above sea level; wind, rain and snow, and the very, very cold were soon to be my daily-bread but, I loved it. Imagine the perfect job-description if the great outdoors is your passion...Get up, have a brew, and then go on a little walk, watch out for the water voles and the sparrowhawks on the way to your rain-gauge. Return to Bleak House before 9am and phone in your figures. Have another brew and a bit of breakfast, then go on a long walk around the Reservoir and across the hills. Don't forget to call at the Youth Hostel for another brew and a piece of cake, oh and while you're there, check the water-tank on the hill, it was a bit of a Devil for emptying overnight. You get the picture, it was the job to die for. Early doors one of my friends asked me, 'Well Woody, what exactly do you do?' and I replied, 'I get up each morning, put the kettle on and look out of the window and if the Reservoir is still there, I'm okay'. And that, was basically that; there I was, a young lad with a beautiful wife, living in a wonderful 19th Century folly of a house, which came free, a Land Rover and someone drove up on a Thursday to pay my wages in cash.

With my bonny down to a few embers, I heard the voice of a child from over the perimeter stone wall which backs onto St James Church, "Hey Mister, hey Mister", but when I looked up there was no one to be seen. As I carried on sweeping, "Hey Mister, hey Mister!" rang out again, only this time accompanied by giggling. I assumed it was young children who were shouting over the wall for a game, and then ducking down out of sight so decided to surprise them. The next time they shouted, "Hey Mister", I ran up the hill, jumped over the wall and was just about to go, 'Boo!' when I realised that there was no one in sight. There was no car driving off, the fields and churchyard were empty, and no sign of the kids along the track which leads up to Loft End Quarry.

Bemused but not really concerned, or troubled in anyway, I assumed that the kids had run off faster than I thought, and were hiding somewhere laughing to themselves.

For the first time since moving into Bleak House I found myself alone in the graveyard, and although I had driven past on the Salt Road which runs in front of the Church gate, I had never actually set foot in the place. I use the term, 'alone', loosely because after a quick walk around I discovered that the graveyard was full of children, including a brother and sister who died either side of Christmas Day in the 19th century, and almost every gravestone told a miserable and unhappy tale. Having said that, there was a contented tranquility about the place and it felt like I had stumbled into a crowded playground at break-time. As I moved fronds of dead bracken aside and traced names of children carved in the headstone with my fingers I remember thinking, 'rest easy young one', as I read each name.

Vincent Fox Gee of Crowden Hall Died April 8th 1913 aged 5 years.
Frank Crossland of Crowden, Died January 10th 1901 aged 14 years.
Eli Whitehead of Woodhead, Died 1884, aged 18 years.
Margaret Anne of Crowden Station, Died June 8th 1875 aged 9 years.
Mary Ann Chadwick, Died 1850 aged 11 years
Thomas Chadwick, Died 1851 aged 7 years
Joseph Chadwick, Died 1852 aged 9 months.

So much sadness in a small patch of earth, and yet in my three decades at Bleak House, the place was full of joy.

Walking down the stone steps from the Church Yard that morning, I recall the vista was stunning, still is, looking out over the tops of the Bleak House impossibly tall chimneys towards Shining Clough and Bleaklow; to the right Torside Reservoir and in the distance the distinctive outline of Mottram Parish

Church seven miles away, while to the left, the view I have never tired of, Woodhead Reservoir and the hillside's curvaceous contours beckoning me. On this occasion, and for one more year yet before the Railway Line closed for good in 1981, a diesel engine pulling ten or more wagons in it's wake, slicing through the Valley as the Steam Locomotives had done for over a century before. As for admiring the views I was in good company, Queen Victoria had travelled on the line, and was said to have been very impressed with the newly built chain of five reservoirs, the largest in the world at the time, a Victorian Wonder. It is not known whether she was amused or not when they entered the smoke filled and claustrophobic Woodhead Tunnel a few minutes later which was constructed in 1845, and at three miles, thirteen yards (4,840 m) one of the longest in her Majesty's Empire.

Once through the awkwardly hung wrought iron gate, with thoughts of more coffee and a bacon butty the now familiar call of, "Hey Mister, hey Mister", stopped me in my tracks. Against the back wall of the graveyard there were two children, a boy and a girl. The girl, the tallest of the two was holding a baby. They did not move, nor say a word but, they were smiling. Each child was dressed in their Sunday best and as clear as day, like a high definition black and white photograph pulled from a very large glass-plate negative, standing out in stark contrast to the relative colour of the day including the small patches of heather which had crept under the wall for shelter from the moors above, the yellow grass tussocks and a faded brown wreath which lay at a jaunty angle on a nearby tomb.

It was easy to suppose at the time that the children who showed themselves were the Chadwick's but, I never found out for certain.

Chapter Two:
Pawdy Blanche at the Crowden Rifle Range via Wexford.

The first time I saw him was a distant view, and he was dressed in what appeared to be early 20th Century British Army uniform, and he was walking briskly, although with a pronounced limp, towards the Rifle Range Butts. 'Butts' is my term and I'm sure there is a more accurate description, perhaps platforms or terraces. Crowden range opened in 1899 and for the use of some of the Manchester Volunteer Battalions. 177 linear yards of markers' galleries were constructed, from which about 50 targets could be displayed. The furthest distance fired was 1000 yards and the range closed in the 1960s. Apart from the military, civilian clubs also used the range and arrangements were made from time to time with the railway company to set down or pick up shooting parties.The butts were made from railway sleepers and positioned strategically in terraced rows above the Rifle Range building and billets, now the Youth Hostel and Outdoor Pursuit Centre at Crowden.

The Butts allowed the soldiers to lie down and fire over the Crowden Great Brook at a range of traditional targets of the circular red, white and blue variety, and also, I have been told, targets with the outline of a man. Local legend also has it that, during the 2nd World War, some wag, trying to inject a little humour into the situation, substituted the regular targets with pictures of Adolf Hitler, much to the amusement of the regulars but, landing him a hour or two in jankers for interfering with the King's Property. The term jankers appears to be first recorded after the Boer War, 1899-1902, and for certain before the Great War, 1914, and may have originated from a much earlier reference to 'janglers', soldiers in chains carrying out laborious and repetitive tasks, such as peeling potatoes, or cleaning floors. If I was a betting man my money would be on the term 'Janker Wallah' as the original source of the expression, a Hindu term that refers to a fellow who does menial labour.

Ironically, for this tale, as it concerns an Irishman, the bugle call for any miscreant to get up and begin cleaning the latrines, or peeling potatoes, was known as 'Paddy Doyle', whoever he was?

Some of the Officers were not above bending the rules themselves though, 'do as I say not as I do' type of thing, and I found the evidence to prove this as I uncovered in 1981, and continue to find in 2017, bullets which came from hand-guns. I believe the Officers could not resist having a pop themselves, whereas in real-life action these weapons were only for short-range use. Out on the hill no one was watching and it was too good an opportunity to miss, no pun intended. There are also a couple of random inch-thick sheets of metal with holes punched in them which must have come from something a little bit more substantial than a Royal Enfield. The broken up shale scree received most of the fire opposite the butts, and it is here that the business end of the bullets keep showing up as the rain gently washes away the years to reveal more.

My prize possessions are the bullets which hit this soft ground and stayed intact, as most of the finds are smashed to smithereens.

One ex-army guy I met in the early 1981, Mr Brocklehurst, painted a particular vivid picture of how, when the Officers were not looking some of the men would try their hand at shooting white hares and red grouse from half a mile away, and if successful with the game bird, a veritable ticker-tape of feathers filled the Valley, before alighting on the Great Brook, and drifting off as a large raft of down towards the weir and Woodhead Reservoir beyond. Mr Brocklehurst described the resultant flurry of feathers as, "It wer' like one of them Snow Globes tha shakes at Christmas tha knows!" Mr Brocklehurst wasn't done there as there was always an addendum to everything he said, and usually it involved further information on whatever was talked about, whether you wanted it or not. On balance I always did.

"It wer' the Frogs that started it tha knows, same as a say, and they filled the globes we tinsel, they shud ah come from Tinsel!" The latter had Mr Brocklehurst chuckling, as Tinsel is the shortened name of Tintwistle four miles down the road from Crowden. As for his very un-pc description of the French, in mitigation, he lived in different times.

"Ay lad, it's 'cos they ate frogs tha know, scruffy beggars", "I've eaten them", I replied, "And they were lovely with garlic". "Ah well, same as I say, you're a scruffy beggar an' all tha knows". Of course he wasn't about to stop there.

"Aye, same as I say, it were int' 12th century, or thereabouts when't Monks in France had been telt tha canna eat meat on Fridays until yon crafty one telt the Catholic Church that frogs were fish so that they could ate 'em, aye them Left-footers, crafty lads them ya know, and if that did'na work there wora atime went they'd ate Barnacle goose, cos the same as I say, they reckoned yon burds hatched out from barnacles on't side ot ship tha knows".

Almost without breathing, Brocklehurst managed to throw in the reason why Catholics were known as Left-footers as well, and one more reason as to why the Catholics were 'crafty', "Aye, same as I say, it were to do wit' spades tha knows".

According to Mr Brocklehurst the saying turns on a traditional distinction between left- and right-handed spades in Irish agriculture. It has been used as a figure of speech and often, sadly, as a term of abuse to distinguish Protestants from Catholics, 'He digs with the wrong foot.' Most types of digging spade in Britain and Ireland have foot-rests at the top of their blades; two-sided spades have foot-rests on each side of the shaft and socket, while an older style had only one. Two-sided spades may well have been introduced by the Protestant 'planters' in the sixteenth century. By the early nineteenth century specialised spade and shovel mills in the north of Ireland were producing vast numbers of two-sided spades which came to be universally used in Ulster and strongly identified with the province. One-sided spades with narrow blades and a footrest cut out of the side of the relatively larger wooden shaft continued in use in the south and west. The rural population of Gaelic Ireland retained the Catholic faith and tended also to retain the one-sided spade and 'dig with the wrong foot'.

Moving swiftly on, and me just managing a 'yes' and a 'no', Brocklehurst returned seamlessly to the snow globes, "Same as a say, at turn o't 20th century went Doctor asked a fella calt Erwin Perzy, to make the Edison light bulb brighter for his operating room in't Vienna. Yon fella Perzy knew a cobbler who'd filt a globe wit water and shoved int' front ot' candle to magnify light. So Perzy filt the water globe first wit' tinsel, then wit' white grit but that dinna work and bits flawted ta' bottom", said Brocklehurst.

It seems that the effect Perzy created with the white grit fascinated him because it reminded him of falling snow and he persevered and he made a miniature of the Basilica of the Birth of the Virgin Mary (to this day, the basilica is the most important pilgrimage site in Austria). Using pewter from his medical instruments shop, Perzy created the miniature. He then decided to place the miniature in the glass water globe with the white grit. The first snow globe was invented, and the rest as they say.

I miss the Old Guys who walked Crowden, and was so lucky to have met them as a young man, soaking up their tales like blotting paper, and ironically I was able to share stuff I knew about wildlife with them, so it was quid pro quo arrangement. I quizzed them, and they were very gracious in their questioning of me. Not that I was any great expert then, or indeed now but, I did have some knowledge of natural history, having spent all my life in small villages, in England, Scotland and of course, Ireland, where my days were spent happily, climbing trees, and falling down them; swimming in Lakes, and nearly drowning in them, and of course, running up mountains and getting lost in them. A wonderful way to grow up. It meant that, I had some good ammunition for a story-barter, you show me yours, and I'll show you mine kind of thing. My trusty hip-flask, a gift from a short-sighted German Hunter on the hills above Loch Ness, was always topped to the brim with a good malt, and proved very useful for prising stories from my erstwhile companions. This particular Herr was a pain in the rear end who managed to put a neat crease across the roof of my deerstalker friend's prized Daimler when he took an ill advised shot at a Roe Buck. Revenge was taken slowly when we explained to him that he had wounded the deer, which looked to be a fine specimen and that we would take him back to the Hotel, the Culloden as it happens, with it's wonderful whisky bar full of the rarest drams you could imagine, and return later with the dogs to track his beast. Little did he know that we had an assortment of roe buck trophy heads in the deep freeze at home, and that once defrosted no one would know the difference, least of all our German hunter, and he was over the moon when we delivered his 'Silver Medal Head' the following morning. It should be noted that, he missed the deer by a mile, the dogs stayed at home while we visited the Dores Inn, and that his trophy was to cost him a premium on his fee. We laughed all the way back to Loch Ness Side with a big tip, the repair money for the 'Jag' and the priceless memory of the German waving us off with the thistle we had given him in the left hand side of his hat band. We told him that it was a Scottish tradition, to urinate on the thistle as a signal of a successful hunt. We had also presented him with a sprig of pine which has been dipped in the deer's blood for the right hand side of his hat, in the German tradition.

Mr Brocklehurst, chuckled at the story as he was not fond of the Germans and he was able to offer in exchange an explanation as to who, the aforementioned limping Soldier at Crowden might be, and this was forthcoming after I described my second, and third sighting to him in early April 1980. I remember the time of year because I was busily learning Irish Songs for my first paid public performance as a folk singer, at Crowden Youth Hostel, when the

Soldier appeared, and although this might sound corny it literally was, out of nowhere, and began to join in on the chorus of Galway Bay. "Hi, how are you?" I asked, "Tip, top Sor", he replied before marching off in what appeared to be a hurry but, it transpired in time that he always walked that fast, in spite of his impediment. " 'Twas drilled into me Sor', said Pawdy of this habit. I did insist that Pawdy stop calling me 'Sor' but he replied, somewhat apologetically, "I can't help it Sor".

At around 8.55am on the morning I met Pawdy, bearing in mind all the 'levels' needed to be phoned in to the North West Water Office by 9am, I was fortunate that I could see from my bedroom window that there was a thin layer of ice on Woodhead Reservoir, and even after a short time in the job I had learned to listen to the water flowing over the lip of the wonderfully crafted stone weir and guess very accurately how many millimetres above top-level was going over, or 'Overtopping' as I heard one retired Waterman say.

I confess that I was fond of my bed in my twenties and once again, being late up I had guessed that no rain had fallen and the small weathervane I had crafted in the courtyard enabled me to suss out wind-direction very easily, and my wall mounted thermometer enabled me to complete the job in two minutes instead of the half an hour if I had dragged myself from my comfy pit. At this stage my wife Moira had already left for work and I was in the wilderness sweet-shop on my own, it was literally just me and the Valley, although I soon had plenty of company.

When I actually did do my job, it was a ten minute walk to the rain-gauge from Bleak House, my eyrie in the hills, and I feel a little bit of retrospective guilt here. Stan Arnfield, my lovely Boss, would be mortified at my dereliction of duty, especially if I knew that I would regularly telephone Frank Thorpe, the Waterman, at Torside, the next Reservoir down in the Longdendale chain and ask him how much rain he had recorded. If Frank said there had been 5.6 mm, I would add a bit on, as historically, and even though only a mile or so up the road there was always more precipitation at Woodhead. This was fact because I had access to the large bound record-books of Woodhead Reservoir Keeper's going back to the early 20th Century, so for example I can tell you that March 1909 was notable for some very cold and snowy weather. On the 3rd, around 15 cm of snow fell at Woodhead and the maximum temperature was only 0.3°C. Over snow cover, the temperature fell below minus 8°C. on the night of the 4th/5th, but on the 6th, snow turned to rain and gave a total of nearly 20 mm. Further snow fell until mid month, but it then slowly became milder. Temperatures were above average during the last week with a high of nearly 15°C. on the 29th. In these micro-histories were the lives and times of every one of my predecessors, and most of the entries were handwritten in pen and ink. By the time I arrived we were down to biros and a green-covered A5 lined notebook, and although much smaller I still managed to squeeze in the daily-levels and a veritable cornucopia of information that, someday, someone, somewhere will read with the same appetite as I devoured the originals.

As I made my way over the hill to Crowden, there was a light dusting of snow and I wasn't looking forward to operating the valve which allowed water to pour into Crowden Great Brook, because unless you had gloves on, which I didn't, your hands would stick to the frozen iron-work. The released water came from the water course which encircles Crowden and by lifting the valve, the water by way of an underground pipe of around 24 inches in diameter would shoot down into the small residuum lodge at the base of the weir. These lodges, most often situated at the base of the Reservoir Weirs were built to catch the silt before it went any further down the system and they were occasionally drained to be emptied.

The first time I had to drain the residuum lodge below Woodhead Reservoir, was a revelation and a first hand experience to be savoured as it allowed access, both on foot and even by Land Rover into the tunnel under the Woodhead Dam, and a close up view of the butterfly valves. They looked pretty strong but there was a mighty pressure of water on the other side. I am sure there is a formula for working this out but, you've heard what my maths was like. These valves could be operated electrically from the valve house near Bleak House, and in case of emergency, it was still possible to operate them manually with a team of men and some very large iron 'spanners' for want of a better word.

As soon became the norm at Crowden I became distracted and left the task momentarily when I spotted a dipper on the leaping-weir. These weirs were designed to wring every last drop of water into the reservoirs at a time of shortage and this just to satisfy the all-powerful Millowners and keep the looms spinning. Simply, if there was plenty of water coming downstream, the water flies over the gap, however if the flow slows down significantly then, it drops down into the water course and thence to Tintwistle and beyond. Simple Victorian Engineering at its finest. As for the dipper, nothing simple about these beauties, and they would soon be laying eggs in a nest of their own hanging beneath the stone work of John Frederick La Trobe Bateman and his work force. The construction of what was at the time, the largest chain of reservoirs in the world began in 1848 and was completed in 1877.

So there I was, singing my heart out, breath on the air, and just when I reached the last line of the second verse of Galway Bay, the Soldier appeared again, and joined in with a lovely harmony on...

'And watch the barefoot gosoons as they play.'

If you ever go across the sea to Ireland,
Then maybe at the closing of your day,
You can sit and watch the moon rise over Claddagh,
And see the sun go down on Galway Bay.
Just to hear again the ripple of the trout stream,
The women in the meadow making hay,
Just to sit beside the turf fire in a cabin,

And watch the barefoot gosoons as they play.

'Lovely that mate', says I on hearing his fine voice, and me with my very own trout stream at my feet, and Pauline and Wendy, at the Outdoor Pursuit Centre ready to dish up a lovely breakfast and a cup of Earl Grey. Sorry, I took milk with it then. For some reason, and for the life of me don't ask now but, I thought it nothing unusual to encounter a Soldier in a uniform from the Great War on a cold morning at Crowden. And neither, for that matter did I think at the time, how come I hadn't seen him approaching me and how on earth, had this uniformed tenor arrived stage left as if by magic.

Mr Brocklehurst had said, "Aye lad his name is Pawdy Blanche, same as I say, I remember it sounded like Danny Blanchflower, yon famous Irish footballer when I first spoke to him tha knows".

"Pawdy joint British Army to escape havin' nowt at home, and he telt me that he came from a little village in Wexford near'bout Kilmore Quay. he can sing that lad them Jesuits knew a harmony or two".

Mr Brocklehurst, explained that the man who introduced him to Pawdy, was nicknamed, Old Fez, which was short for Fazackerley, and he was born around 1870, in Crowden Village itself, at that time, a hamlet with a hundred villagers. Old Fez was able to remember stories from locals who were around when George 111 was on the throne, and in fact, his favourite tales were about boxing, with him asking and answering the same question a hundred times. 'Wen't was first time boxers used padded gloves in't ring, the Jessies?' He'd ask, '1818 is correct!', before you had time to answer.

Poor King George 111 still had two years to go on the throne at that stage, knew nothing about boxing and was already off his rocker by all accounts. Reading between the lines, and only to be confirmed later but, Old Fez and Pawdy were in regular communication for a number of years. However, that said none of this can account for, why it was me that saw him and indeed was able to speak to him on my morning Patrols many years after he had died, and further that this type of encounter would come to be my daily bread during my twenty eight years at Crowden.

It was thanks to Pawdy that I discovered the treasure trove of spent bullets on the far side of the valley from the rifle butts, and this after I had asked him about several large patches of bare soil which seemed a little incongruous in amongst the heather and coarse grasses. "Are ye t'ick or something?' laughed Pawdy, "That's where the targets were, and the ground is full of lead, nut'an, and I mean nut'an, will ever grow dare'. The following day I went to investigate and sure enough, on closer inspection the ground was indeed full of lead, and I'm talking tons of the stuff, and the bullets were mostly mangled where they had hit a piece of stone, which immediately made me think what would happen to a person if one of these hit a rib or a thigh bone. There were some pristine examples where the bullet had obviously hit soft ground, and then many years later had come to the surface again, a little bit of history in everyone one of them. I returned home to Bleak House that day with a collection of bullets filling both pockets, and I still have many of them but, after the first few visits, I became more discerning and only kept the finest examples, and typically these were about an inch long and had to be unmarked, with a lovely verdigre colouration, which is simply a bright bluish-green encrustation or patina formed on copper or brass by atmospheric oxidation. Best of all although smaller, were the bullets fired from the Officer's pistols. The models used at Crowden was Webley Mk IV revolver, produced by Webley and Scott in Birmingham, the standard issue British pistol, with some 300,000 produced during wartime. The Mk IV model, which debuted at the close of the nineteenth century, was a 11.6mm calibre weapon and proved immensely reliable in wartime conditions even among the muddy trenches of Flanders Fields.

When I asked Pawdy if the Officers ever hit the targets he said, "You're codding me, dey couldn't hit a whale in a bath and dem innit!" he answered.

A great deal of practice was required before the Webley could be used accurately since it jumped on firing. Despite its high reputation British officers generally preferred the use of a captured German Luger because it had a longer range.

Mr Brocklehurst was a bit of an expert on the subject, ballistics being a particular interest of his but then again he was the font of all knowledge in Crowden, or rather, 'Same as I say'. The larger bullets found in the ground at Crowden come from the British Lee-Enfield 0.303-inch rifle, which was issued to all the regulars of the British Expeditionary Force as they marched into France in August 1914. To give the rifle it's proper name, it was known as the 'Rifle, Short, Magazine Lee-Enfield Mk III', soon abbreviated to SMLE and then almost immediately nicknamed 'The Smelly' by the Tommies. Although the SMLE Mk III was introduced into British service in January 1907, it was simply a modified version of a service rifle from 1888.

It was at this juncture that you knew Mr Brocklehurst was more than just an amateur with a passing interest in rifles. "It wer' 1871, anth' Army wer' usin' th'owd Martini-Henry rifle, which fired a 483-grain, .450-calibre lead bullet from a necked-down .577in cartridge case tha knows. It wer' a reet good, Tommy-proof rifle but then wurst 'append. Yon Frog wit name Paul Vielle come up wi' a nitroglycerine powder in 1884 and mad' it best part useless tha knows", he said.

Mr Brocklehurst was right again, he mostly was, and with the introduction of Vielle's powder, every other military rifle became obsolete overnight. Vielle's powder produced very little smoke to betray the rifleman's position and could be used to drive copper-jacketed 8mm bullets at velocities in excess of 2,000ft per second. The adoption of the 'Modele 1886 Lebel' rifle by the French immediately prompted every other major power to start to develop a small-calibre, smokeless-powder magazine rifle.

By this time, the British military authorities had become aware of the work of a Swiss officer, Colonel Eduard Rubin, who had been tinkering with small-bore rifle bullets propelled with tightly pressed charges of black powder. In 1888 Britain bought 350 of James Paris Lee's patent rifles chambered for the .303 Rubin cartridge, which had a rimmed case and its bullet held centrally by a washer. After some further development, Britain's first .303 service rifle, the Lee-Metford Mk 1, was adopted officially on 22 December 1888. This combined the Lee's action and its eight- round magazine with William Ellis Metford's seven-groove rifling and a modified version of Rubin's cartridge. In 1895, the rifle was modified again with an enhanced 10-shot magazine, improved five-groove rifling developed at the Royal Small Arms factory at Enfield and a smokeless cartridge that used cordite as a propellant. This was the first in a long series of .303 Lee-Enfield rifles.

The Long Lee-Enfield, as it became known because of its 30in barrel, was the standard British rifle throughout the Second Boer War (1899–1902). It was supplemented by a carbine version with a 21in barrel carried by the cavalry. The Royal Irish Constabulary had its own special carbine; this version would accept a bayonet, which was used in some instances for crowd control.

"Them Boers wi' their Kraut Mausers, could shoot ye dead before tha' got out o' tha' bed", said Brocklehurst. He was referring to the advantage the Boer Fighters had over the British with their high powered and very accurate German rifles. Although the Lee-Enfield had a 10-shot magazine it had to be loaded with individual cartridges, which took time, whereas the Mauser's could be loaded with five cartridges by means of a charger in one go. The faster rate of fire combined with the Mauser's ballistically superior 7mm cartridge enhanced the Boer's already impressive marksmanship skills.

After the Boer War, the military sought to remedy the Lee-Enfield's shortcomings by a little bit of tweaking here and there, thereby avoiding the cost of developing a full blown new model from scratch and the 'Smelly' arrived. As

Mr Brocklehurst explained in his inimitable fashion, "Thowd Downing Street lot wer' as tight as a duck's arse tha knows, mek do and mend but it wasna a bad weapon".

The idea was, to provide a standard rifle for all the services, infantry, cavalry, artillery, engineers and the Royal Navy. The resultant weapon was capable of being loaded quickly with two five-round cartridge chargers. The bayonet would no longer be supported by the barrel but instead was fixed to an independent nose-cap with "ears" to protect the foresight.

The new universal rifle had a 25in barrel, a 10-round magazine and a Japanese-inspired sword bayonet with an evil looking 17in blade and the barrel was now encased in a wooden hand-guard. Although the SMLE was only an updated version of an earlier rifle, it was to become the quickest-firing and most effective bolt-action battle rifle of the 20th century. The British regular soldier was expected to be able to fire 15 aimed shots a minute from his rifle. The SMLE's effective range in competent hands was about 400 yd. However, it was fitted with long-range sights calibrated from 1,600yd to 2,800yd. These were intended for mass volley fire when large bodies of men fired at large targets, such as an artillery battery at long range. The cleaning kit – a brass oil bottle and a pull-through – was carried in the butt.

Both Mr Brocklehurst and Pawdy would talk for hours about the Great War, and basically they were like big kids who loved a good tale about fighting of any kind. They told me that in the mid-19th century that Woodhead was well known as a location for bare knuckle fights because those involved were able to slip over the county borders to avoid the police. Thanks to Glossop Heritage Society for this report, from the 'Glossop Record' of March 12, 1864, is of one such fight:

'Prize Fight At Crowden Brook.—One of those scenes which are a disgrace to humanity, took place in this village on Wednesday morning last. The pugilists

were two Manchester men, named Alexander Stewart and Ned Quinn. For upwards of two hours they battered each other, till they were both completely exhausted. Mr. James Bohan, county police constable, from Tintwistle, arriving on the spot, rushed into the ring and stood between the combatants, and stopped the fight. Both men were badly hurt; their faces were hacked in a most shameful and brutal manner. The men attending the fight appeared to be from amongst the lowest grades of society. Both men had to be conveyed to the railway station. It is high time that these brutal and debasing occurrences should be put down'.

Pawdy disagreed with this view but did think that there should be some kind of limit on how many rounds there should be, and how much damage one man should face before the fight was stopped.

Back at 'home' Pawdy had been smitten since the age of 12 by a young girl from a nearby farm, Mary Lannigan. As kids they played, as all country kids do, in the hay, down by the river, at the market and after Mass on Sunday but there came a change, and Pawdy felt awkward as Mary began the transformation from a young girl into beautiful woman. Where at one time the chatter never ceased between them, Pawdy could not summon one word. He said it was as though he'd gone mute overnight, "Twas an ommadawn I was".

Mary was a typical Irish colleen with a head full of ringlets, wrapped in paper, milk white complexion and freckles, blue eyes to crack open the gates of Heaven, and never a thought for a boy. It was to be an unrequited love, because as much as Pawdy wasn't able to talk, Mary became too ill to leave the house for months as she was struck down by tuberculosis and died a miserable and very sad death at seventeen years old. This was not unusual during the early 1900's but Pawdy would never get over the loss of Mary.

Pawdy was a good looking young man himself but, his Gabriel Oak candour and bashful nature which he retained into manhood, left him open to ridicule by his more streetwise comrades in the Army. At just over six feet tall, with the reddest of red hair, and more freckles than you could shake a stick it, more ammunition for Micky-taking, and with the broadest shoulders and longest reach of any soldier in the British Army, Pawdy was on a loser the moment he got on the boat, and embarked for his first night in an Army Camp in England. He was shy, he was huge, he was ginger but, most of all, he was a Paddy, and over here.

To put Pawdy's story in perspective, we need an overview of why Irishmen joined up to fight alongside the British. It is estimated that around 200,000 Irishmen enlisted during the so-called Great War. Grandpa Bill often said, "There was nothing 'great' about it, I can tell you".

There was no conscription at the time, and many of the men joined as volunteers during the War. Pawdy with the wisdom of hindsight claimed that Irishmen enlisted for a number of reasons including, the perceived justice of the cause against the Germans but, Ireland was deeply divided in 1914 between the Nationalist and Unionist political groups and local considerations played an important part for many of the men.

The establishment of an Irish 'home rule' parliament in Dublin had been the Nationalists main political goal for most of the 19th century, were encouraged to join the war effort by their leader John Redmond in September 1914, as he was convinced that they were honourably defending small nations such as Belgium. He also thought that the British may then feel honour bound as 'Brothers In Arms' to continue with commitment to Home Rule.

It was a gamble, by Redmond, who mustered the majority of the Volunteers, and many thousands paid a heavy price, with an estimated 40,000 Irish dead. Their sacrifice would also help to seal Redmond's political eclipse. As Pawdy said, "It seemed like a good idea at the time to be sure".

This becomes a bit personal for me now, as I have discovered that it is possible that John Redmond was a relative on my Dad's side, and Redmond's family live in Wexford, as did my Great, Great Grandmother. As with many families, this fact seems to have been the skeleton in the cupboard as I distinctly remember as a young boy that there was a certain antipathy between some of my Mother's side, who all decamped to Leicester in the late 40's and early 50's, and my Father's family. This was partly down to the mood of the day when shops and lodging houses could get away with signs outside their doors saying, 'No Blacks or Irish', and also because my Grandfather was in the British Army. Ironic then that I discover after a little family-tree climbing that Grandpa Will's Mother in Law was from Southern Ireland.

From 1912 the Unionists had organised an armed 'Ulster Volunteer Force' (UVF) to oppose home rule and secure the union with Great Britain, so they were not about to stand by when Great Britain itself went to war. The Unionist and almost wholly Protestant 36th (Ulster) Division came into being. The Nationalists on the other hand, mostly Catholic, joined two of Lord Kitchener's 'New Army' divisions raised in Ireland, the 10th (Irish) and 16th (Irish) Divisions.

Some Irishmen had no interest in politics and were simply after a bit of 'craic', and this was true of so many young men from the U.K. who joined up for a bit of fun, a dare or because their mates did, as with the so-called Pals Regiments. In Ireland, Tom Barry, later to become an IRA commander, enlisted in June 1915 'to see what war was like, to get a gun, to see new countries and to feel like a grown man'.

James Connolly, the socialist revolutionary, later to be shot in his chair as he couldn't stand up because of injuries received during the Easter Rising, said that it amounted to 'economic conscription', as there was no work in Ireland, and that, for example, a labourer could double or triple his pay by joining up. Francis Ledwidge, poet, nationalist and trade union organiser, joined up after an unhappy love affair. The juxtaposition of a Dublin slum, or a rural turf-roofed cottage in Wexford, against the backdrop of Passchendaele, Suvla Bay and the ill-fated assault of Gallipoli, where many of the Irish boys were bound, must have been impossible to process in a young soldiers mind, and any deprivations back home, perceived or otherwise, would soon have seemed a better bet.

Pawdy, who was both poor, lovelorn, and many miles from the 'home-house', was spared the Turkish fire-power, and was billeted in the Rifle Range at Crowden, after falling, he told me he was tripped, on the gangway as the troop-ship arrived in Liverpool. With a broken ankle, Pawdy said he was, "Of no use, to man, nor beast", and was removed from the ranks and taken to nearby hospital in Bootle to get fixed. What should have been a simple job, became more complicated when the wound developed an infection and subsequent sepsis. Pawdy nearly lost his leg up to the knee but, fortunately the infection subsided and his leg was saved although he was left with a permanent limp. "I was lame as a crippled donkey, and ran like a spancelled ewe", was how Pawdy described the effects of his injury. The latter relates to the practice of "spancelling," when farmers would use a short rope to tie an animal's left foreleg to its right hind leg, thereby hobbling the animal and stopping it from wandering too far. This practice was especially useful in the areas where there were no fences or stone walls to keep the livestock enclosed.

It is unlikely now, after all these years that, we will ever understand how Pawdy came to be stationed at Crowden, as his comrades decamped to Basingstoke but, I live in hope. Initially, Pawdy was devastated to have missed the 'excitement' of travelling to Turkey but, he was surely one of the lucky ones, as many of his fellow Irish Volunteers would soon face the horrors of war.

The 10th Division, which Pawdy had joined, came into existence as a result of Army Order No. 324, issued on 21st August 1914, which authorised the formation of the six new Divisions. It was formed of volunteers, under the administration of Irish Command. After initial training at the regimental depots, the units of the Division moved in 1915 to the Curragh, Newbridge and Kildare, where training in Brigade strength began.

In May 1915 the Division moved to England, which is when Pawdy had his 'fall', and was inspected by Lord Kitchener at Hackwood Park, Basingstoke, at the end of the month. On 27 June, the Division received orders to prepare for service at Gallipoli. I told Pawdy I was learning two songs at this stage about the battles in the Dardanelles, a location where so much Irish, British and Australian blood was spilled, to not much gain. The Dardanelles, which was an area of major strategic value to all sides of the War, is a narrow, natural strait and internationally-significant waterway in northwestern Turkey that forms part of the continental boundary between Europe and Asia, and separates Asian Turkey from European Turkey. One of the world's narrowest straits used for international navigation, the Dardanelles connects the Sea of Marmara with the Aegean and Mediterranean Seas, while also allowing passage to the Black Sea by extension via the Bosphorus. I enjoyed telling Pawdy the lyrics of a song named, 'Salonika', as some of the lyrics could have alluded to him but, he wasn't amused..

'Oh me husband's in Salonika and I wonder if he's dead,
And I wonder if he knows he has a kid with a foxy head,
So right away, so right away, so right away, so right away,
So right away Salonika, right away me soldier boy'.

'And The Band Played Waltzing Matilda', written by Aussie Eric Bogle, really hit the nail on the head with regard to the tragedy of the whole campaign, where thousands of Soldiers were sent to their death on open beaches with nowhere to gain cover and the Turks dug in with machine guns and cannon.

'And how well I remember that terrible day
How our blood stained the sand and the water

And of how in that hell that they called Suvla Bay
We were butchered like lambs at the slaughter
Johnny Turk, he was waiting, he'd primed himself well
He showered us with bullets and he rained us with shell
And in five minutes flat, he'd blown us all to hell
Nearly blew us right back to Australia'.

On 6th & 7th August 1915 the Division landed at Suvla Bay, less the 29th Brigade which went to ANZAC Cove. Anzac was the term used for soldiers from Australia and New Zealand. The main body made an attack on Chocolate Hill, on the 7th August. The Hill was so-called because the scorched grasses and scrub appeared chocolate in colour.

On 29th September 1915, the Division withdrew from Gallipoli and moved to Mudros, and on 4th October went on to Salonika.

From 1915 to 1918 the Division suffered a total of 9,363 officers and men killed, wounded or missing in action. One Irish Voice from Gallipoli said, 'When people back home talk of 'fighting to the finish', well give 'em a day of this and they'd be peace-mongers for the rest of their lives'. A second Irish Voice reported, 'Beautiful morning and not a breath of wind, and a slight haze which rapidly disappeared. The River Clyde, (The Troop Transporter) beached according to plan at 6:30 , none of us felt it, just a slight jar. Two companies of Dublin's were towed to shore and were met by terrific rifle and machine gun fire. They were literally slaughtered like rats in a trap. A third Irish Voice, Lieutenant Drummond Fish, a well known Artist who was with the 10th Division in Suvla described the scenery, 'The colours were the most wonderful thing about Gallipoli. There were mornings when the hills were as rose as peaches - times when the sea looked like the tail of some gigantic peacock, and the sands looked like great carpets of glittering cloth of gold - the place an inspiration in itself, and if beauty could have stopped a war, that scenery would have done it.'

As improbable as the latter description may be, in the face of such utter slaughter, my Grandfather, William Wood, 'Bill', was a contemporary of Pawdy's, and had joined the British Army before the Great War, and he also was able to see beauty in the face of the 'Beast'.

Just over one hundred years ago my, 'Grandpa Bill' was saddling up his horse, fettling his lance and polishing his brasses; the day to day stuff you would expect of a 12th Lancer. Riding into war was probably far from his mind. However, everything changed on the 28th July 1914, and both Will and his horse, 'Floss', boarded a troop ship and headed for France.

He never spoke about the carnage, and his stories centred on the futility of sending horses into this 'new kind' of war, his efforts to look after Floss, and how he was fascinated by the countryside and the wildlife in it. He was especially interested in how the land could heal itself, and that the animals could carry on their lives in spite of the war raging all around them. He was a countryman, like me, my Dad, and my Sons, and indeed Pawdy, his eyes and ears were awake to the sounds and smells, some familiar, some exotic; the birds, trees, butterflies and the flowers of Flanders fields.

I loved the stories of his 'ride-outs', as he called them, as they headed for the front line through Belgium and France, although some had tragic endings. It was during these conversations that his love of the natural world shone through.

In and around the Somme, he spent many weeks waiting 'behind the lines', always ready at a moment's notice to be called forward, and it was during this time that his horse, Floss, was requisitioned for other duties. Unlike the horse in Morpurgo's, 'Warhorse', Floss was spared the rigours of hauling canon, and she was used for carrying supplies to the front.

Grandpa talked about dragonflies on the marshes, swallows catching insects above the water, and the splash of water voles, as they dived beneath the margin willow and watercress; whether they drowned out the distant sound of gunfire and bomb blasts is another thing.

He joked that they were given no spoons in their field kit, so they had to shoot spoonbills and use their bill to eat soup; I think he was joking but, he also said that the abundance of ducks, storks, bitterns and herons, meant that they never went hungry, and that part of the tale is very likely to be true.

I am fairly sure that he was somewhere in the region of the Cavins Marshes, half way up the Somme River Estuary, an area where saltwater meets fresh. It was here a century ago that sheep grazed on the salt marsh, as they still do today, and a tick on my bucket-list, is to sample the meat of this particular animal as my Grandpa, a butcher for fifty years, once said, "We managed to nab a couple of the sheep that fed on the brackish lagoons and it was the finest meat I've ever tasted", and that recommendation is good enough for me.

He made it back from France, but didn't have much time to relax, and was soon packed off to Ireland just the Easter Rising in 1916. I have a postcard which he sent to his Brother from Dublin, which depicts the damage to O'Connell Street, and thereby began another story for another time.

Pawdy, Old Fez and Mr Brocklehurst, often asked me talk about my Grandpa, they were fascinated and one simple tale from the front-line which tickled them the most, apart from the thought of the Somme lamb, was how Grandpa Will buttered his bread with a bayonet. For the record, he held up the fresh unsliced loaf and spread butter on one end before then cutting off a slice. He continued to do this for the rest of his life, generally with a bread knife, and I've never seen or heard of anyone else buttering bread in this fashion. In explanation my Grandpa said, "It was easier to butter that way because as soon as you cut a slice and tried to butter it, the bread broke up". Makes sense to me. Fez, who had fought in the 1st World War was even more touched by the story of my Grandpa's which involved a march along country roads with a constant danger of entrenched German snipers. Grandpa Will was on the inside of a five abreast battalion, the middle man. They were belting out songs as they did, including Jack Judge's 'It's Long Way to Tipperary' written in Stalybridge, and spirits were good until a couple of stray bullets whizzed overhead. With no order to take cover the men kept on marching and it was then that one of my Grandpa's best pals who was on the outside of the marching line asked if he could swop places. Grandpa Will did as asked and you might have guessed what happened next. The sniper was in an elevated position, a Church Tower it turns out, and within five minutes of the switch a straight head-shot killed the lad who thought he might be safe.

Snipers were taught to harden themselves to what sometimes amounted to shooting sitting targets but many must have struggled as is obvious by this letter home from R.A. Chell, and British sniper in September 1915.

'After about fifteen minutes quiet watching - with my rifle in a ready position - I saw a capless bald head come up behind the plate. The day was bright and clear and I hadn't the slightest difficulty in taking a most deliberate aim at the very centre of that bright and shiny plate - but somehow I couldn't press the trigger: to shoot such a 'sitter' so deliberately in cold blood required more real courage than I possessed. After a good look round he went down and I argued with myself about my duty. My bald-headed opponent had been given a very sporting chance and if he were fool enough to come up again I must shoot him unflinchingly. I considered it my duty to be absolutely ready for that contingency. After about two minutes he came up again with added boldness and I did my duty. I had been a marksman before the war and so had no doubt about the instantaneousness of that man's death. I felt funny for days and the shooting of another German at 'stand-to' the next morning did nothing to remove those horrid feelings I had'.

Both my Dad and Grandpa have long gone but, life goes on, as in the Somme Marshes and I am now a Grandpa myself, to the beautiful Orlaith Edna Wood, daughter of my son Culain and partner Chloe. Grandpa Sean, it's got a nice ring to it. I look forward to telling her a few Great Great Grandpa Will stories.

After my third meeting with Pawdy, it had become a regular thing that he would catch my eye, and we'd exchange waves, and the times we got to have long chats were few but, eventful, as he spilled out his heart to me. On one occasion he described his girl, "She has the smile to fill this valley, and a voice to charm a badger from his hole," and so entranced was I with the story that, one time in the middle of the day, I asked him a question completely oblivious to a party of hikers who looked at me very strangely, and noticeably sped up to pass me by as I appeared to be talking to myself. They obviously couldn't see Pawdy, and over the years, me being fay, fae or fey, lead to a number of long standing relationships. Some people interpret the 'fey' as being spirits of some sort, and they even offer advice on how to interact, personally I believe being 'fey', is just the ability to be able to, in the first instance, see 'them', whatever you wish to call them, and secondly, having the calmness to be able to communicate in whatever way 'they' will allow. It's 'them' that call the shots in the relationship, and 'they' decide when you will see them, although, over the years, out of sheer devilment I decided to call them out but, more of that later. It may be a coincidence, or a happy accident but, with Pawdy hailing from across the Irish Sea, as do my family, with me Mam born in Dublin and the rest of her side from Carlow and Tipperary but, there is an old Irish notion, which could explain the Crowden-phenomenon, without having resort to any pseudo, or quasi religious rationalisation, which in my view is nonsense. Caol ait, pronounced, 'queal acth', is the idea that, there are some places where it is easier to have contact with those who have gone before, and although some writers have tried to flower this up by providing a kind of cliched travelogue of where you can find these locations, these feelings, for example, the Cliffs of Moher, Newgrange and St Peter's Basilica, which by the way are all wonderful places but, they are missing the point, because unless a person has the innate ability to unlock, see through, open the curtain or, more like, feel, these 'thin places' and the people in them, it's a waste of time. Just as, defining, as some have done, a 'thin place', as the gap between Heaven and Earth, and even, as an avenue which leads direct to God. In other words, the notion is sometimes hijacked by Religion, and you can read into that whatever you want. In hindsight, I now recall my schoolboy visits to the Confessional Box of a Catholic Church as my introduction to 'thin places' but, only in the sense that we were told, once the door was shut that, God and the Priest could see everything, and that, woe-betide, the lad that lied, because his tongue would turn black at the altar when receiving communion, and worse, that the Priest would then send him packing in front of the congregation mouth foaming. Those Christian Brothers certainly knew how to put the Fear of God into young kids when I was at school, however, I'm pleased to say that their bullying indoctrination had no affect on me, or at least I don't think it did. In my view, C. S. Lewis came closer to the mark than anyone in describing a 'thin place', his wardrobe, and when I read his observation, *"Someday you will be old enough to start reading fairy tales again"*, I felt very close to him.

Pawdy, told me that, as an Irishman in the British Army, he was abused daily and called all the names under the sun, by both officer and his English peers, and he felt that, like so many of his comrades who enlisted from Ireland that, they were regarded with suspicion, had arisen from the bog itself to cause mischief, and were surely part of the Uprising, even spies. Pawdy was part of nothing but, unfortunately for him, the abuse was similar back at home because, some would never understand why a 'true' Irishman could join the British Army. As a boy I had read Brendan Behan's, Borstal Boy, and the abuse Pawdy faced, seemed pretty much on a par with what was dished out to Behan while incarcerated. I think it hurt Pawdy more though, whereas Behan didn't give a damn. It always amused me that, Behan was surrounded by petty criminals, thugs and burglars, and he was incarcerated for being a member of the IRA and attempting to blow people up. The latter was obviously not humorous in any way, it was just the lack of segregation in those days which bemused me.

Pawdy meanwhile was none of these things, and as I see it, he just wanted to earn a few 'extra bob', as he called it, 'To send home to me Mammy.' I find it strangely comforting that I experienced these meetings, and find it somewhat amusing that, it never did bother me. As you will discover, many of my 'friends', and that is how I came to view them, presented no threat, and if they didn't show some days I was rather disappointed and found myself calling out, "What's up with you?" to no one in particular but, it should be noted that certain individuals showed up fairly often in the same place at the same time. You could set your clock by them to be honest.

It would appear that the reason Pawdy was always on his own was that, he would be singled out on a daily basis to return to the shooting-butts to clear up the spent cartridge cases, and some days they would be in the thousands but, as he told me, it didn't bother him because the Valley reminded him of home, and he'd just sit just up there admiring the view and dreaming of Mary, and something else close to his heart, Wicklow gold, a subject he would often return to.

"Ah Seanean, (As he liked to call me) Wicklow gold is like no other, and I'd be happy for sure with an ounce of her river ore, to make a ring for my Mary". Pawdy told me this in the early 1981, and according to my notes, we were stood by Crowden Little Brook and he had demonstrated how, back at home, he had panned for gold. Since those days I have seen some beautiful pieces of jewellry made of Wicklow Gold, and he wasn't far wrong, a Crucifix presented to Daniel O'Connell, being particularly exquisite, and very difficult to describe, especially in terms of colour but, a kind of soft red yellowy gold, is not a bad stab. This piece is now on permanent show at O'Connell's house at Darrynane Beg in County Kerry, which Pawdy was delighted to hear, as O'Connell was one of his great heroes, and he often quoted the, 'Liberator', as O'Connell was known, "The corrupt higher orders tremble for their vicious enjoyments". He was referring to the landed gentry, British Government and the Queen, I imagine.

"Der' still looking fer da stuff to be sure", explained Pawdy and I discovered that he was right when met a prospector on a trip to Wexford in June of 1981. He was called Willy, as Irish as the day is long but looked for all the world like an eccentric Englishman, dressed in tweed and bent double on the riverbank patiently panning and watching for the slightest glimmer of gold in the water. Willy had one small nugget in a little leather pouch, which to be honest looked like a wizened testicle tied up with a green braid, and this was maybe the size of a child's first tooth. "Wurth a fortune dat Fella", he said.

The hunt for Gold in Ireland continues to this day, and it was only in 2012 when one prospecting company hit, as they say in America, pay-dirt. A Dublin based mineral exploration firm has struck gold in the south west of the country, a find estimated to be worth tens of millions of dollars.

Neil Ring, Director of IMC Exploration Groups told RTE's 'Morning Ireland', television programme that, they had spent $400,000 on sample drilling. "It's a very, very significant high level, high grade find. The concentration of gold per tonne in the sample we have had assayed is 11.3 ounces. Now to put that into perspective, the Clontibret find in Monaghan a few years earlier was 1.24 grammes per tonne. 11 ounces is 354 grammes, so it's a very significant high level, high grade find."

Mid-chapter I took an inkling to visit Crowden again, and maybe see if Pawdy was still there as I was sure he would love to hear about the gold, and I was certain he would be keen to learn of the Ballinesker Hoard of Wexford Gold artifacts discovered in the early 1990's, although thinking about it he probably knew anyway being some kind of spirit and all-that. This find included priceless gold bracelets, fasteners and boxes.

As I jumped into my car, and bearing in mind that, at the time it was nine years since we had moved from Crowden I got to thinking that Pawdy and the others may not appreciate me writing about them, and I mean really overpowering thoughts with all manner of probably ridiculous scenarios running through my mind including that they may wish me to join them for good, and I even imagined all the kids in the graveyard at St James coming out to greet me and each child beseeching with pleading look on their ashen faces not to share my secrets with the world. Discretion being the better part of valour and all that, I recruited my wonderful fiddle playing friend India Shan Merrett and her dog Roddy to come with me.

India was immediately transfixed when I began to tell her some of my Crowden stories, and most of these stories have never been shared with anyone for over thirty years. I wondered whether we would catch a glimpse of my old Pal, Pawdy, mooching near the butts, or whether he'd be playing hard to get, and watching me, watching for him. Back in the day, these eye contact 'look backs of recognition' became my daily bread at Crowden., and not just with Pawdy. On this visit however and much to India's dismay Pawdy did not show but I felt him, especially when I showed India where the bullets were. India like so many before her filled her pockets.

I used to say to Pawdy, with regard to another of my 'friends' the 'Shining Girl' that, 'I'll be looking back, to see if she is looking back, to see if I am looking back at her!" I was messing about with a verse of 'Looking Back' by the Manchester Bluesman, John Mayall, and referring to my first glimpse of this beautiful girl. I said to Pawdy that, he should come and say hello but, he explained that, his kind could usually only move in some kind of perpetual loop, like a bat, following the same figure of eight nightly feeding-patrol for ever. Sounds grim but he seemed relatively happy with his lot, and besides, when I expressed concern over the longevity of his situation he said, "We can let go you know, at any time. We are here because we want to be". This unnerved me a bit but Shining Girl said the same, as she skipped away from me towards her long gone home, "I might see you again Sean, I might not', but more of her soon.

As I write, 9.15am, Saturday 20th May, 2017, 'things' are occurring which are difficult to explain. As you have just read, I had been writing about Pawdy, the Rifle Range and Crowden when my email pinged, so I clicked on my BT Yahoo Account, and there was an email from Ebay, the online Auction Site, alerting me to an item which was ending soon. It was a vintage postcard of 'Crowden from the Rifle Range', and there was a very familiar face in the foreground, 'Shining Girl', my erstwhile companion from Hey Edge is there on the left, with the smile I have already described, a few years younger perhaps as when she appeared to me but, thank the stars for early negatives in all their glorious detail, and with the franking on the reverse confirming 1919, as the date of posting you could accuse me of being smug when I say, I rest my case. I had never seen this postcard before, and I had certainly not bid on the item, and neither had I entered any search for photographs relating to Crowden, or the Rifle Range in recent weeks, so there was not much possibility of so-called 'cookies' tracking my browsing preferences or internet searches. Fortunately, I bid on the postcard and nearly three hours later it was on it's way to me, the best £4.90p I have spent for a long time.

Pawdy once compared his punches to an earthquake, bragging that his straight jabs often, 'Shook a fella to his boots!' and who was I to argue but, he never came across as a fighter, he was quiet, thoughtful, and although he did sometimes become animated and excited when he talked of certain fights, he would soon regain his composure and generally walk off without a by your leave. When I say walk off, one only needed to be distracted by the call of a cuckoo or some other bird, for Pawdy to be three hundred yards away in the blink of an eye, and only occasionally did he look back and acknowledge my existence. It was his Father, James, who had forced him in the direction of boxing when he was in his teens, and this as Pawdy told me was as a challenger to the Incumbent Champion of any travelling country fair, and even though his heart wasn't in it, so he said, it seems that he had a bit of a reputation, and this in turn lead to him being challenged by some of his peers and others when they had drink taken. "Sor I was dangerous but there was no harm in me and if I kilt a man, I'd wear a glove like Dan". It was remiss of me not to ask what he meant by 'wearing a glove like Dan', but the reason emerged during my research for this Chapter as you will discover shortly.

His love, Mary, at this stage, I'm thinking early 1915, had died, and although their relationship had never been consummated, and reading between the blurry-lines and scant mention of her, they had never even been out walking together but, as any broken-heart will know, the love stays.

All things considered, Pawdy, took up the offer of the King's Shilling, and a regular wage, away from Ireland, away from any reminders of Mary, and away from the poverty, only to find himself at Crowden, which he loved. The heather blown hills, brown trout brooks and hawthorn lined 'boreens', were his little home from home, without the trevails. Although 'frying pan to fire' comes to mind as he was ostracised by many of his comrades for his nationality, was was regarded with suspicion by some of the Officers, and he was also ridiculed for his awkward gait. Pawdy's Commanding Officer at the Rifle Range, was a Scot, who described him as, 'The gowk we' a hirple', meaning the 'fool with a limp'. In spite of the persecution, Pawdy insisted that, none of it really affected him, and that day to day life had been bearable at Crowden.

He was resigned to trouble and, so he told me, had developed a very thick skin. For several years, Pawdy, ignored my requests for information on his untimely demise, he thought that he had told me enough and, that he had showed himself to me because he knew I was able to see, 'Behind the door', and further that, 'There's no harm in ye', he said.

I always enjoyed that summation of my character, and still do down the years.

When I least expected it, Pawdy appeared one day as though in a hurry, flying along an old track way between the Rifle Range and Brockholes Sessile

Oakwood. It is an ancient pathway which only becomes really visible in winter when the bracken and disguising grasses have died down. Wooden carts, horses hooves and the feet of Medieval village folk had worn this track into the fabric of Crowden. 'Why the speed', I asked him, 'I have to go,' he replied, 'I may return one day but, you will have left Crowden by then.' 'Doubt it', I said, there's only one way I'll be leaving Bleak House', laughing out loud, maybe it was a nervous laugh, I don't know, but the thought of not living at Crowden seemed literally, unthinkable. The Valley was Heaven on Earth, and the only thing missing was children of our own, why would I ever want to leave. I wouldn't, and that was that.

'You'll see', he said, 'You'll soon be up to your elbows in shite wit' 'tree kids', and then assured me with a kind of riddle, which kept me second guessing for years; 'It will be a blessing when you leave', he continued, 'Because the pictures of your heart will be hanging on the wall'. With that, and me obviously puzzled, until over twenty years later, with two sons, Oisin and Culain, and a daughter Niamh, when we moved into the Old Co-op in Padfield and opened an Art Gallery.

Pawdy began to explain how he met his end, and the tale I now share, was the last thing he told to me and when he walked off, slowly now down the old lane, I never saw him again, it was November 1981.

It came as no surprise to me that, as Pawdy began to spill the beans, Old Fez appeared from the gate leading into the oakwood, now 'Brockholes Nature Reserve, "Hold on Lad', he said, 'I wanna hear this'. 'Come on so,' replied Pawdy, 'You are a 'Walker' just like me, and I tink Sor you have a good idea already do you not?' My head went into overdrive at that, they even have a name for themselves, 'Walkers', I like it, but Old Fez appears to have fooled me completely.

Maybe not intentionally, as for some reason not only did I not ask but, I didn't catch the slightest hint that he wasn't alive and kicking. 'I'll speak to you later', I said to Old Fez with a big grin on my face, shaking my head in disbelief. Pawdy, for his part was also amused, and his parting shot began something like this. 'Right Sor, while on a few days leave from Crowden, I was in O'Donoghue's on Baggot Street, Dublin, with a few of da lads, and we got to talking about boxing, and in particular about a fella with an even longer reach than me, Dan Donnelly. When he died they dug the poor critter up to measure them, and Jasus, worse than that, there's a pub on the Curragh that has one of his arms in a glass case, like a long skinny pike, all wrinkled and wizened with age.' Pawdy then gave me another one of his knowing looks, and said, 'You will know all about O'Donoghue's and the Curragh yourself before too long'. I knew the pub he meant but, wasn't sure what he was inferring, and besides I wanted to hear more about the 'fella' with the long reach, and what it had to do with Pawdy's demise.

Donnelly was an ungainly 6 foot 6 inch boxer who, having worked for a trainer at Maddenstown on the Curragh of Kildare, ended up defeating the English champion George Cooper in what was considered the prize-fight of the century in 1815. Donnelly's arms were so extraordinarily long that he could reputedly button his knee breeches without stooping. Thousands of gentry and country-people alike gathered to witness his victory. The fight took place in a hollow near the Athgarvan end of the Curragh, where it is commemorated by a small limestone obelisk.

Donnelly was born in the docks of Dublin, Ireland in March 1788, the ninth of his mother's 17 children. He had worked as a carpenter earlier in his adult life.

He fought at a time when boxing was of the bare-knuckles variety and bouts had no time limits. He took part in only three major fights, winning each of them. His first triumph was over Tom Hall at the Curragh on September 14, 1814 in front of 20,000 spectators. His second victory on December 13, 1815, at the same location and with a similarly-sized crowd, was his most celebrated and a source of Irish pride because his opponent, George Cooper, was from England, which still ruled Ireland at the time. Donnelly broke Cooper's jaw in the eleventh round of the 22-minute match, and collected the prize of sixty pounds.

A squat, weather-beaten, grey monument surrounded by a short iron fence marks the exact site, which has been called Donnelly's Hollow since the bout. The inscription reads: DAN DONNELLY BEAT COOPER ON THIS SPOT 13TH DEC. 1815.

In his third and final fight on July 21, 1819, he defeated Tom Oliver in 34 rounds on English turf, at Crawley Down in Sussex.

He had a reputation for being a gambler, a womanizer and a drunkard, so he wasn't all bad then. After his victory over Cooper, Donnelly was the proprietor of a succession of four Dublin pubs, all of them unprofitable and Fallon's Capstan Bar is the only one still in existence.

He died at Donnelly's Public House, the last tavern he owned, on February 18, 1820 at the age of 32. An oval wall plaque commemorates the site of his death and he was buried in an unmarked vault at Dublin's Bully's Acre cemetery, near the Royal Hospital Kilmainham. Unfortunately for Dan, his grave was no place of rest and the interest in his unfeasibly long arms only grew with his death, and as Pawdy said, his body was soon removed by grave-robbers and sold to the highest bidder, a Dublin Surgeon.

One of his arms subsequently found itself in Scotland at the University of Edinburgh's medical college, where it was disinfected, lacquered and used in anatomy lessons. It was next exhibited at an English travelling circus before returning to Ireland in 1904 when Texas McAlevey, a Belfast bookmaker/bartender acquired it to first put on display at his bar, before relegating it to the attic of his betting shop. James Byrne, the proprietor of the Hideout Olde World Pub in Kilcullen, County Kildare received it in 1953 from a wine merchant who had purchased it just for fun. This was where the mummified arm would be showcased for the next 43 years. The trophy limb was the subject of a February 20, 1995 Sports Illustrated article. Desmond Byrne, son of the late

James and current owner of Donnelly's arm, removed it from public viewing in 1996 when he sold the Hideout.

Pawdy, knew about the legend that was Tom Donnelly and had decided that a visit to the Hollow was in order, not least to pay his respects to Dan Donnelly, and he was accompanied by a couple of drinking partners from Dublin who were a little sceptical about the whole thing. With money in his pocket, porter in his belly and a couple of days left on leave, before he was to return to England, Pawdy hired a driver to take them out from the city, and it is here that the story becomes a little hazy, not least because by the end of it Pawdy was dead.

Reading between the lines, and piecing together the bits that Pawdy could remember, it seems that, after a few drinks, in the bar, the very pub that it in time would display Donnelly's Arm from 1953, things got out of hand, no pun intended.

As the saying goes, 'boys will be boys', and after talking about the huge wagers which were placed by the Dublin elite on Donnelly's fights, Pawdy threw down a challenge to his fellow drinkers, and also to a couple of 'young bucks', who happened to be in the pub at the same time. "Ten shillings to the lad who is first to run to the rim of the Hollow to Donnelly's Stone three times, and then back to the bar and drink a pint of porter!" shouted Pawdy.

They were off, and even with his 'gammy' leg Pawdy was doing well but, his efforts were short-lived, and although we will never know whether his Mother's, "It'll end in tears Pawdy", came back to haunt him, he slipped and fell head-long against the metal railings surrounding Donnelly's Memorial Stone. No more than a foot high but, Pawdy's head was no match for the unforgiving cast iron, and he collapsed onto to the grass, little rivers of blood spread out around his head like a giant red halo. Pawdy told me, "The last words I heard came from one of the other fellas as he turned me over, "Jasus lads, da big fella, he's stone dead!"

Parts of the Pawdy jigsaw were still missing and even Old Fez, wasn't sure how Pawdy, came to be at Crowden. Fez had said that he would love to know more but went on to say that, "Pawdy Blanche was not the only odd-bod to arrive at the Rifle Range tha knows". Riddles followed by even more riddles was the order of the day with the 'Walkers'.

Pawdy's earlier riddle, concerning the Curragh of Kildare and O'Donoghue's Pub in Dublin was solved much faster than the puzzle he threw my way about having children and owning an Art Gallery. A matter of months after my last sighting of Pawdy I received a phone call from a well known musician from Manchester, Eamonn O'Neal, who was interesting in forming a Irish band. He had already teamed up with the Ushers including Caroline on fiddle, Angela on banjo and young Paul, sixteen at the time, and he wanted myself and my singing partner Martin Coult to join. I would like to say it was me but, I think Eamonn came up with the name, 'Curragh', and although the original band only lasted for twelve months in one way another the name has stuck with me for nearly forty years, latterly the Curragh Sons, as in the Sons of Curragh, and over one thousand performances.

It was on our first tour of Ireland in 1984 when O'Donoghue's pub featured on the itinerary, and although we were due to play at Kevin Conneff of the Chieftains club, Slattery's, on Capel Street later that day, we all piled into O'Donoghue's for a lunchtime music session downstairs and a few pints of Guinness. It would have been very rude not to, as this is where the Dubliners started out and every Irish Musician worth their salt had played in Slattery's at some stage. Paying homage to the Masters. There are a few Irish bands and musicians who I would rate higher than the lads from the Dubliners, perhaps Paul Brady, Planxty, the Clancy Brothers and Tommy Makem but, as they were the first group I ever saw aged 10 at the De Montfort Hall in Leicester, and also because we always include one or two of their songs in our set-list to this day, these boys are up there for me. The craic at Slattery's was, if you were any good then you got invited upstairs for sandwiches and a few more pints of Arthur's finest drop. So smiles all round when we were beckoned to the hallowed ground of fame and joy of joys, and no pressure then, as the Dubliners were there in person as well as covering the walls.

We were kind of awestruck I suppose that afternoon as Ronnie Drew held court in that neat little boozer by St Stephen's Green, "Sing me your heart's favourite", he said to me, and when I chose to sing the Ewan MacColl song, 'Freeborn Man', he smiled as wide as the mouth of the Liffey. After an hour or so Ronnie made his farewells and left me with a pearl of wisdom which I like to think I have adhered to all my life.

"Sean", he said, "If I had all the money I had spent on drink, I'd spend it on drink".

Pawdy did not show but I reckon he could have been there somewhere in the fabric of the building singing along but, with so many folk in there I couldn't 'pick up on him' anywhere, and I did try.

I dedicated this book to 'Me Mam' Claire, and that was before I discovered a remarkable gift from beyond her woodland grave on the book-deadline day Friday 24th November 2017. She had kept the programme from the Dubliners concert fifty four years ago, and not only that it was signed on the front cover by Dominic Behan, Brendan's brother, and on the back cover by the Dubliners themselves, Barney McKenna, John Sheahan, Luke Kelly, priceless, and Ciarán Bourke but no Ronnie Drew. He was in the bar obviously.

Chapter Three:
First Contact with the Shining Girl:

The 'Shining Girl' first appeared as a blur in the distance, and although from where I was standing, I thought she looked like a girl of teenage years, I could not be one hundred percent sure, as she skipped and marched along the Salt Road singing out loud to herself. I had caught sight of her as I tramped in the mud of the old trackway which led to Hey Farm, it still does in fact. And although most of the walls of the farm buildings were intact, save for the stone roof slates, which had been removed and stacked at the back of the house during the 1st World War when the incumbent farm-hand enlisted. This de-roofing was common practice at the time, so that the owner of the building would be exempt of any tax, as the farmhouse was uninhabitable. Thirty odd years later I still remember this short poem which I wrote, most inappropriately in my North West Water Diary, after my first visit one of many hundreds to Hey Farm.

> *There's only one wall still standing,*
> *And the roof has long fallen in but,*
> *The House and it's Spirit are living,*
> *And I'm sitting here thinking of them,*
> *Knowing full well that*
> *One day,*
> *I too will be gone.*

Eight years earlier when I was living in Argyll, I met a lovely old man, who gave me a lift when I was hitchhiking between Lochgilphead and Oban, and he wrote a short, Highland proverb in the back of my sketch pad, and wished me well in my life. His words, like mine, are simple and prophetic.

Breac à linne, slat à coille is fiadh à fireach - mèirle às nach do ghabh gàidheal riamh nàire.

A fish from the river, a staff from the wood and a deer from the mountain - thefts no Highlander was ever ashamed of. I would like to add one more autobiographical line to this proverb from my play with songs, The Angel On O'Connell Street, (2107) *'At least once steal beauty in your life'.*

Funny how these things stay with you. My first wife Moira and I tried to buy Hey Farm from North West Water but, they would not sell as the property was inside what they called the 'Water Catchment Area', or in other words, the rain which fell on the farm and surrounding land eventually reached the Reservoir and they were very strict about these things. Eventually a local farmer took out the eaves and re-roofed the farm with tin sheets for a sheep shelter and used the flagged byre for shearing and the like. At least the place was being used but it would have been an amazing place to live, still would.

I was delighted to discover during the writing of this chapter that Hey Farm has a name check in the aforementioned *'The Extent of the Lordships of Longdendale' (1361)* which with one small reference and the name on a map of the Valley dates the place to several hundred years earlier than I had first thought.

The little farm on the hill had become a regular haunt of mine, not least because it was in an ideal position to watch the world go by, and perhaps more importantly, to spot any bosses who may have been scouring the Valley for me, as I could see the main A628, the now disused Railway Line, and the single-track road beyond the tracks which meandered towards Lodge Farm where the Gamekeeper lived. I would get a phone call later in the day from Stan Arnfield along the lines of "Hello Sean, we came up today as we needed to operate the valves at the Dam but, we couldn't find you to get in", he said. "Yes, I saw you, I was unblocking a load of debris half way up Shining Clough, it was getting dangerous, and it took me hours to shift it. It was about one-o'clock and you were just turning up the Holmfirth Road?" I replied, "That's right," said Stan, " Don't worry I had a key anyway and it only took me five minutes." So there I was, happy as a sandboy, still stealing beauty and timber, poaching that trout and eating the venison. Sound advice from a Highlander in 1971.

I remember however, feeling a slight pang of guilt, with flask and sandwiches in hand, wheatear for company, skylarks overhead, and being paid for the privilege. It didn't take me long to ascertain that the bosses did not go in for much walking, and a little subterfuge was the order of the day as a modern-day Reservoir Keeper.

There was a small plantation of pine between myself and the Shining Girl, and the trees were referred to as, an 'amenity planting', a great idea in theory but, they need looking after, and unlike the dead trees which I complained about further down the Valley, many of these needed thinning out, and a few relict ash and one lonely sessile oak setting free to see the light of day once more.

Fortunately I had my binoculars with me, and trained them on the girl, the Shining Girl, and she appeared to be around seventeen, or eighteen years old, and it did not occur to me what she might be doing on her own at Crowden at 1pm on a Monday afternoon in May 1980, and in hindsight, neither did it enter my head that, my actions may have appeared somewhat suspicious. But then again, why would it, I was not spying on her, it was my job to observe who was entering the 'Water Catchment Area' on behalf of North West Water, and obviously at this early stage in my tenure I was at least attempting to show due deference to the long line of punctilious Water Men who came before me.

Shining Girl must have sensed that I was watching her, and she stared right back up the hill in my direction and down through the mirrored lenses of my expensive Swarovski eyeglasses, into immediate and devastating eye-contact and from there, plummeted, deep and deeper into my cave-like soul, and thence to bounce around uncontrollably like a drunken speleologist in all of the hidden spaces of no return, sump to muddy sump, and back again.

Her eyes were the blue of cornflowers, and as dazzling as dappled early morning sun on a trout stream; clear and lustrous, as the brightest day in Bright Town, and her hair the colour of a field of ripening barley, rippling like curly kinetic staves as she moved through the air. She was 'shining' for sure, and kind of floating and so was I; there is a word for it I'm sure but, I was a gonner with the strangest sensation in the pit of my stomach. Eviscerated comes close, as does the more prosaic 'gralloched', Highland once more and meaning the removal of innards, and this normally on the hill to make carrying the carcass home much easier. There was nothing humdrum about this episode, this micro-moment in my life, and I was the Monarch of the Glen brought to my knees. This old stag has been laid low twice subsequently but for different reasons, when my first wife left after twenty years, and then my second wife, Nicole, decided to up sticks after another twenty years in 2017. Both relationships with so many successes and fun, and children who I would die for but, I guess it's a tough assignment living with me with a head like a sieve and plagued by Van Gogh's Curse. Having said that they both know they were and always will be loved, and you can't say fairer than that.

Shining Girl, understood intuitively the effect she had upon me and as I raised the glasses once more, her smile issued the coup de grace.

Leaning against the lacerated trunk of a tipsy sitka spruce, I was hoping for an unaided glimpse of Shining Girl's progress, and my nose came to rest by a bubble of oozing resin, the unctuous nature and comforting smell of which has stayed with me ever since but, more importantly on this occasion, the wind had dropped enabling me to hear what she was singing, which also allowed me to understand the significance of her dramatic marching and skipping.

The song, she informed me, during our first conversation a week later was, *'The Wreck of the Hesperus'*, with lyrics written by the American Poet, Henry Wadsworth Longfellow, and recalled the sinking of a merchant ship of the same name in 1839. My dad had used the expression to describe my bedroom and other things he thought were a mess but, I never thought to ask what he was referring to.

It could never be described as a simple song, and it was not the sort of ditty sung in the school playground of her younger days but nevertheless, the Shining Girl, was giving it all she could in terms of performance, hence the marching, the skipping, and the flourishing of hands as a fully paid up performer in an old time Music Hall. The kind of show which were very popular in the 19th and early 20th Century.

"My Father used to play the song on his upright piano, in a rather staccato fashion, which is why I got the idea to sing and dance like an Italian marionette whenever I am singing it", she told me. However, she could equally have told me that, the moon was made of chocolate, and that my first delivery would arrive by spaceship the next day and I would have believed her.

Shining Girl felt a strong affinity with the 'tragic daughter' in the song, and she performed it rather well. She was a showgirl and as I later discovered, her 'uncle' had taken her to a local theatre, in Ashton Under Lyne on a number of occasions, and she had also seen the world famous, Buffalo Bill & His Outriders extravaganza.

Buffalo Bill Cody was also a constant companion of my childhood, along with Davy Crockett, Wyatt Earp and other fictional characters such as Tex Tucker and Roy Rogers but, Cody was the real-thing; a rider for the pony express, a frontier scout, a buffalo hunter, and a veteran of the so-called 'Indian Wars', and probably the most famous American of his day.

Shining Girl said, "The number of people in Glossop, trebled overnight, and all of us Valley Folk walked the seven miles just to see the spectacle".

On the morning of the 17th October 1904, Buffalo Bill and his Rough Riders, piled into the town after performing in Ashton Under Lyne two days earlier. Eight hundred men, women and children; cowboys, native Americans, including Sioux, Cheyenne and Cherokee; blacksmiths, doctors and cooks; five hundred horses and a host of wagons and equipment. Mottram Moor, as busy as it is today.

The Town Worthies would have been nervous, as they would have heard that 'Charlie Little Soldier', in his full native regalia, was found worse for wear on the streets of Derby, two Native Americans had died in another town, and the Grand Master himself had been seen relaxing with a pint of Bass Ale in Burton. Derek Slack, of Glossop, was also told of an incident by his grandfather, when Buffalo Bill went into the Norfolk Arms, Glossop, and saw a West Indian cricketer called Olivera, who played for Glossop and was very popular in the town. Apparently Buffalo Bill called for him to get out, whereas the regulars picked the show-man up and threw him out instead.

The visit was partly funded by Samuel Hill Wood, who went on to finance Arsenal Football Club, and the show included Sitting Bull and Annie Oakley. It is said he stabled some of his most valuable horses in stables behind the former Roebuck Inn on Whitfield Cross. The 'Show' was set for the fields of Pye Grove.

There was more to Shining Girl's so-called 'uncle' than meets the eye, and reading between the lines, because she would never be completely explicit about their trips in his 'motoring car', as she called it but she did explain how she felt trapped, like the girl in the song, and that she could never tell her parents, particularly her father. "He wouldn't believe me", she often said whenever I broached the subject.

The song describes an ill-fated voyage through winter storms, when the Captain brings his daughter on board the Hesperus for company. The Captain ignores the advice of one of his more experienced hands, who fears that a huge storm is about to hit. When the storm arrives, the Captain ties his daughter to the mast to prevent her from being swept overboard. The situation goes from bad to worse, and she calls out to her dying father as she hears the surf beating on the shore, then prays to God to calm the seas. The ship crashes onto the reef at Norman's Woe, off the coast of Gloucester, Massachusetts, and sinks. The next morning a horrified fisherman finds the daughter's body, still tied to the mast and drifting in the surf. The poem ends with a prayer that all be spared such a fate, *"on the reef of Norman's Woe."*

Longfellow combined fact and fiction to create this poem, the inspiration being the great storm which had ravaged the north east coast of the United States for 12 hours, on January 6th, 1839, destroying 20 ships with a loss of 40 lives. "The Wreck of the Hesperus" is based on two events: an actual shipwreck at Norman's Woe, after which a body like the one in the poem was found, and the real wreck of the Hesperus which took place near Boston. You can't beat a good bit of artistic licence but, when I actually read the lyrics for this book, I found that the song could have portrayed Shining Girl, as though Longfellow had read my earlier word picture of the beauty which she indeed was.

> *It was the schooner Hesperus,*
> *That sailed the wintry sea;*
> *And the skipper had taken his little daughtèr,*
> *To bear him company.*
> *Blue were her eyes as the fairy-flax,*
> *Her cheeks like the dawn of day,*
> *And her bosom white as the hawthorn buds,*
> *That ope in the month of May.*

The skipper he stood beside the helm,
His pipe was in his mouth,
And he watched how the veering flaw did blow
The smoke now West, now South.
Then up and spake an old Sailòr,
Had sailed to the Spanish Main,
I pray thee, put into yonder port,
For I fear a hurricane.
Last night, the moon had a golden ring,
And to-night no moon we see!"
The skipper, he blew a whiff from his pipe,
And a scornful laugh laughed he.....

I will spare readers the full nine or ten verses but, suffice to say, the Captain ignored the advice until it was too late, and it was within the lyrics that I spotted so many metaphors for what was happening with Shining Girl's so-called 'Uncle'. I just wished I had learned them at the time of our 'contact', then perhaps she could have 'left' the hillside earlier than she did because, it was several years before she sat me down and painted the full picture, which she had been trying to allude to in her own genteel fashion. In a scenario similar to those played out daily on our TV screens, she had been abused by Uncle Jack on countless occasions and although obviously when I met her in the early 1980's, it was much too late to do anything to help her, as she was long dead, I think Shining Girl was very pleased to be able to, finally share her story, and on reflection, it was soon after this revelation that our contact ceased for a time. I did miss her and thought about her every day until she came back.

The song concludes with...

At daybreak, on the bleak sea-beach,

A fisherman stood aghast,
To see the form of a maiden fair,
Lashed close to a drifting mast.
The salt sea was frozen on her breast,
The salt tears in her eyes;
And he saw her hair, like the brown seaweed,
On the billows fall and rise.
Such was the wreck of the Hesperus,
In the midnight and the snow!
Christ save us all from a death like this,
On the reef of Norman's Woe!

In hindsight she had first tried to tell me something had been happening with her 'uncle', soon after I realised that she was a 'walker', which was almost immediately, and more interestingly, many years later when I discovered that she did not have to walk too far from her family home at Enterclough to spill the beans, as the house was a stone's throw from my vantage point at Hey Farm and five minutes from the track which skirts the top-side of the closely planted pine.

To that point in 1992, when we bought Bleak House, the first private owners of the iconic property, so named by long gone residents for obvious reasons, Enterclough to me, was a bend in the A628 where the clough went under the road and into the watercourse, or if necessary, and at times of heavy rain, via sluices into the Woodhead Reservoir. There are a series of valves at this spot which I would be instructed to operate from time to time, and I assumed, wrongly it transpired, that Enterclough was simply, where the 'clough' or gully, 'entered' the reservoir. As the first people to purchase Bleak House, it turned out that when it came to paper-work with regard to the property, there was none but our Solicitor, Tony Wright, of Aspinal & Wright in Glossop, he is a tenacious kind of guy who wouldn't take no for an answer, and he eventually turned up a remarkable hand-drawn plan for the site which Bleak House would eventually stand in. The management of Manchester Corporation were obviously lining up their ducks for when the reservoirs were to be built, and had earmarked a raised spot on a bend in the road, with good views of the valley where the reservoir would eventually be.

Across the top of the plan, was the name Tollemache, finely drawn, and in the best Victorian handwriting. He was the landowner, who dropped lucky when it was decided to construct the reservoirs, and he owned a large portion of the valley, a bit like winning the mid-19th Century 'Big One'. The Bleak House was not shown but, the plan, extended beyond the small parcel of land intended for the property, and Hey Farm, the Salt Road, and the bend in the Toll Road, later the A628, were all there, and then, bingo, as I traced the line of a small track leading directly from the side of the Salt Road, and out across the valley, where the water would be. It was heading for the Lodge Farm, before falling off the edge of the faded paper but, passing the distinct outline of several houses bunched together fifty or sixty yards down a slope and beyond where the sluices now sit and there it was, in sepia tones, the words Enterclough. Shining Girl's family, before Bateman had left his mark lived in the small hamlet of Enterclough, and somewhere under one hundred and fifty years of silt stands the remains of their house.

Shining Girl explained, "Father talked very fondly of the house at Enterclough, and apparently the whole family were very upset when they were forced to move down to Crowden, as nice as it is. I was always drawn to the area. Even when I was alive I enjoyed sitting where you sit at Hey Farm, and imagining father, and my grandfather going about their business. Like you I am able to see other 'walkers' but, never as far as I am aware have I ever seen my grandparents, so hopefully they are at rest".

Top Left : Sean, age 3 at Southend

Top Right : The 'Bird Room', St Martin's, 1975

Middle : Sean at 18, Achnamara, Argyll

Bottom Right : Sean and Scarba, Didsbury Intake 1979

Top Left : Bleak House

Middle Left : St James looking towards Torside Reservoir

Bottom Left : St James and Bleak House, Chris Peate

Top Right : Crowden village circa 1905

WOODHEAD FOOT PATROL
(1st DRAFT)

PATROL W.2.

From the Keepers House proceed down to the Etherow Residuum Lodge Number 2
inspecting sluices etc. Proceed alongside the masonry spring watercourse
in a westerly direction to Crowden Upper Weir and examine the springs near
the old rifle range. Continue down to Crowden Lower Weir inspecting the
works in the vicinity. Return to the spring watercourse and continue to
Ash Tree Farm site then return to Crowden. Attend to the sewage pump as
required. Return to the line of the Millowners' watercourse and follow it
through to Etherow Pool Weir and thence on the Derbyshire side, visiting the
various wells and springs, manholes on the foul water pipes etc., below
Woodhead embankment. The screen filters in the Brown Springs supply tank
must be examined and cleaned with the inlets being cleared of weed and
floating debris. Check that the ram is in working order. Examination must
also be made of the water which issues from the original Reservoir discharge
tunnel at the mid-point of the embankment. Any unusual discolouration must
be reported immediately to the Engineer. Continue down the main road to the
quarry about 200 yards from Wilmer Clough East stream returning by the Skew
Arch and Paper Mill Spring to Crowden Station and the embankment. Return
home to Keepers House.

Top : Patrol Route   Bottom Left : Sean on Torside Edge 1980
Bottom Right : Sean at 26 with Griselda, Golden Eagle, Bleak House 1980

Irish enlistment poster

Top Left : Shining Girl at Crowden early 20th Century

Top Right: Rifle Range Crowden early 20th Century, Shining Girl on the left.

Middle Right: Rifle Range Target Practice

Bottom right: Rifle Range circa 1930's

Top Left : The Angel

Top Right : Woodhead Reservoir overflow circa 1930

Bottom Left : Crossley 1909

Bottom Right : Margaret Wagstaff and her daughter Christine outside the 'Cafe' at Crowden, circa 1910.

Top Left : Woodhead Road outside Tintwistle

Top Right : Casa Bateman, Albufera

Middle right : Kenny Leveret and Wendy Marsden 1981

Bottom right : Midden Find, snobs, marbles and majolica

Chapter Four:
Shining Girl, Spain and Swamp Rats:

Shining Girl's 'Uncle' was no relation at all but rather 'a friend of the family', and it would appear that he first abused her soon after the turn of the 20th century when, I'm guessing, she was six or seven. Her uncle was around sixty years old at this time and had known Shining Girl's grandfather, before ingratiating himself with Shining Girl's father and mother.

Her uncle's car, was the talk of the region, a Crossley, which must have looked out of place at Crowden, when her seven litre engine roared into the village. I have to confess I had never heard of a Crossley motor car, but not only have discovered facts and figures to swell the heart of any vintage car buff, I also turned up some tantalising strands which knit quite seamlessly into the fabric of my story, well almost anyway.

The first Crossley cars were introduced in 1904 built to a design by the company Chief Engineer, J S Critchley, who had previously been with Daimler, and his associate, W. M. McFarland. The intention was to build an 'English Mercedes'. The first car available was a 22hp, shortly followed by a larger 40hp, both models had 4 cylinder engines cast in two pairs and featured chain drive to the back axle, and had many advanced features including pump cooling, lightweight pistons, an automatic carburetor and internal expanding brakes. As was the custom of the time the cars could be supplied complete, or in chassis form which resulted in a wide variety of coachwork. Until the opening of the dedicated Crossley Motors factory in 1907 production is believed to have been limited, actual production numbers are not known, with many components being bought in, and one report describes the chassis of these being *'..built by one of the leading French makers'*. At least one 22hp (4760cc) model is known to have been exported to Australia in 1905, and a 22hp engine was also supplied to Henry Ford who fitted it to one of his cars.

Cars were entered in the Tourist Trophy Races as early as 1905 but with little success. However in April 1906 Charles Jarrott used a 40hp Crossley to set the London to Monte Carlo record. His record was beaten a month later by a Rolls-Royce but he regained it for Crossley for a while in 1907.

What is thought to be the sole survivor of this era is the massive 1909 40hp (7 litre) model on display in the Manchester Museum of Science and Industry. When I first read that, I thought I had really dropped lucky but the trail to link the Shining Girl's Uncle to this particular vehicle went cold on me. I suppose, as the eternal optimist, I should take comfort that, the initial provenance of the car, is unclear, and it is only, 'thought', to have been owned by music hall star, Marie Lloyd. This knowledge set me off a thinking, actually hoping out loud, that there was some connection with the Crossley again, not least because the Shining Girl had mentioned her trip to the Liverpool Empire in 1914, to watch a performance by Lloyd. Shining Girl appeared grateful to her 'uncle' for this trip out but, we should bear in mind that, these days (2017) it is well known that many 'abusers' turn out to be known to the families, and they groom their victims. Some abusers get into the minds of the victims so much that, they become almost 'grateful' for the attention. Shining Girl did fall into this category but at the same time she also told me that she hated him. Having seen the upholstered bench seat in the back of the Crossley, I can only but shudder at the thought of Shining Girl's degradation in the relative opulence of the luxury coach-work. I actually gave the Shining Girl a hug on one occasion when she alluded to what went on in the vehicle and became very upset at the memories. I remember thinking, it was odd because the hug 'worked', in that, I didn't just grasp thin air and actually felt her body.

It is nigh impossible to understand what it must be like to be a victim of abuse but for certain a nightmare to feel the necessity to play the game, act out a lie and stick to the story you are instructed to tell or else. Having said all that, Shining Girl still harboured some kind of 'feelings' for the bastard of an 'Uncle'. She even repeated one his favourite stories concerning the 'near the knuckle' performances of Marie Lloyd, who was well known for her risque innuendo and downright smut on stage, a kind of early 'Carry On Girl'. The story goes that, as a result of complaints, Lloyd was summoned to perform some of her songs in front of a Local Authority Committee. She sang "Oh! Mr Porter", "A Little of What You Fancy", and "She Sits Among the Cabbages and Peas".

The numbers were sung in such a way that the committee had no reason to find anything amiss, although when the Committee, 'got', the joke in the latter song, she retitled it, "I Sits Amongst the Cabbages and Leeks", which they missed completely after protests, and, I'm presuming, they missed completely that she was having one more laugh at their expense.

As for what became of the Crossley, it is known to have been bought second hand in 1912 by Sir Thomas Tacon, then the High Sheriff of Suffolk, and remained in the family until 1952 when it was bought by Mr Bill Westwood who kept it until 1995 when the Museum of Science and Industry in Manchester acquired it.

When Shining Girl's uncle came calling, he invariable pulled up outside the Commercial Public House which was first on the left as you entered the village from the Tintwistle side. He would typically have a couple of beers and then walk along the lane, of no name which runs by the present day campsite, and call at Shining Girl's house, where her mother would offer him tea and cake before he walked off back down the lane with Shining Girl at his side. 'Uncle' had personal tragedy to play on, and I'm guessing the fact that he had lost both a son and a daughter in quick succession, and then his wife, caused the 'family' to feel sorry for him. Shining Girl never criticised her parents once.

The story was that she 'did' for him, which was a colloquial term for cleaning and perhaps a bit of simple cooking. When I chanced at interpreting the 'did' into a more sinister meaning, Shining Girl, would walk away and, if really cross, just not be there. I would like to say 'disappear' but it never felt like that, because it was obvious to me that she was still there, and had just decided to, not let me see her. I never once brought up the subject of her uncle's actions but, was always prepared to listen if she wanted to talk about it. She never did, except for the very early days of our time together, and then only hinted at it, and even when I once became a little frustrated with her, advising that if she got it off her chest she could 'let go', and finally have some peace, she snapped back and said, "I have told you before Sean Wood", (It wasn't good news when Shining Girl used my 'Sunday Name', not good at all) "I could 'go' now, if I so wished, so please just be here, and I will be as happy as I can be". I wasn't going anywhere, I had two lives, one with the living, and another with the walkers, what could go wrong?

As a matter of interest I listened to other songs of the day intent on singing one or two to Shining Girl to watch her reaction but shuddered when I heard the lyrics of one of the most popular Music Hall songs of the day...'After The Ball'.

> *A little maiden climbed an old man's knees—*
> *Begged for a story: "Do uncle, please!*
> *Why are you single, why live alone?*
> *Have you no babies, have you no home?"*
> *"I had a sweetheart, years, years ago,*
> *Where she is now, pet, you will soon know;*
> *List to the story, I'll tell it all:*
> *I believed her faithless after the ball."*

"Bright lights were flashing in the grand ballroom,
Softly the music playing sweet tunes.
There came my sweetheart, my love, my own,
'I wish some water; leave me alone.'
When I returned, dear, there stood a man
Kissing my sweetheart as lovers can.
Down fell the glass, pet, broken, that's all—
Just as my heart was after the ball."

"Long years have passed, child, I have never wed,
True to my lost love though she is dead.
She tried to tell me, tried to explain—
I would not listen, pleadings were vain.
One day a letter came from that man;
He was her brother, the letter ran.
That's why I'm lonely, no home at all—
I broke her heart, pet, after the ball."

Although Tin Pan Alley was established in the 1880s, it only achieved national prominence when Charles K. Harris's 'After the Ball' sold two million pieces of sheet music in 1892 alone. The sentimentality of 'After the Ball' ultimately helped sell over five million copies of sheet music, making it the biggest hit in Tin Pan Alley's long history. The song was a tearjerker, a melodramatic evocation of lost love. No surprise Shining Girl did not see it the same way.

If I recall correctly one particular day in June, the morning had begun as normal, and all of my levels, rain, temperature, wind and water-depth, had been phoned in to Bottoms Office, and I was heading for Hey Edge and the woods on the HolmFirth Road looking for long eared owls which were nesting there. This was a glorious piece of English countryside, long eared owls calling in the night and visible during the day if you were prepared to disturb them now again and watch their ear-tufts stick up in alarm at your presence. I wouldn't normally do this around nesting time and there is a big fine attached to knowingly moving about near a nest site of protected birds of prey, and quite right too. It was fairly safe to show people, now and again where the long-eared roosted though, and as for the diurnal, or daytime flying owl, you could never gauge when they would show up but it was always an absolute joy. By the reservoir side, or 1,000 feet up on the moor, this gem of a bird would fly into my life on a daily basis as they quartered the hillside for short-tailed field voles, sometimes almost in my face if I ventured too close to the nest on the ground, and one time in the calm after a snowstorm, eye to eye before veering off with a quiet 'boo, boo, booing' and hitting into a drift feet first before flying off with a vole hanging from its beak. That will do me I thought at the time, a standard morning at Crowden, and the arrival of the owl was only bettered by a small flock of redpolls, like drops of blood on a sheet as they skittered past me

I use the term 'standard' loosely, because Shining Girl soon appeared, which was always a pleasure and accompanied me for half an hour or so. Her 'loop' seemed to be a mile either side of Enterclough, North, South, East or West, not a yard further, and although I never saw her 'bump' into some invisible barrier once the mile was reached, she would walk no further and as much as I tried to encourage her, "Come on," I said on this occasion, "Let me show show you the long-ears", that was it, and she would just stand there looking forlorn. The pleading look to fall for like your favourite puppy dog eyes ever, and I had fallen for her and 'them' the first time I clapped my eyes on her.

It was around 10 am and very warm already, so I sat down on a clump of inviting but, more importantly, dry purple moor grass on Ancote Hill and Shining Girl as if by magic was suddenly there sitting by me. On some occasions, I could see her walking towards me, while at other times she would call out and wave. A number of times she was accompanied by a gamekeeper who had lived in a cottage next door to Shining Girl at Enterclough. "That's William you won't hear a word from him because he is dumb", she said, "He knew my grandfather and has 'walked' for sixty years or more since he shot himself by accident. Or at least that is what they say, although some say that he got into a fight with some of the workers at the Woodhead Tunnel who he thought were poaching, and that one of them turned his own gun on him during the tussle. I think he is 'walking' because he cannot bear the notion that folk may think he was so stupid". Shining Girl went on to talk about William's disquiet when his house also vanished beneath Woodhead Reservoir, and it is very tempting to conclude that the following extract from the writings of Bateman, which I first read in Tom Quayle's seminal, 'Reservoirs In The Hill', refers to William's cottage.

5th May 1849
'A cottage and outbuilding, the residence of one of the Duke of Norfolk's gamekeepers will be covered by water. The Duke's agent, Mr Tomlinson has applied to me about it as they are anxious to make arrangements for building another. The value they put on the whole is £200.'

William had also put in a number of solo appearances for me at this stage, the first as he walked on the Salt Road while I was, as per normal, on the track to Hey Farm a hundred feet above him. He was at the bottom of the woods and me at the top, both of us heading in the direction of Bleak House. He appeared to be your typical 19th century gamekeeper: bowler hat, starched wing collar and tie, tweed waistcoat and jacket, with plus fours buttoned at the knee, four buttons, and shiny leather boots, shotgun over his forearm, canvas game bag over his shoulder and two spaniels at his heel. I had already had 'contact' with a number of walkers but wasn't sure if William, who was not identified to me at this juncture, was not an actual 'living' gamekeeper because aside from the bowler hat the North West Gamekeepers, including Gordon Woodhead at Crowden dressed the same way in the early 80's, and come to think of it, many gamekeepers still do in 2017.

There was only one way to find out and that was to sprint on ahead of him and hide behind a wall and watch for him walking past, which I did, and pretty smartly then as it was around four stone ago and I could run like a gazelle. Peering through the gaps in the dry-stone wall, I guessed that I was at least fifty yards in front of him only to hear one of his dogs bark fifty yards the other side of my position. He was a walker alright.

Gordon Woodhead on the other hand as far as I could see, went everywhere in his Land Rover and like many of the bosses and other North West Water workers, Gordon was always a little wary of me, not least because I had given gamekeepers some stick in my wildlife columns. I was the kid who became a Waterman out of nowhere, and worst of all I wasn't phased about opening my mouth if I thought something was wrong. A good example of this would be my protestation about Gordon's Gibbet which adorned the wall of the garage near his house and stunk to high heaven, in the summer buzzing with flies and dripping with maggots. Traditionally these 'Gibbets' consisted of every so-called piece of vermin that a keeper had killed, and they were strung up, hung up and laid out for any passing Master of the House, or in Gordon's case any boss, to prove that the job was being done proficiently. If you were to agree with this job description, Gordon was very good at his job and the menagerie of dead stuff included, weasels, stoats, foxes, crows and rabbits attested to his skills. My argument at the time, and still is for that matter is that, if he left the first three on the list alone, they would have taken care of the rabbits for him. To be fair to Gordon, we got on very well with a mutual respect for each others knowledge and point of view and I will always be grateful for his phone call which betrayed his genuine love of the countryside when a tiny merlin had pulled down a full sized racing pigeon, twice it's size, in flight. By the time I reached Crowden, the little falcon boxing well above its size, was sitting on the dead pigeons chest with 'welcome to my office' written all over its face.

On another occasion, 6th November 1980 to be precise, Gordon, shot-gun in hand was in the vanguard as a posse of 12, including three Policemen, an Engineer, two Farmers, one bewildered hiker and assorted outriders advanced along the Old Salt Road behind the roadside cottage, High Stones Lodge, it was the Dirty Dozen coming to my aid.

Half an hour earlier I had been driving along the same road after being told there was a fire near Crowden, when I came upon six or seven brand new cars parked at all kind of precarious angles in a field of boulders. On pulling up to investigate I turned off the engine only to be greeted by the sound of chanting coming from a nearby plantation. It was in a foreign language which I could not understand and there was a man leading the singing with some kind of short verse, and then the others, sounded like fifteen to twenty people, both men and women, would all respond with a heartfelt refrain. Climbing from the Land Rover I crept to a nearby wall and peered through a gap in the stones and the sight which greeted me sent a shiver up my spine and brought to mind the stories I had been told about Devil worship at St James Church. I believed the tales of Black Masses and of Pentangles and the word, Satan, being daubed on the walls in the blood of chickens, were told to me to put the 'frighteners' on the 'Young Waterman', and they worked, 'Give me the harmless Chadwick's anyday' I thought to myself as I watched the cloaked and hooded figures dance around in the wood. The reported fire was certainly there and was blazing and crackling away as I watched on, wondering what on earth to do. My mind was made up for me seconds later when two big men with even bigger beards emerged from the trees with what looked like two large swords apiece in their hands. 'Bloody Hell, it's a sacrifice', came into to my mind as I scuttled back to the Land Rover to radio for help. The radio crackled into life like a spitting sausage in a frying pan,

'101 to Bottoms, come in over'...'Bottoms to 101, what's up?' asked John in the Office. I explained the situation and John immediately galvanised the aforementioned troops, 'Bottoms to 101, make sure the gate is open please, over'.

Gordon arrived first with a 12 Bore shotgun loaded and ready for action on his arm, and was soon joined by the 'Bobbies' who advised him to 'crack' the piece and be sensible, which he reluctantly did and we were soon joined by the rest of the posse and marched purposefully towards the action. 'Action' might not be the best word to describe the events which unfolded before my embarrassed eyes, because much to the amusement of the gathered throng, the Devil Worshippers, were actually Iranian Nationals celebrating the 1st Anniversary of Khomeini's rise to power and, wait for it, the swords turned out to be kebab-skewers that they were cooking meat on over the fire.

The best and possibly most typical Gordon Woodhead story which has always tickled me and made many people smile, relates to the time when he found a dead hiker while patrolling the old coach road between Pikenaze Farm and Saltersbrook in his dirty green Defender. Armed with a short-wave radio, but maybe because he was in a black-spot near to the Woodhead Tunnel air-shafts, the perfect location for sightings of golden plover, dunlin and the occasional dotterel. I never mentioned these birds to Gordon for obvious reasons. They were my secret, as were the peregrine falcons which had already begun to prospect the valley for nesting sites after an absence of fifty years or more. I had already spotted the evidence before seeing my first peregrine in the Valley, and the distinctive v-shaped notches taken out of the woodcocks breast bone lit up my day. I didn't tell Gordon the dead bird was on his patch though.

Whether the radio worked or not Gordon did not use it, opting instead to shove the deceased hiker, rucksack, walking stick and flask into the back of the 'Landy' and proceeded to deliver him to the depot at Tintwistle. By chance I happened to be picking something up from the Yard when he pulled up, "Hey lads, come and see what I have found, can you phone the police please but don't bother with the ambulance it's too late". When the police arrived they complained that Gordon had removed the body and Gordon quick as a flash said, "I'll take him back if you want".

On this occasion on Ancote Hill, Shining Girl was just 'there' as I looked to my right, and I began a two hour conversation with her about everything and nothing. As I have already said, this was a common and garden every day event, for me at least, and she asked me about the owls and the like as I drank my coffee and finished off a bacon buttie. "Do you want a bite?" I teased, knowing full well that she never ate, or drank for that matter, and said, "It's not for me this eternity lark, I find it hard enough to wait until the next day for more bacon, never mind not eating it for ever more". "Look", says she, "I enjoy watching you enjoying your food, which you seem to rather a lot, and to be quite honest that is sufficient. I do not miss eating, I do not need to eat but there is nothing stopping me remembering what it was like to eat when I was alive". "What was your favourite food then?" says I, "Hare", she replied, "Ah, now you're talking, my dad is a butcher in Leicestershire, and we would often have a brown hare dropped off at the shop." Shining Girl asked me if I had ever tasted mountain hare. Having spent many times in the Highlands, especially in the woods above the village of Dores on the eastern shore of Loch Ness, I had certainly enjoyed mountain, or blue hare, to some tune; barbecued, smoked, and the best ever, cooked in a wood burning oven with red wine and anything else you could find until the gamey flesh fell off the bone.

The mountain hares on the hills above Crowden and Woodhead Reservoir, which Shining Girl was familiar with had been brought down from their native stronghold in the Highlands, during the 19th century, before being released onto the moors to provide a different kind of 'shooting' for the local gentry and their friends but, it was soon realised that shooting mountain hares was like popping off ducks at a fairground. It was basically too easy because of their habit of laying-low, and very still, before loping off thirty yards or so, before habitually stopping and looking back in the direction of the guns. Easy targets, and even more so in the winter when snow was on the ground, as during the colder months the hares changed their pelage to white, and therefore when there was no snow on the ground, the poor creatures stuck out like sore-thumbs against the dark brown peat bogs. Perhaps surprisingly, because the same shooters were quite happy to walk through a wood and shoot pheasants, some of which were only just out of the pens after being fattened up with peanuts. In their wisdom they decided that the mountain hare was no fun, so stopped shooting them. Since then the hares have flourished, and are now a regular sight on the hillsides from Bleaklow and Black Hill, to Kinder Scout and the Snake Summit.

In very bad winters they would come down the wall at Bleak House, where I fed them carrots and cabbage but, this was also a dangerous time for them on the roads, and many of their numbers became roadkill which I have to confess was a double-edged-sword for me. Sorry for the fate of the hare but, delighted to take the animal home for my tea. They were nearly always just clipped and most of the hare edible. Shining Girl thought this was disgusting, and to be honest, she wasn't the only one that disapproved of my unusual 'hunter-gatherer' antics. My taste for roadkill had actually begun in the Sutton Bonington, Leicestershire, where my dad was the village butcher from around 1965 to 1998. Two villages, originally Sutton and Bonington, joined up sometime before a reference in the Domesday Book and eventually became the longest village in England, or so they say. The village is basically one long road with a few lanes running off it, and with farmers and commuters the road was fairly busy even in the 60's. The maths of cars and abundant wildlife using the same road is fairly obvious and provided me and the lads with a road-kill larder of the kings and the only thing we ever turned our noses up at was foxes, we preferred to give Reynard a proper Viking Funeral complete with railway sleeper, sticks and straw, before pushing him with great ceremony into the River Soar, much to the chagrin of passing barge skippers. Just to reiterate, our menu items were dead when we picked them up and I wouldn't normally dream of eating curlew or lapwings but as my mother would often say, 'Waste not, want not'.

My dog Scarba, who accompanied me at all times on my ramblings in Longdendale, had by this stage become accustomed to the walkers and fairly often she knew they were around before I did. She was wary, and you could see her fur was ruffled but she was accepting. There was however one occasion early on in my tenure as Reservoir keeper when Scarba was not so forgiving. I had walked to the rain-gauge and then via the back road, walked across the Woodhead Dam to gauge the water level. Crossing the road and climbing the stone steps which lead to the main road and Bleak House, as I would do many thousands of times in the coming years, I turned to the final flight only to see a hooded figure crouched on their haunches in the gateway. I stopped in my tracks and tried to make out whether it was a man or woman without much success. Whatever it was that morning it was unnerving especially when I said 'Good morning' nervously and received no reply, only the sound of a wheezy chest normally achieved after smoking eighty Woodbine a day for forty years. As it neared 9am, the witching hour for phoning in the morning's levels, I turned to make sure Scarba was sitting to heel as usual but, she had gone and as I looked up to find her, I just caught sight of her running for dear-life, rounding the corner on the far side of the dam and heading towards Glossop. My whistle which normally brought an immediate response was to no avail, and several oncoming cars blared their horns at Scarba as she sped past them in the opposite direction, tail between her legs and bit between her teeth.

An awkward moment followed as I made to pass the foetal figure muttering some inane greeting with regard to the folly of sitting on a cold stone step at Woodhead on a winter's morning. "Shall I get you a cushion?", or something equally as barmy. If I am to report this accurately, which is obviously what I want to, then the person, I'd swear a woman, raised her head slightly as I squeezed past and revealed her bright green eyes from within the depths of her hood. Her eyes were tiny but piercing. I can write about this now with no concern but on that morning, as I crossed the road I was genuinely frightened and drenched to the skin from sweat.

Her parting shot in between those heavy, heavy rasping breaths was, "Manion, Manion". I relayed the tale to Shining Girl, and she claimed no knowledge of the woman, or who Manion might be.

I called in the levels and rushed to the north east facing front room window and she was still there and remained at the top of the steps for a further hour. By this stage I had showered and changed and was sure of one thing, I wasn't venturing out while she was still sitting there, and it was only when Scarba poked her head sheepishly into the kitchen two hours later that I discovered she was gone.

I wasn't going to mention what went through my mind as I waited in the kitchen for her to go that morning but, honesty being the best policy and all that. I imagined that the front room was two feet deep in blood and if I went back to check on her again then the blood would flood the house. Down all the years I am very aware that this encounter may sound far-fetched but, nothing of this nature happened again and she was never sitting on the top step in my time. Scarba however, from that day on always jumped through the cast-iron railings before the gate and dived head-long into the brambles and bracken emerging halfway down the steps before carrying on as normal.

She was a great dog, a German shorthaired Pointer who couldn't point. She did however have a 'soft' mouth and brought back a young blue hare from the hill one morning. Without a clue where she had brought him from, we decided to rear the creature and called it Kenny, after the television comedian Kenny Everett. It was funny at the time.

She was called Scarba after the Inner Hebridean Island of the same name, which is covered in heather and ferns and during the autumn and winter the island, one up from Jura, is the same colour from a distance. That's her with me on the front cover.

Kenny grew strong and behaved half dog and half cat, with Scarba and our cat Myrtle who moved in from the Youth Hostel as mentors, all three of them sleeping in the dog's basket. It was a unique experience to watch the hare gradually moult out his summer coat and turn completely white before Christmas.

It was during our conversation on that fine morning, that Shining Girl said that I reminded her of her grandfather in the culinary department, and she felt sure that one particular recipe of his would be right up my street, 'Swamp Rat Stew'. Obviously I was intrigued, and although her memory of the ingredients were vague she was fairly sure that it did not contain rats. It turns out she was wrong.

Shining Girl's father used to tell this story as his party-piece, as did his father before him. I have used the tale many times in recent months but when writing it for the page, it is a real challenge to achieve the same and very effective punch-line but, here goes. Be patient this is no shaggy-dog story, Scouts Honour.

You see, the Grandfather had spent some time in Southern Europe, an amazing rarity in the late 19th century, legendary in fact in Longdendale, because as we have already heard, travel from Crowden was generally best avoided and most Valley-folk were homebirds. To add to the unusual nature of this event, he was away for over a year on a job and although there is nothing unusual about working away from home these days it was headline news back then.

On his return he had brought back for his wife some distinctive hand painted bright blue earthenware Majolica bowls, another scarcity in the Valley, as in they were unique and never seen before. Shining Girl explained that her grandfather could not wait to cook up his version of 'Swamp Rat' to share with some of his friends who were regulars at the George & Dragon public house, which was situated across the road from the Holmfirth turn-off, and he used one of the largest of the Majolica dishes to transport the food.

Shining Girl explained, "Grandfather returned from the pub a little tipsy, and was asked by his wife how the food had gone down. Apparently he burst out laughing and said, 'It didn't lass, I droppt' the bloody dish on't flags, an't only regular to tayste it wer't dog!"

As I said, Shining Girl could not accompany me to watch the owls so I said my goodbyes, still smiling at the thought of the pub-dog getting stuck into the 'Swamp Rat Stew' and left her sitting on the heather as I negotiated Oaksike Clough and Oaksike Bridge, before crossing over the A6024, climbing a gate to check on a few regular spots for pollution. There was none but I recorded the licence plate of the burned out car on the lay-by, and ticked off a couple of teenagers for swimming in the residuum lodge below Pikenaze Farm. I had to admire the lads, as firstly it was a school day and secondly they had cycled all the way from Glossop, a good seven miles.

Here you have a classic example of my working day as a Reservoir Keeper. Job done in ten minutes, owl-time for two hours and as it happens a good half-hour trying to photograph a dipper in the lodge. The dipper is one of my top-ten Valley birds, a great character of the waters edge, and sometimes deeper, and they always constructed a nest beneath the walkway across the weir. About the size of a football, and always out of sight, unless you knew where to look, skillfully attached to the concrete and metal construction, by some miraculous weaving and wedging.

'A chocolate brown and white bibbed wonder', is how I described the bird, the size of dumpy starling in the Manchester Evening News and the Sunday Times in the early 90's, and that is an evocation I'll stick with, and not just because of their ability to walk underwater in their search for larvae. They achieve this feat by walking against the current, the flow keeping them submerged.

However, this was nothing compared to a very rare and probably unique hunting method, which I have not found recorded anywhere else in bird-literature and Research, a Crowden one-off courtesy of yours truly.

I had spotted the following opportunistic feeding behaviour in January 1983, several months prior to the meeting with Shining Girl on Ancote Hill. The residuum lodge was frozen over, and had been for a few weeks and both kids, and adults I'll wager, had been throwing large stones to try and break ice, and succeeding with some of the coping stones purloined from the nearby dry-stone walls. This vandalism was also recorded in my notebook with the comment, 'Another job for Tommy Gardner'. Tommy was one of the team of North West Water, wall-rebuilders who walked the valley daily, putting right the walls which were constantly being knocked down by bad drivers.

While leaning against the railing of the weir-bridge, and admittedly throwing a stone or two of my own at the ice, a dipper popped out of one the holes which had been previously made by trespassers. He or she, they are both identical, shook off excess water and proceeded to, the clue is in the name, dip up and down eight or nine times before shooting off over the snow covered ice to the far banking.

Dippers hunt by sight, and have a third white eyelid known as a nictitating membrane, which protects the eye when they are submerged but the behaviour I witnessed, was surely learned, and not used by all dippers. This bird, then flew off to the edge of another hole in the ice, dipped and bowed, and with great aplomb dropped into the water, only to pop out of another hole twenty feet away, after being underwater for around ten seconds. An amazing sight for sure, and was only bettered when the first individual was joined by another adult bird, which proceeded to adopt the same technique, and with the same amount of success. Neither bird ever re-appeared on the ice without something or other wriggling in its beak. I'm not renowned for giving animals names, apart from dogs, cats and Kenny Leverett but I did nickname these birds Pingu and Pinga when I told, and retold the story.

During that May 1983, a slow-moving trough of low pressure gave a wet day on the 1st, and the temperature on the 2nd failed to rise above 11C. The end of the first week was warmer but it then became cool, breezy and showery. There were some heavy, thundery showers, but during the last week the weather generally improved, and temperatures rose, and on the 25th it was sunny all day but with a cool northerly wind. On the 31st, the temperature rose above 20C, for the only time in the month. This was the day I was talking to the Shining Girl, and dipper watching, and although I spotted her a few times in the following weeks, there were no conversations and two months later, my first wife Moira and I flew off to Majorca for a two week holiday in the North East of the Island, in the small touristy-town of Alcudia.

The place was fine then although now a hell-hole with karaoke blaring out from every Sports-Bar and six different sports on six different televisions, all melding into one impossible mess of a sound. In '83, yes, there was karaoke but, there was still wonderful 'local' restaurants away from the strip, which were used by Mallorcans and served the most amazing food. After the first few days on the island, the words of Shining Girl and by default, her father, would come back to me in quite remarkable circumstances during a series of discoveries to make one guess at happen-chance, coincidence, fate and serendipity in one fell swoop, or indeed to wonder whether they happened by design, or augury. No matter, because whether predicted by second-sight or some other divining it blew my socks off.

It was our first foreign holiday together, and we were far from loaded but determined to eat well, drink lots, and for Moira to read loads of books, and for me to hire a bike and cycle the miles of trackways across the labyrinthine S'Albufera, the largest and most important wetland area in the Balearics. The marshland is a former lagoon separated from the sea by a belt of dunes, which for many centuries – but especially in the last two as a result of human influence has filled up with sediments converting it into an extensive floodplain. The Natural Park affords protection to some 1708 hectares of marshes and dunes.

S´Albufera traces its origins back some 18 million years, but the present wetland was formed less than 100,000 years ago, and the current sea dunes are even more recent, being around 10,000 years old.

The basis of S´Albufera´s ecological richness is water. The virtually permanent inundation of much of the Natural Park provides favourable conditions for vegetation growth and variety according to the depth of water, proximity of the sea and type of terrain. The range of plant species gives cover and food to a multitude of animals, which in turn are food for many more. S´Albufera derives a large part of its water from rain falling on some 640 square kilometres of north and central Mallorca, by way of seasonal streams, known as 'torrents', and also springs from subterranean aquifers which are known as 'ullals'. Seawater intrusion during the summer months has a particular effect on the vegetation and fauna.

The marsh vegetation is dominated by reed (Phragmites australis), saw-sedge (Cladium mariscus) and reedmace (Typha latifolia), large emergent plants growing in the flooded areas. Also important are the species which live submerged in the canals, small lagoons or 'llisers´ and flooded marshes. Among the most notable are fennel pondweed (Potomogeton pectinatus), spineless hornwort (Ceratophyllum submersum) or duckweeds (Lemna sp.) The more brackish areas, where salt water mixes with fresh to create a potent 'soup' supports rushes (Juncus) and glassworts (Salicornia and Arthrocnemum). The main trees are white poplar (Populus alba), elm (Ulmus minor) and tamarisk (Tamarix africana).

In some of the drier area there are a wide variety of fungi recorded, 66 species so far. One of these, the toadstool Psathyrella halofila, was discovered new to science in 1992 and is still only known from S'Albufera.

There is also a wealth of fish, twenty nine species to be precise, and the majority marine in origin. The most numerous are the eel (Anguilla anguilla) a Mallorcan staple for centuries, and also a variety of mullet species. Among the amphibians the marsh frog (Rana perezi) population stands out, and reptiles include the water snake (Natrix maura) and European pond terrapin (Emys orbicularis). The most abundant mammals are the rodents (rats and mice) and bats (8 species), including important rarities such as the Barbastelle (Barbasterella barbastrellus).

The number and diversity of invertebrates is enormous. The most notable groups are the dragonflies, spiders and, above all, the moths – of which more than 300 species are currently known.

S´Albufera is the only site in the archipelago where over two-thirds of the total number of bird species recorded in the Balearics have been seen, 271 different species.

The 61 species breeding in the marshes include Black-Winged Stilts, Kentish Plovers, Glossy Ibis, Spoonbills and Flamingos, and I was blessed in 1983 to see flying overhead Black Vultures, Bee-eaters, Ospreys, Night Herons, Scops Owls and Eleonora's Falcons within a short walk from my hotel balcony and I could not believe there was no one else about.

The latter, named after a 15th Century Sardinian Princess, for me the jewel in the crown for the Island, and without doubt the bird I had really come to see, not least because I had read that they came in the evenings in large groups to prey on the dragonflies and beetles which are so abundant on the marshes, and also because of their sheer beauty, especially the dark morph of the bird, like a slim and longer tailed dark brown peregrine, and perhaps their delayed breeding to capitalise on the hundreds of thousands of migrating songbirds funnelling past the Spanish Islands before crossing the Sahara. It has recently been established that some of the migrants, if not killed and eaten immediately are stored alive in crevices in the rocks at the nest sites. Not for the squeamish that one. The young also fledge at this time, and learn to hunt from the nest sites on the cliffs before they set off on their long journey to their wintering grounds in Madagascar.

I was lucky enough to witness the Eleonora's over the marshes, fifty of them at least, and if there was a collective noun for such a phenomenon, which there is not I claim a 'Veneration of Eleonora's' as my own invention.

Shining Girl was a distant memory as I soaked in the sights and sounds of the marshes and having ticked off many of the birds I wanted to see within the first two days, I began to take a bit more notice of what was around me, the whole picture, you might say. The bicycle I had hired was not the best, a cumbersome piece of kit and my inner-thighs had taken some hammer and had become rather chaffed. Vaseline duly applied on the third day I walked into the marshes.

First up, on that morning, was a brace of hoopoes a bird I would later record outside Crowden Youth Hostel and which would also be the subject of my first article to appear in the Sunday Times in 1988, which for me, was a great achievement on it's own but when my words were accompanied by a black and white image of the bird taken by Eric Hosking, the undisputed King of bird photography at the time.

It was while, chasing down a dusty lane trying to photograph the little blighters, that I was stopped in my tracks on a small stone bridge which straddled a murky, milky white dyke. By the side of the bridge was a very familiar cast iron valve-wheel, and on further inspection a cast iron sluice gate identical to the ones I used daily in Longdendale, and what's more the masonry work appeared to be a carbon copy of similar constructions in the valley.

Curiosity aroused, I went on to discover all manner of stonework and water-workings across the length and breadth of the Reserve, before finally checking out a stone building I had already seen several times but ignored, and all was explained. It was called Casa Bateman. The drainage of the Albufera Marshes it turned out, was one of La Trobe Bateman's overseas commissions, when his own Company, the Majorca Land Company, were employed by the Island's

Government to reclaim the vast area of wetland, and put it to good use. Casa Bateman, (Bateman's House) was originally part of the 'works' but, as of the early 1980's had been turned into a small museum.

Bateman, who went on to buy the marsh, was revered and criticised in equal measure for his efforts. In the first instance he brought jobs but, one publication of the time, if my translation is accurate said, 'The rich but unhealthy territory of the Albufera was more or less a common treasure of the local villages until 'the English' arrived'. The 'English' referred to, were obviously La Trobe Bateman and his workforce, which included Shining Girl's grandfather and a number of Bateman's trusted engineers, stonemasons and other key workers.

As most people in rural areas hesitate to embrace change until it is forced upon them, Crowden included - why would you want your Valley filled with water - whereas the Mallorcan locals of the Marshes were probably most fearful of losing the annual arrival of eels. These slippery critters teemed into the marshes in mid-January around the Feasts of Saint Anthony after their long and mysterious travel from the Sargasso Sea to the island, and slithered inland along the channels of the Albufera, to which the former Arab population gave the name al-buhayra, the 'Little Sea'. It's ironic, Crowden gained five 'mini-seas' and lost land, while Albufera lost a sea and gained land.

Having said that, another publication around the same time, the Revista de Obras Públicas, characterized the Albufera as 'An extensive and gloomy reed land, in whose mist there hovers the dreadful image of death.'

This struck me as being very similar to early descriptions of Longdendale, when writers more or less said 'There be dragons' and I wouldn't bother unless necessary.

This gloomy observation may have referred to the endemic malaria of the marshes, the mosquito-borne disease which, some historians claim, brought down the Roman Empire. The term malaria originates from medieval Italian, *mala aria,* or 'bad air'. The disease was formerly called ague or marsh fever due to its association with swamps and marshland. Malaria causes symptoms that include fever, feeling tired, vomiting and headaches. In severe cases it can cause yellow skin - as it develops in the liver - seizures, coma and death. Symptoms usually begin ten to fifteen days after being bitten. Bateman predicted a reduction in malaria when his works were complete.

The works were described as Pharaonic, in the manner of the Pharaohs across the Nile Delta, and involved the construction of 138 km of channel widths of between 4 and 60 meters, 13 siphons, 40 km of roads, 11 bridges, and a sea jetty of 300 meters. He ambitiously aimed to reclaim 1,700 hectares but fell woefully short, and only 280 hectares were suitable for cultivation. The main cause was the porosity of the soil allowing the infiltration of seawater, while the design was focused on avoiding flood water run off from the interior of the island. It was a complete economic failure. Bateman packed his bags, financially stung by the whole episode, briefly passed on the business to his son, before all of their 'interests' in the land were liquidated.

On the plus side, the incidence of malaria was reduced.

The local workers hired by Bateman, often complained about the conditions imposed on them, sometimes, even in song. It is not reported what Bateman thought of this, if indeed he ever heard it.

Ja comença a fer gotetes
i es torrent que ja se'n ve:
Mal s'endugués s'Enginyer,
es taulons i ses casetes!

The first drops of rain have arrived,
the stream started to grow:
May the devil take the engineer,
the boards and the barracks!

Shining Girl's grandfather had managed to avoid malaria but, had seen several of his English counterparts suffer. "My father described them as 'gibbering wrecks', and no use to man nor beast, when the symptoms returned back in England', she said.

Reading between the lines, her grandfather rather enjoyed his time on Majorca; the pay was good, compared to working in Longdendale, the sun shone and he particularly loved the food and wine. As I said, he was a rarity in a tiny hamlet in North Derbyshire, he had been on the Continent whereas many had never been beyond Glossop.

Oh to have been a fly on the wall when he told of his Majorcan culinary adventures in the George & Dragon at Crowden; apparently he loved to describe in detail the preparation and, the eating of, the 'rates de marjal', the 'swamp rats', which fed on rice grown in the marshes, and from which, 'rat with onion', was made. The dish was also named, Sa Pobla, after the town of the same name, which sits behind the marshes of Albufera, the 'marjal', refers to the fertile plains of irrigated agriculture which sat between the village and the lagoon. Bateman had been tasked with bringing this vast brackish lagoon under control. Personally I am pleased he failed, as Albufera is still one of the best areas in Southern Europe for birdwatching, with the added benefit that malaria is now under control, at least in this location, while still proving to be a scourge in other parts of the world. The great man can rest easy that he will never be forgotten because as recently as 1955, a street in Sa Pobla, was given the name Bateman commemorating his works in Albufera de Mallorca.

I have heard that rats are still hunted in the marshes near Valencia, where they are prepared as 'arros amb rates de marjal' (paella with swamp rats) or as a 'Espardenyà, translated as 'worthy of a prince'.

I suppose in times of hardship, rats will have been a welcome addition to the menu, and a good friend of mine from Galway can recall a local man who ate them on a regular basis and he called them, 'house rabbits'.

Back in Crowden in the late 19th Century, Queen Victoria was still on the throne, and although the works on the reservoirs were complete there were no shortage of jobs, and many of the itinerant workers returned to their own homes, some to Ireland, and the locals were employed en-masse by Manchester Corporation to care-take the Longdendale Chain, Bateman's pride and joy. With the Mallorcan disaster swept under the carpet, Bateman went on to receive every award going for his engineering works, and he would surely have been delighted when 111 years after his death, on 15th September 2000, a Blue Plaque, was unveiled on the deepest air shaft of the Mottram Tunnel, a 3,100-yard (2,800 m) long pipeline connecting the valleys of the River Etherow and the River Tame. The plaque is inscribed:

John Frederick La Trobe Bateman
(1810–1889)
Pioneer – Water Engineer extraordinaire
Brought water to the taps of Tameside and Manchester by constructing the six mile long chain of Longdendale Reservoirs from 1848.
At the time these became the largest reservoirs constructed in the world and Europe's first major conservation scheme.
Completed in 1877, these waters have never run dry. This plaque is located on the deepest air shaft over Mottram Tunnel, measured at some 200 ft below.

On our return to Crowden from Majorca, the first person I spoke to about Bateman's connection with the island was Tom Quayle, followed by every other North West Water employee I came into contact with, probably until they were sick of hearing about it, and here I am still talking about it thirty four years later. Two things I kept to myself until now were, my contact with Shining Girl, and the other walkers, and secondly, my further investigations into the tales of her grandfather, principally his story about the Majolica pots he brought back from the Island for his wife. I just thought it an improbable story serving rat-stew to your mates in a public house by the side of Woodhead Reservoir. I was, it would have to be said, a 'Doubting Thomas' but, Shining Girl insisted it was true and when you think about it, what did a dead girl from Crowden in Longdendale have to gain by telling me, a very much alive young man, a pack of lies.

A couple of weeks later, I literally sat up in bed and said to myself, 'majolica', and therein, for me anyway came the substantiation of this entire book, not that I needed to prove anything to anyone you understand, as I'm a simple storyteller telling a story but, oh boy, you couldn't make this stuff up. In the Irish tongue of my mother, I am a 'seanchaí', a traditional Gaelic storyteller and historian. The word seanchaí, which was spelled 'seanchaidhe' before the Irish-language spelling reform of 1948, means a bearer of 'old lore'. I'll take that.

The name majolica is thought to have come from the medieval Italian word for Majorca, although an alternative explanation is that the name may have come from the Spanish term 'obra de Mallequa' meaning luster-ware that was made by Moorish craftsmen from Malaga. The term majolica refers to a certain type of ceramic that is created when unglazed pottery is first fired at 1,100 degrees Fahrenheit and then a series of glazes was used to create an intense translucent colour. Majolica pottery techniques were first developed in the 3rd Century and majolica was very popular during the Victorian era. Majolica has a tin glazing that creates a brilliant white, opaque surface for subsequent painting. The colours were then added as metallic oxide glazes and the pieces were then fired again at a lower temperature.

Pottery that emerges from a kiln has a dull, bland surface that is porous. A subsequent glaze firing at a lower temperature produced a smooth, bright, and colourful surface that is not porous and holds liquids. Glazes are in essence a type of glass that when heated binds to the clay to form an impervious layer. Glazes were made from a number of ingredients that were blended together and mixed with water to hold them in suspension. Various minerals were used in majolica glazes such as ground granite, limestone, flint, quartz, sand, lead, and clays. Metal oxides were added for color. Alimony and vanadium oxides were used to obtain yellow colours, chrome oxides for green and pink colours, cobalt for blue colours, the copper oxides for green colours, iron oxides for orange colours, manganese oxides for purple and brown colours, nickel for grey colours,and tin oxides for whites and black colours.

The morning after my majolica-awakening, I saw Moira off for school measured what I had to measure, and made straight for the site of the George & Dragon. The place had been demolished a number of years earlier, over sanitation issues but I reasoned that somewhere near the site, there would have been a midden, which is basically a dumping area for kitchen and other domestic waste. Shell middens, found in the white sands of Ireland's west coast regularly, as the dunes erode, reveal the remains of early Beaker Man's dinner in the shape of limpet and mussel shells, and even on occasion the bones of the first domesticated cattle. The word 'midden' is likely from early Danish, mødding, and the Swedish mödding.

I had dug in middens behind the Achnamara Residential School in Argyll, where I had worked as a volunteer during 1971-72, and had discovered all manner of medicine bottles and terracotta jars, not to mention, personal items such as combs and clay pipes. Ten years later, I had done the same, by the Clough adjacent to Hey Farm, with similar finds.

As I rounded the bend by Enterclough, Shining Girl was by my side, and before I could say a word, she said, "I know where you are going Sean Wood, and I know what you plan to do". I remember laughing at hearing my 'Sunday Name' again and asking her if she would come and help me. As I searched for a midden, Shining Girl thought it amusing, to call out, "Freezing, Warm, Very

Cold", as I began to excavate, what I thought, were promising areas to dig but, when she shouted, "Boiling Hot", as I landed upon a location which looked like a man-made spoil heap in a dip by a relict hawthorn hedge, I began to dig in earnest.

I was disappointed at every turn, and the first half hour turned up all manner of detritus from the mid-20th century, and every bit of it smashed, including many Bovril Jars. As I was getting disheartened although determined to get to the bottom of it, literally, I spotted a local farmer, Ryder Howard, crossing Nine Holes Bridge in his tractor with front loading bucket. With no need to attract his attention, as he had already seen me I ran to the wooden gate to beckon him in. "Do me a favour Ryder, come and shift a bit of muck for me will you?" I asked, "No problem", he replied, and he chugged across to the midden in his old but, trusty John Deere which was held together by bits of wire and ill-fitting bolts. No worries though, as it did the job in grand style, and very soon we were down to the a piece of ground which had not seen light of day since Napoleon shot his bolt.

Shining Girl was watching on as Ryder did his bit, before clearing off down the road, slowing every car in his wake and I reckon, taking great delight in the 'doing'.

It should be said here that Ryder Howard changed the face of vehicle accessories one sunny afternoon on the track above Pikenaze Farm, at Woodhead when I saw the same tractor rattling over the brow of a hill sporting a very odd looking mascot on the bull-nose bonnet as he scattered a covey of red grouse in his wake. From a distance it was difficult to ascertain what exactly the bouncing pink effigy was but, I was fairly sure it was a blow-up female doll, and as he came closer, close enough to see the big smile on his face, it was indeed a shiny sex-toy, and my farmer friend pointed enthusiastically towards his prize as though I could have missed her. He was before his time was Ryder, as the 'pimping' of tractors had not been dreamed of in the early 1980's. She was a happy looking lady, with lipstick as red as a cock grouse's wattle, framing her wide open mouth, and what appeared to be a matted wig stolen from a bald Uncle glued to her nether regions. Her name was, Ellie, it said so on the back of her neck. Expensive she was not, and at the risk of being lewd with no pun intended, honest, she would have gone down with the slightest bit of pressure. Very poor quality.

Ryder explained that he had found the 'doll' blowing around the heather (stop it) and thought it would be a bit of a laugh to tie her up-front with baling twine. The things you see when you have not got your gun. This was 'League of Gentlemen' stuff, long before the popular television comedy show, which was filmed in Hadfield aka Royston Vasey, was ever aired, and when some of the writers of the programme were still at school. The likes of Reece Shearsmith and Mark Gatiss would surely enjoy the postscript to this less than edifying tale.

After a couple of days Ryder tired of his new plaything and discarded poor Ellie in an open-sided farm building, and you might have thought that was that but you would have been wrong because the following April I received an excited call from my Farmer friend. "You're into birds, you'll have to come and see this, you just won't believe it", said Ryder. And he was right, I wouldn't if I had not seen it myself. You may find this hard to swallow but, a male wren had made a nest in Ellie's open mouth, and the female, with her head just visible was happily sitting on a clutch of eggs laid in Ellie's throat.

The things you see when you have not got your camera.

Normally the male wren constructs several nests and his partner then selects her favourite, and the only clue as to why she chose Ellie from his selection can be found in the bird's scientific name, Troglodytes, meaning 'cave-dweller', from the Greek trogle. Depending on where you look, variously described as someone or something that lives in a hole or mouse-hole, a cave goer or a cave diver, referring in this case to the tendency of wrens to enter small crevices and similar areas as they look for food and nest sites, one who creeps into holes.

Originally the word was used to describe a prehistoric cave dweller from the African Red Sea Coast.

As for unusual nest sites, readers of my columns have always kept me informed of the latest weird and wonderful locations, including the blue tits that utilised a bullet hole in a wall in Salford, the bullet reputedly fired from a Kalashnikov aka AK-47, and the more pastoral but equally inventive coot, who climbed aboard a shopping trolley in Glossop Brook.

Sifting through the midden, without the patience of an archaeologist, it didn't take me long to work backwards from 1815, and my heart raced when the August sun of 1983 reflected from a small patch of blue peeking out from the muck, damp and dust of time. Discarding the spade I fell to my knees, now the careful excavator, and uncovered a piece of majolica from a broken plate. No trace of the 'rates de marjal' but, I was overjoyed, like Tony Robinson of 'Time Team' fame on helium..

Shining Girl gave me one of her knowing looks and without thinking, I pulled her close to me and kissed her full on the lips. It was like an electric shock without the accompanying pain and I wanted more.

Chapter Five:
History of the Valley in a 'Midden'.

There was a bunch of other very interesting artifacts which came to the surface as I scratched about in the dirt for pieces of Majolica, my 'blue gold', which part-told the story of the George & Dragon and England itself, from glass medicine jars and coloured glass marbles, to pot 'snobs' and what was left of, what I thought at first, a bowl, with the image of a robed lady standing on a globe with a background of clouds, and part of a 'saying'...SHALL BE CAST AWAY, in a scroll over her head. Intriguingly, my initial research suggested that the full inscription came from the Native American, Iroquois Constitution, and would have read, SELF INTEREST SHALL BE CAST AWAY. However, I then got the experts from Glossop Heritage Trust in on the job. The pottery fragment, most fittingly, was part of a 19th Century tankard, which had a lid to keep the flies from your beer and the complete wording was, THE SWORD SHALL BE CAST AWAY.

Snobs is a traditional children's game played the world over for which there is no formal organising body. Consequently, rules vary from country to country and place to place. The game is also known by a variety of names including Jackstones, Chuckstones, Dibs, Dabs, Fivestones, Otadama, Tally and Knucklebones.

All that is needed to play the game of Snobs is five small clay squares. Alternatives to the squares can be pretty much anything of a similar size - originally sheep knucklebones were used.

To start a turn, the player throws five snobs into the air with one hand and tries to catch as many as possible on the back of the same hand. The snobs that were caught are then thrown up again from the back of the hand where they came to rest and as many as possible are caught in the palm of the same hand. If no snobs end up being caught, the player's turn is over.

If, however, at least one snob was caught, the player prepares for the next throw by keeping one of the caught snobs in the same hand and throwing all remaining snobs on the ground. The player then tosses the single snob into the air, attempts to pick up one of the snobs that was missed and then catches the snob that was tossed, all with the same hand. The player repeats this until all the snobs have been picked up.

That done, the player throws down four of the snobs again, throws the single snob in the air, attempts to pick up two snobs with the same hand before catching the tossed snob. This is repeated again and a final toss sees the player picking up the last snob. The process is then repeated for three snobs followed by one snob and finally, all four snobs are picked up before catching the single tossed snob.

For skilful players, the game can continue in an agreed way with further permutations and challenges according to the player's whims. For instance, the other hand could be used to throw, the player may have to clap hands before doing the pick up or perhaps slap both knees.

I remember, hazily after fifty years that, once we had worked our way through the preliminary stages of the game, we used to throw the snobs in the air and try and guide them between open fingers.

Shining Girl, proved to be a mine of information about children's games in Crowden in the late 19th and early 20th Century, as did one Arthur Brocklebank, who I will introduce exactly as he introduced himself to me. I had decided to investigate again the St James Chapel graveyard as there was always something different to see, not least a little carving here, or a missed name there, and I had brought with me a wax crayon to try and get a 'rubbing' of an Angel on the edge of one of the flat-gravestones. These stones must have taken some shifting two hundred years ago, and most of them are now skew-whiff with heather sprouting from beneath like a natural cushion for their weight.

The Angel came out really well, and as I was on my knees making a green version, a pair of well polished black shoes appeared in front of me; above the shoes, the start of a neatly pressed pair of black trousers, which gave way, as I lifted my head, to a slightly more creased mid-region, and then to an over-long black jacket, a rough pair of hands and thence to a collar and tie, followed by a craggy benevolent face, topped with a massive shock of white hair, and he reminded me of my dad a bit. At a guess the man was around seventy years old, slightly built, but with a healthy glow to his face and, I guessed slightly ill at ease in a suit. You could say, he was all trussed up, and on his way to a funeral.

"Good morning", I said, before the stranger replied with an engaging smile, "And the same to you lad", he replied, "'Tis a grand morning tha knows but, North Easterly gets reet under tha bonnet!"

I explained what I was doing, although it was fairly self-evident, and asked if there was a burial due at St James that morning. "Nae lad, tha canna plant any moor in there tha knows, it's full 'tut brim", he said, "Thy'd n'er get a babby in". Charming I thought but he was probably right, and apart from a hand-full of locals, including Retired Waterman, Eddie Davies, in the early 80's, and his wife Lil, sometime later, the graveyard is chocker. I should also give a mention to Bob Blackburn, another Waterman whose ashes were scattered around his wife's memorial near the Church Door.

Mr Brocklebank chatted away at length about this and that while I was still prone, trying to produce the perfect rubbing. He waxed lyrical about skylarks as one particular bird serenaded the pair of us on high, and why wouldn't he, larks are a proper sound of Old England. The collective noun for the skylark, an exultation, is probably the perfect description, a feeling of triumphant elation, jubilation, a rejoicing. Arthur Brocklebank agreed and proceeded to demonstrate his knowledge of collective nouns for birds. The kind of game I like.

Arthur sat on the stone steps of the Church, while I perched on the edge of the Angel Tomb. "These steps are at exact same height, as steps on yon Mottram Church tha knows", said Arthur. I didn't question him on that small piece of local folklore, as I had heard the story before, and I also knew that the original wooden church had been built as a 'Chapel of Ease', by the landowner, Edmund Shah, 500 years earlier. In other words, he made it easy for far fetched parishioners to attend services instead of traipsing the seven miles to Mottram.

I said, "I think my favourite collective noun is a 'Tok of capercaillie', "A what?" Laughed Arthur, "What on earth is a capercaillie, it sounds like a dance?" I explained that it was a large cousin of the Red Grouse, which was only found in the Highlands of Scotland. "As big as a turkey, and they have to launch themselves from a branch, and drop a few feet before getting airborne". I was exaggerating slightly but they are big rascals. "Be some eating on them then, not like yon skinny moor cock", said Arthur. He was referring to the Cock Red Grouse which are found all over the moors at Crowden, and sometimes on the back wall at Bleak House. "Aye, that'd be a covey o' grouse", said Arthur resuming the game. "Your turn lad".

"Okay, a 'bazaar' of guillemot, and a 'confusion' of guinea fowl?" I offered. To anyone who knows their birds, these two collective nouns, are a close, second and third to 'toc', the former because they crowd together in their thousands on jagged cliff faces, and the latter because, guinea fowl with their fat bodies and peculiar little heads, seem to scatter hither and thither in no particular coherent fashion. I'll never forget one time in the south of France, around 2012, not so far from La Rochelle, when a group of us were staying in the fading Chateau of a fading French pop star. Not least because after the long drive I bagged the turret bedroom, which was reached by a cast iron spiral staircase. I was knackered, and plonked the suitcases down and lay on the bed. After a quick snooze, half an hour tops I sat bolt upright to find a woman and a girl, side by side at the end of the bed, 'French-walkers', both in Victorian dress with gaunt faces staring at me, and unlike their Crowden counterparts, they put the fear of God in me and I never went back into the room during the next seven days. I even got one of the other lads to bring down the suitcases, feigning a bad back.

The Chateau was shabby but the building, a stunner, and the grounds remarkable, and although I may sound like a big-softy on this one, there was no way I was looking up at the turret bedroom window because I knew they were watching me. Fortunately, the local wine helped, and on my first afternoon outdoors whilst tucking into a pig's trotter in jelly, and a plastic bottle of deep and thoughtful red, I could hear what, might best be described as a 'swishing sound', starting off slow and building to a crescendo, before dying down and kicking off again. Intrigued, I wandered off down the lane in the direction of the sound. All was explained half a mile later, it was a multi-thousand 'confusion of guinea fowl' on a farm, and the noise was simply their synchronised dashing, first one way, and then the other across the field.

Obviously, this had not happened when I first spoke to Arthur but, he was stuck again which was no surprise as the furthest he had ever been from Crowden in his entire life was Glossop one way and Holmfirth, just over the hill in Yorkshire the other but he did come back at me gamely with, "A bobbin of robins", which I thought he must have made up but, he was correct. I tried Arthur with one of my jokes at this stage, as we seemed to be getting on very well. 'What are you left with if a puffin flies off?' "Don't know", says Arthur, 'Nuffin!" says I. It was a tumbleweed moment.

"Anyway", I said, "As we're playing a game of sorts perhaps you can help me with these?" pulling assorted items excavated from the George & Dragon midden, including the three pot snobs, the glass marbles, spent shells and assorted decorated crockery, from my North West Water issue, grey jacket, which was always bulging with something or other from my daily patrols.

Arthur was delighted with these finds, and was palpably back in his school-days as he handled the marbles. "Oh my days," he said excitedly, "I had some 'merps' exactly like these when I was a bairn, and older to be fair, and in fact I still have them; and when I say exactly, I mean the same type and size, because each glass marble is an individual, and they will never match completely a bit like the eggs of birds".

It was noticeable that Arthur, lost some of the local accent when talking about marbles and the like, which is something I have observed with some of my own Irish friends at times, and thinking about it, my own, 'phone-voice' is a smoother and more articulate version, some people call 'posh', compared to my more usual Rugby Club pared-back Anglo Saxon.

Arthur to his credit, knew his stuff when it came to marbles, and when I interrupted him in full flow, to ask about 'snobs', he said, "All in good time, all in good time". He was on a roll, see what I did there, and it proved to be a fascinating hour. As ever, my note book of the day shows my recording of this conversation were fairly accurate. When it comes to marbles Arthur was my latter-day 'Google'.

Marble like objects have been found in archaeological digs all over the known world, and the British Museum in London has both Greek and Roman marbles dating from 200 years before the birth of Christ, as well as some Egyptian examples found in a child's grave dating from the Early Dynastic period 3000 BC. In North America marbles in a burial mounds, from as far back as 6000 BC.

"I've done a bit of research myself, you know", I explained to Arthur, "And what I love is, the fact that a favourite game in the 14th century was – 'nine holes', and I found these marbles, fifty yards from Nine Holes Bridge!" The actual game of Nine Holes is played with a bridgeboard. Players take turns shooting their marbles through the arches in numerical order. Arches that are shot through out of sequence don't count. A successful shoot through the correct arch entitles the shooter to an additional turn. First player to send his marble through all nine holes in the correct order wins.

"Aye lad but, it's nothing to do with Croden, and did you know, a kind of 'Nine Holes', was played by the novices at Westminster Abbey, and in the first bay of the North Cloister, by a stone bench near the Prior's Seat, you can seet' t'holes fer aiming marbles at; I would like to see that", said Arthur.

My small collection from the George & Dragon midden, range from roughly made pot marbles around the size of a walnut, to several beautifully coloured glass examples of a standard marble size, one a transparent dark amber with white striations, a white with emerald green infusions, a tiny light blue, and the largest, a cloudy plain glass with a clear seam around the circumference. All very precious to me.

Paintings by many Dutch artists from the 16th century show children playing the game of marbles. One by Pieter Bruegel painted in 1560 shows over 200 children playing some 80 different games, including marbles titled 'children's games' and it can be viewed at the Kunsthisrorisches Museum in Vienna. There are also Dutch tiles in Delft wear that show different marble games; these blue tiles were used as decoration around fireplaces, and as early 'skirting boards', in the larger houses of the time. The grander the house the more sophisticated the Delft. The Douce collection held in the Bodleian Library, Oxford, contains scores of old prints showing Flemish children at play. One of them by Jacob Cats (1625) show 13 games being played, with marbles in the middle foreground.

I explained to Arthur that I had seen a painting by the Dutch Painter, Adrian Van Ostade (1620 – 1685) entitled 'Musicians at a cottage door', which shows a rural scene from the 17th century, in which two small boys can be seen playing an early ring game.

"Aye", Arthur replied, "There's an old poem from yon back, which could describe me at Croden School, as I wasna' the best and a, 'dunce at syntax, but a dab at taw.' Arthur then proceeded to explain the game of Ring Taw, 'taw' being the marble used to aim with.

" You draw a circle ont' ground, a few feet across, and mark 'taw line' about six feet away, then each player puts in about five marbles. You then take it in turn and the first player must hit the marbles out ow'ta ring and keep yon shooter outside o't ring too. An't players keep any marbles they hit out o't circle. Any shooters left in't circle become targets for'tuther players. If a player has no more marbles to shoot, they are out o't game, and game is over when all't marbles have been knocked out o't circle".

It occurred to me whilst writing this book that, a 'midden' such as the one at the George & Dragon, and another I found near the clough at Hey Farm, not only provide a visual history of the Valley but the history of mankind through dumped objects. My kind of cack-handed archaeology.

As Arthur and I continued the discussion, Shining Girl, as she sometimes did, began to show herself from the back of St James Church, I winked in her direction and smiled, as first she appeared on the Mottram side, and then immediately on the Woodhead side and then three feet behind Arthur. I wondered for a second whether Arthur would, or 'could' see her, when as if he was reading my mind said, "Don't mind her," answered my question, "She's a Will o' the wisp' that one". I was secretly very pleased that Arthur knew about Shining Girl, at least I wasn't on my own I thought.

Arthur did not elaborate and continued with his potted history of marbles instead, Shining Girl meanwhile had gone again. "There are numerous mentions of marbles in European literature", he said, "And in 1729, a certain Samuel Rogers wrote this verse in his 'Pleasures of Memory'.

'On yon gray stone that fronts the chancel-door,
Worn smooth by busy feet, now seen no more,
Each eve we shot the marble through the ring

When the heart danced, and life was in it's Spring'.

Funnily enough I knew one other piece of writing by Rogers... *'To know her, was to love her'*, which pretty much sums up my feelings for the Shining Girl, however crazy that may sound. My contact with the walkers was plain and simple every day life and times at Crowden and nothing out of the ordinary, well let's say, not after a year or so anyway. I had become accustomed to them by then but, it should be noted that generally the only people I spoke to about the walkers, were the walkers themselves, and dear Arthur by acknowledging the presence of Shining Girl gave me great comfort and confirmed that I was not seeing things.

Arthur continued to demonstrate his knowledge and told me about the contents of a book he had read about the Battle of Trafalgar.. "It read, 'A wounded seaman aboard the 'Conqueror', his leg shattered, lay on deck calmly playing marbles with stray grapeshot while waiting to be carried below', said Arthur.

Fifty years after Trafalgar, (1805) glass marbles made their appearance, most of them coming from small German glasshouses, and the reason for this sudden mass production and export was due to the invention of the Marble Scissors, a small hand held device that rounded one end of the cane or rod that made the marbles, while cutting the other, so making them round.

I asked Arthur if he knew how my glass examples were made and of course he knew chapter and verse, "Colouring-agent is placed in the furnace with the scrap glass, unless they are to be clear but, for the internal colouring, the melted colouring-agent is streamed into the liquid glass as it emerges from the furnace", he said.

The history of marbles was interesting but, the game came alive for me when Arthur described how it was played at Crowden in the 19th and early 20th

Century, I'm guessing the same time that some of my examples found their way into the George & Dragon 'midden'.

"Keeps, was my favourite marbles game, because if you were a good shot any marbles you were able to knock from the ring', you kept, and I was pretty good. Some schools in Glossop banned 'Keeps', because they considered it was a form of gambling, and they tried to stop us playing it at Croden School but they couldn't follow us home, could they?" laughed Arthur.

"I'll see thee later lad," Arthur announced abruptly, "I'm of t' Caf in Croden", he said, suddenly reverting back to his broader local accent.

"Okay, nice talking to you but, there is no cafe in Crowden?" I said.

Arthur did not answer but rather lifted himself up from the stone step and walked nimbly through the gates and headed down the single track slope towards Crowden and the main A628. I gathered all my 'rubbings' and crayons together and went to climb over the back wall into the Bleak House garden. I cannot recall why but, something made me walk back onto the track and watch Arthur's progress down the hill. He was nearly at the bottom by the time I saw him, and he stopped briefly to look at something in the verge, before momentarily looking back in my direction and giving me a nod and setting off briskly once more. He was twenty feet from the main road and showed no signs of slowing up, and although the 'Woodhead' was nowhere near as busy and dangerous as it is today, it was still a much used highway in 1983, and there were a few wagons and cars driving each way as Arthur approached the junction.

Before I had time to shout out, Arthur had kept up his pace and just walked out into the road. I suppose now, in a way, time stood still because the vehicles kept on moving and there was no honking of horns or the slamming on of brakes, and seconds later Arthur appeared unscathed on the other side of road.

I was a mixture of surprised, shocked and incredulous at what I had seen but, in some ways this was just one more unusual occurrence in my first three years at Crowden, and I put it to the back of my mind.

Several weeks later after I had written about St James Chapel in one of the local newspapers, I received a small package through the post from one of my readers. Reader response and communication has always provided the very life-blood of my writing and this early letter was a good example of this. The lady began by telling me that her family, the Brocklebanks, had once lived in Crowden and that some members of the family were buried there, while others had been married or christened in the Chapel. Her letter made for very interesting reading, as did the funeral cards for some of her relatives but, nothing could have prepared me for one of the black and white photographs. Although it was a poor photocopy it clearly showed Stone Row, once called 'New Row', a line of five terraced houses, which by the time I had moved into Crowden was the Youth Hostel. As it happens they are now private houses again.

Standing outside one of the houses, was a group of people, one a rather large lady, a couple of children and two men. One of the men was Arthur Brocklebank, and he was wearing the same black suit. Painted on the wall of the cottage behind them, in big white letters, TEAS. Arthur, as I suspected after his Houdini-like crossing of the A628, was a walker.

No wonder he had seen Shining Girl, and it was still just me and them which kind of suited me.

As for the Cafe, I also had its existence confirmed in 1998 when I received a couple of letters from Mrs Christine Whiteoak, of Royton, also prompted by reading one of my articles, and they were packed with amazing stories about Crowden and some of the characters who lived and worked there, including a quarryman called 'Yorkshire Jack'. Readers will hear more of him in Volume 2 but, more importantly for this chapter, Christine gave me a picture of her great grandmother, Margaret Wagstaff, outside the cafe with her daughter Hannah. Margaret ran the Cafe, and how can I put this, was larger than life. Christine explained, "Margaret died in 1913 and if you read the report from the Glossop

Chronicle, she had eight coffin bearers and my late father told me she weighed 26 stone when she died".

Chapter Six:
From Hey Farm to Windy Gap in County Kerry.

By now, I reckon readers will understand that as far as I am concerned, Crowden and Woodhead are parts of a special valley in so many ways, and although I could make a comprehensive list of the local attractions, which would obviously include the views, Shining Clough; the wildlife, ermine; the history, when it was the 'Head of the Wood', and mentioned in the Domesday Book, and without doubt there would need to be special mention of the walkers. However, perhaps surprisingly, early on in my tenure I discovered, and not just with regard to Pawdy Blanche, or even the Irish Navvies, who built the original Woodhead Railway Tunnel, many dying in the process and more of them in Volume 2 but, there is a tangible 'personal experience' link, direct to Ireland which I cannot even begin to explain thirty years later. So best of luck with this.

On holiday in County Kerry in the delightful little hamlet of Darrynane Beg, a bit like Crowden in terms of size and scattered homesteads, and also in the sense that in days gone by many more people lived in the area. I'm talking hundreds, instead of tens. The ivy and fuchsia-covered stone ruins bear witness to a once bustling town-land, where tenant farmers, seaweed collectors and fishermen would meet up at the local market in nearby Caherdaniel, or further afield in Kenmare, and occasionally even further when they might travel the forty miles to Killarney itself. The pubs are still there as are the Catholic Churches but, the people long gone. There's a cue there for all manner of political and religious discussion about things like the Great Irish Famine, 1845-

1852, but, Paul Newland, long time fiddle player from my band the Curragh Sons summed the situation up rather nicely for me when he said, "Big churches and small houses, what's that all about?"

On the slopes of Mount Tullig, about half a mile west of the Caherdaniel village lies a fine stone staigue fort, or Caher, and although both the village and the fort were not named after Daniel O'Connell, I would like to think they were. O'Connell, often referred to as, 'The Liberator', or 'The Emancipator', was an Irish political leader in the first half of the 19th century. He campaigned for Catholic emancipation, including the right for Catholics to sit in the Westminster Parliament denied for over 100 years, and the repeal of the Act of Union which combined Great Britain and Ireland.

O'Connell's plea to the British Parliament in 1847 went unheeded but by then it was probably too late anyway.

'Ireland is in your hands, in your power. If you do not save her, she cannot save herself. I solemnly call upon you to recollect that I predict with the sincerest conviction that a quarter of her population will perish unless you come to her relief'.
Daniel O'Connell to the British House of Commons, 1847.

His Darrynane House mentioned in the earlier chapter about Pawdy Blanche, has the Wicklow Gold Crucifix on show, and also the finest dining table I have ever seen made from 7,000 year old bog-oak, with an amazing pair of carved Irish Wolfhounds as table legs. The 13th Commandment should read, 'Thou shalt not covet Daniel's Table', but oh my word, I do, I do.

On our first full day at Darrynane we decided to head for the hills, and one hill in particular, Eagle's Hill. At 549 metres, I just knew that the view would be stunning and certainly perfect for an eagle to nest and survey the scene below. There were no eagles on our visit but the hill was not given the name by accident, and at one time golden eagles, or even the magnificent white-tailed sea eagle, would have nested on the rocky crags close to the summit.

White-tails were once a common sight around Britain and Ireland, with many place-names demonstrating this, such as Lough Erne in County Fermanagh, 'erne' being an old name for eagle, however in the last few hundred years both types of eagle suffered massive declines. Draining of land and the felling of forests for agriculture reduced the amount of available habitat, and the remaining few birds were persecuted and hunted for a bounty.

The last breeding pair of white-tails in England were found on the Isle of Man in 1818. They persisted much longer in Scotland where persecution was the biggest threat. The increase in sheep farming and movement of the human population to coastal areas lead to further conflict with poisoning rife. Egg collecting ensured the final extinction of the species as a breeding bird in the United Kingdom when the last specimen was shot on the Isle of Skye in 1916.

Thanks to a successful reintroduction programme, the species is now breeding all over the Western Isles and along the Western Seaboard in Scotland, and there are high hopes regarding the birds reintroduction to both England and Wales.

It was a similar time-frame in Southern Ireland and the last white-tail to grace the slopes of Eagle Hill was well over 100 years ago. The Irish White-Tailed Sea Eagle Programme was established in 2007 when 15 young eagles taken in Norway were released and a further 20 in 2008. In 2007 one chick was fitted with a GPS Satellite transmitter which gave excellent hourly GPS Fixes near the release site and up to 8 kms into the mountains but, it was soon found poisoned. Wind turbines and illegal shootings have added to the woes accounting for many more birds. In 2015, 31 years after my first visit, I was invited to write about the first successful hatching of a white-tailed eagle in County Kerry for over a century, and again after the chick's much recorded maiden flight.

One bird was hatched in Killarney National Park by a pair which had failed twice previously, and the other was hatched near Kenmare by a pair in their first attempt, a mere flap or two from Derrynane thanks to the eight foot barn-door wings of the white-tail.

In spite of the setbacks with over 30 birds lost, the Irish breeding population of white-tails is now spread across four counties, from Glengarriff in West Cork, to Connemara, Co Galway, with Lough Derg near Mountshannon, Co Clare, being the most successful hatching location. In early 2017 a regular reader of my wildlife columns sent me a video clip of a 'big bird' he had taken by the roadside in the far north west of Donegal; he thought it may be a golden eagle but, much to the delight of the reader and myself it was unmistakably a white-tail. The birds are known to wander and this individual could have come up from Connemara but, there is a real possibility that the bird may be part of the thriving population in the Western Isles of Scotland. The bird was not tagged which means it could be from an unknown nest, and thereby demonstrating the complete and lasting success of the Scottish reintroduction programme started by John Love in 1975. Fingers crossed for Ireland I say.

Back in 1984, we set off on an old 'green road' to the scattered village of Behaghane. The trail now part of the 'Kerry Way' climbs through a boulder field leading to the foot of Coad Mountain where there is a split in the trail. We followed the higher path accompanied by a pair of kronking ravens. Their appearance made me think of Arthur Brocklebank back in Crowden, and although, at this stage I had not seen him for a few months, I resolved to start our collective noun game again with an 'unkindness of ravens'. Ravens were also nesting near Crowden at this stage, as they still do, on the gritstone edges of Torside Clough.

The highest point on our walk that morning was 385m above sea-level at the aptly named, Windy Gap, between Glenmore and Caherdaniel, the views were stunning both ways, in one direction to the coast, and beyond somewhere on tiptoe, to the quite remarkable Skelligs, while inland brought the promise of some rough walking but, then the joys of the heady heights of Ireland's highest mountains. Carrauntoohil is the Boss, at 3,406 feet, and the central peak of the Macgillycuddy's Reeks range. The ridge northward leads to Ireland's second highest peak, Beenkeragh, while the ridge westward leads to the third-highest peak, Caher. Carrauntoohil overlooks three bowl-shaped valleys, each with its own lakes. To the east is Hag's Glen or Coomcallee, to the west is Coomloughra and to the south is Curragh More.

I have a theory that J. R. R. Tolkien was inspired by some of these Irish place names when it came to creating his magical kingdoms and characters in, 'The Lord of The Rings', Carrauntoohil, and the Macgillycuddy's Reeks being fine examples. Macgillycuddy a Clan Chief, and with Carrauntoohill, sounding even more Tolkien-like in Gaelic, Na Cruacha Dubha, meaning 'the Black Stacks'. In their topography, the pinnacles bear some comparison to the author's description of Minas Tirith..

'Carven by giants out of the bones of the earth, Minas Tirith serves as the last bastion of man against the might and menace of Sauron. Its seven walls of ancient stone rest at the knee of Mount Mindolluin, at the end of the White Mountains. From its towers, it is possible to look out south, beyond the Anduin river to the sea, or north, to the fires of Mount Doom'.

The 'Towers' in Kerry, are the mountain edges themselves, natural lookouts to the Ireland's own Misty Mountains. The range is composed of Devonian red sandstone, which has been substantially modified by geological ice action, notably in the form of sharp peaks and corries.

I also believe the author was likely to have visited Connemara in County Galway on his travels and for readers with a mind to follow things up, the topography around Galway Bay and Connemara is remarkably similar to the coastline of Middle Earth, just saying; and while I'm on a roll, Tolkien was surely inspired by some of the place names in the Peak District as I am fairly sure that I cannot be the first to have thought this everytime I drive past Wormhill, Stony Middleton and Flash.

There is a good chance that Windy Gap would have been used somewhere in the Mountains of Gondor if Tolkien had ever experienced walking across it, and just like us, he would have been completely caught off guard.

It was a fine day with no breeze and we had already discarded our waterproofs, and the noon-time sun had me huffing and puffing like a steam train, and then we hit the Gap. A sudden and powerful gust seemed to come from nowhere, one foot in, one foot out and it was, to all intents and purposes the 'Okey Cokey', of mountain squalls, in out, in out, shake it all about, or to give the experience more voracity…

'A squall is a sudden, sharp increase in wind speed that is usually associated with active weather, such as rain showers, thunderstorms, or heavy snow. In our case, a squall was definitely, 'an increase in the sustained winds over a short time interval, as there may be higher gusts during a squall event, usually occurring in a region of strong mid-level height falls, or mid-level tropospheric cooling, which force strong localized upward motions at the leading edge of the region of cooling, which then enhances local downward motions just in its wake'.

The 'step in', and 'step out' of Windy Gap, calm, storm, calm, storm, is a natural happening I was so pleased to experience but, just as the sudden wind which rushed through the Bleak House courtyard in Chapter One, was followed by the voices of dead children, the gusts of Windy Gap, proved to be the precursor of one of the strangest and most 'unnatural' affairs of my time in Longdendale.

A matter of feet from the Gap, calm was restored with just the hint of a mild zephyr caressing my face, and a little further the only clue to the maelstrom close by was the sudden undignified upward flight-pattern of a surprised gull heading seaward.

With more time on our hands, and a handy Black's of Greenock two-man tent which we had left at home and plenty of supplies, we would have gone on to 'Mordor', and left behind the relative comfort of our little thatched cottage and wildflower meadow for a few days but, I had left a rack of bacon ribs on a very low light, and I was due to sing that night in the Blind Piper Pub in Caherdaniel. So instead, we plonked ourselves down on a few rounded boulders, broke out the sandwiches and just soaked up the scenery.

I was distracted momentarily from the distant vistas by the clacking call of a stonechat, one of the few insectivorous birds to tough it out through the British winters. The southern balm of County Kerry ideal. They make an alarm call that sounds like two pebbles being struck together, hence the name and you cannot mistake them for anything else, the adult males are relatively easy to spot with their conspicuous collars and rusty breasts, although you could confuse the female with their cousins, the whinchats. and were once thought to possess clandestine powers, inspiring poets such as WH Auden.

> *...lonely on fell as chat,*
> *By pot-holed becks*
> *A bird stone-haunting, an unquiet bird'.*

And yes this bird was noisy, or as Auden described it, 'unquiet', so I got off my haunches to try and take a photograph as he 'gave-out' from the bouncing stem of a flowering gorse bush. There followed a short-lived game of hide and seek, where I'd train my lens on him only for the little blighter to shoot off as the shutter was pressed, and it was I who got fed up before him. As I replaced the lens cap and turned off my trusty Canon an unusual shape in the undergrowth caught my eye. The formation was an anomaly amongst the time-moulded, Henry Moore-like free-form boulders, and the sensuous curves of an Irish hillside. It was an angular configuration of what looked like flat stones, beneath a carpet of moor grass and on closer inspection this proved to be the case.

As I tugged at the mat of grasses the root base was very shallow and close to the surface and the whole lot lifted up like a duvet, which fortunately stayed in one piece, allowing me to look underneath. I shouted to my wife Moira, "Hey, come and look at this, and see if you can get a decent picture", she shouted back, "What is it, I'm comfortable here thank you".

"It looks man-made", I replied, "And in fact, it seems to be lots of flat stones placed in the deliberate outline of an arrow, starting with small stones at the 'arrowhead', before gradually giving way to much larger stones, maybe, the size of a breadboard at the rear. I'm guessing the whole construction is pointing due-west, for whatever reason".

My commentary did the trick, and with the photographs duly taken, and the 'carpet' laid carefully back in place, we were about to call it a day and head down to Caherdaniel, when a lone blackface sheep appeared over the brow, walked past us without a by your leave and believe it or not, went down on its front legs, and as it turns out evidenced by the drops of water falling from its muzzle took a drink.

The blackface, is a Scottish breed very well suited to the mountains of Kerry, I think a he but both sexes have horns and the fleece on this individual was growing in a thicket around the nether regions. Either way the animal needed some encouragement to move, so I could see where he or she was drinking from. The source of the sheep's water supply was a small well, and although it was unmarked in the usual tradition of Holy Wells in Ireland, on the stone at the front of the well was a finger- worn 'sign of the cross' (signum crucis) which must have taken many thousands of penitents, hundreds of years to create as they knelt and recited, either in their heads or verbally, the Latin blessing *in nomine Patris et Filii et Spiritus Sancti*, or words to that form and effect referring to the three persons of the Christian Trinity usually followed by an 'Amen'.

At the risk of being impolite and I am not sure of the provenance of a memorable but, irreverent skewing of the *'signum crucis'* but, when I was attending De Lisle Catholic Secondary Modern School in Loughborough, Leicestershire, we often used our own version with the attendant hand signals of, 'Spectacles, testicles, wallet and watch'. I first heard it from family friend, Jimmy Finnegan, and it kept us lads amused, that is, until the day we were caught laughing with our shoulders bouncing in unison at the back of the School Hall during Mass. Mr Brennan, the Deputy Head, who had overheard our 'blasphemy' hoicked us out in front of the gathered throng and gave us a couple of strokes each of the cane. Thankfully the punishment was administered on the hand as the school had finally abandoned caning on the backside several years earlier and not before time, as this was 1968.

As for the 'wells', there are hundreds of Holy Wells all over Ireland, many of them still in use, and most, unlike our remote and hidden gem which I cannot find recorded in any literature, are close to Churches and Villages. They vary greatly in appearance, some are very simple decorated only with rounded river pebbles, others are highly ornate and adorned with holy statues, medals, pictures, rosary beads, flowers and candles. Many of the wells have become famous for their alleged power to heal diseases and this is usually attributed to a Patron Saint.

When Catholics were forbidden under the Penal Laws to assemble for Mass in churches, altars were erected beside some Holy Wells and Mass was said there in secret, sometimes on the pain of death.

There was no such suffering that night in Caherdaniel and the locals were highly amused at my attempts to describe the windy turmoil above Eagle Hill, and while most of the throng knew about the well, there was only one old fella with no teeth and a Bobby Charlton comb-over knew of the stone-arrow but he passed out before I could get any sense from him.

'Sing us a song young fella', shouted an 'old wan' called Mick, and he shushed the packed pub for my next song. They would have quietened down anyway, it was that sort of place, they just loved a good song especially one with a story. I gave them one of my own, 'My Lovely Dublin Lassie', which I penned around 1983, with song-writing partner of the time, and long-time buddy, Martin Coult, he was a great talent who drifted away from the music scene, and indeed my life, much too soon and he is greatly missed.

After we had recorded the song, which has proved strangely prophetic lyrically, we sailed off to Dublin thinking the streets would be paved with recording contracts. We thought we had cracked it when I blagged our way into the offices of one Michael O'Riordan, of Ritz Records. "I can do something with that lads", he said, and for the icing on the cake we then met Pete St John, who has gone on to be one of Ireland's foremost songwriters with many great songs to his credit, including the anthemic 'Fields of Athenry' and the 'Rare Ould Times'.

My mother, Claire, a Dubliner, always loved this song, and even though we didn't 'crack it' in Dublin that day the song lives on and was recently included, March 2017, in my play with songs, The Angel on O'Connell Street'. Sad to say that, my Mum passed away in April 2017 but, she knew the song was still going, and was quietly pleased by that fact.

That night in the 'Blind Piper' was the first time I had sung the song in public since it had been written, and with no guitarist, I performed it a cappella. You could hear a pin drop.

I remember when I met you so many years ago,
Your hair in dark brown tresses on your shoulders did flow,
When I looked into your eyes, I had to let you know,
You`re my lovely Dublin lassie and I`ll never let you go.

As the years they rolled onward, our family did grow,
Two sons and two fine daughters, a fair wind did blow,
How a man could have such fortune, I swear I'll never know,
You're my lovely Dublin lassie and I'll never let you go,

Our lives were full together and we loved each other so,
Our children now had children, how you let your pride show,
But then death crept in one morning, like the first winter's snow,
You're my lovely Dublin lassie, why did you have to go.

And now at sixty-seven I'm so weary and slow
As each and every day now your image comes and goes,
When I think of you my darling, well the tears they do flow,
You're my lovely Dublin lassie, and I'll never let you go.

If you can sing or play an instrument in Ireland, it's like having your own Passport into the very fabric of the country, the Heartland, and mine was 'stamped' on each page with Guinness that night in Caherdaniel.

"Funny that", I said before dropping off back in the cottage, "You would have thought that everyone would know about the well".

Time moved on, as did we, and after one more night in one more straggle of houses called Kilmacow in Kilkenny, we found ourselves back in Bleak House with one more story to tell, a tale with more questions than answers.

Shining Girl was the first to appear on my return but she did not come near enough to talk to, and I watched with interest as she rounded the bend below the conifers at the side of Hey Farm before dropping from sight, and then appearing soon after leaning on the gate to St James five hundred yards in the other direction. It was a 'trick' she had used many times before so it came as no surprise to me but, I had anticipated talking to her about our trip to Ireland and the Windy Gap mysteries. I remember thinking that, maybe she was annoyed with me for leaving her to walk the hills alone, and her reticence that morning was down to a little fit of girly pique.

I cannot deny that, the very notion of a beautiful but very dead girl, a walker, being jealous of my time spent away from the valley and maybe even because I was with someone else is absurd. Whether that was the case or not she was real to me, and although others will have their own thoughts Crowden was alive with the deceased.

Half an hour later, after a cursory mooch through the wood with nothing much to brag about in the way of wildlife, I climbed up the hill to Hey Edge. It was, without exception, a steep pull and all your pipes would be working flat out but, you were always and I mean always, guaranteed blue hares, red grouse and meadow pipits so the effort was unfailingly rewarded. I was fit then, very fit, and was once more playing in Glossop Rugby Clubs 1st XV, so every bit of climbing and meandering through the valley was a top-up allowing me to hit the ground running at the start of the season. I even set myself ambitious targets, such as, and yes the lonesome job of a Waterman allowed for talking to oneself, 'Right, here we go", before setting off with a distant boulder as a target and then placing my index finger on my temple to gauge how quickly my heart rate would return to its normal sixty beats a minute and then concluding the successful mission with, "Nice one Woody".

With one more target accomplished including an ungainly scramble over a six feet high stone wall, surprising a hare on the other side as I dropped to my haunches; "Bend your knees Woody," I said before landing followed by, "Go on you beauty", as the hare stretched his long legs and loped off.

Hey Farm was always a good place to take a breather, and this day was no different, that is until the distant but, distinctive call of the stonechat carried over from the edges of the nearby clough. "That'll do for me I thought", just back from County Kerry to hear the same dulcet tones of the bird in my own back garden. Seconds later another stonechat, this time from somewhere behind the house, shortly followed by yet one more from the slopes below me, it was a 'chat-fest'. As well as talking to myself in the hills it should be noted that, a smile was rarely off my face, and this was one of those occasions. The chats were only bettered by a cuckoo up to no good, while for the cherry on the cake, a peregrine from out of nowhere flashed into a group of racing pigeons three hundred feet above the reservoir flinging out its talons at the last second, and hitting one the birds with such force that it was decapitated; the head spinning towards the water as the powerful falcon flew off towards Crowden with one more meal for the fledglings. Tough life and death for the pigeon but, an awesome sight for any birdwatcher and whilst this particular individual was a gonner, the rest of the party shook up maybe, kept going to some 'loft' somewhere, their 'fancier' one bird down.

Yes, Woody was grinning again.

A minute or so after the falcon's show, Shining Girl appeared momentarily amongst the trees to the right of where I was sitting, she said nothing but gesticulated in an urgent fashion towards the house behind me. I turned to see what was pertaining but, saw nothing untoward and looked back to ask what the fuss was about. She was gone again.

A loud crash in the small stone flagged byre made me jump up with a start. It sounded like the roof had fallen in and all the stone-tiles had smashed on the floor, except that, there had been no roof-tiles since they were removed in 1914, and the last time I saw them, they were stacked neatly at the back of the farm covered in nettles, and as my poem said, *The roof has long fallen in'*. On investigation, I discovered that there were six of the largest roof tiles laid out on the floor of the byre, they were neatly in a row, side by side, with the edge of one, resting on the edge of the next. None of them were broken.

Something similar had occurred when I was around five years old when we lived above a butchers shop in Leicester. In the tiled entrance to the flat on the first floor, there were two rows of old fashioned oval meat plates, some had hunting scenes and others were Willow Pattern, while the largest of the plates had a picture of a wild boar emerging from a wood.

There was a loud commotion one night as though all the plates had fallen and smashed onto the unforgiving floor six feet below the shelves, and I recall climbing out of bed to investigate. As I sat out of sight on the landing my mum and dad talked excitedly about what had happened. "I don't believe it John not one of them is broken", said my mum", "God knows", replied my dad.

Back at Hey and before I had chance to weigh up the implications of the find of intact stone roof slates, there was another noise from outside the farm, this time a kind of speedier and more amplified stone chat call, like an actual stone-mason chipping away loudly with his hammer. Although alarmed, there was no alternative but to check it out and I do confess to being a little apprehensive as I left behind one mystery to walk into another. The second proving to be unfathomable to this day.

On the grass, laid out in identical fashion to the stones by the Holy Well in County Kerry, was a neatly and methodically constructed stone arrowhead. The Crowden version made from the roof-tiles at the back of the farm. The whole affair was shallower than the Irish version, as the rocks by Windy Gap were more like those that would have been utilised for wall building but nevertheless, as in Ireland, smaller pieces were used at the front of the arrow, with whole roof-tiles being used at the back, and yes you may have guessed, the arrow was pointing due-west.

Discretion being the better part of valour I made for the comfort of my own four walls and the Bleak House kitchen, resolving to go back up to Hey Farm as soon as possible to photograph the stone-arrow. Luckily for me, my chunky chum, Oaf, long time friend and Sister Prop Forward from Glossop Rugby Club had arrived at the house before I had to return to Hey on my own. He was actually driving to price a decorating job in Stalybridge but, decided to drive the seven miles extra from Glossop on the Woodhead Road, for a mug of tea and any food that was going. He knew there was always a feed to be had at my house, and on a lighter note, I think this was the day that he broke his own record of how many slices of a Warburton's Toastie with butter he could eat with one breakfast. It went like this: Three before the breakfast arrived on the table, four while he was eating it, followed by a final two slices to wipe up the delicious tomato, egg and bacon juices, which had come together on his platter like a Jackson Pollock. Just the 'nine' slices then.

With his arteries clanging shut after three thousand calories, which had included all those available in half a pound of butter, Oaf wasn't keen for a walk but I insisted and relayed the story to him as we retraced my steps back to the farm, no more than one hour later.

"Come and have a look at this," I said, with that false sense of security one gets when you are accompanied by another person in a tricky situation and was just about to stand by the arrow-head and point to the construction with a triumphant, "Da, derr!" but it was gone. Thankfully, for many reasons not least my own sanity, there was a perfect yellow arrowhead amongst the green grasses where the stones were lain, which would indicate that the formation had been there for at least two or three days. Oaf, as observant as ever said, "There's nowt there Woody". Neither were there any stone slates in the byre, however I was fairly confident that there would be photographic evidence of both the stone arrow-head from beneath the green-duvet in Ireland, and now as I snapped away at the anemic lemon version at Hey Farm. The next morning the film was duly in the post to the photographic developers popular at the time, Max Spielmann, First Class.

As I said earlier, 'Best of luck with this one', and I wish that there was a rational elucidation which I could offer by way of an interpretation. No such luck

I'm afraid, and I cannot even suggest that this occurrence is linked in any way shape or form to any other story I may share in this book, it's a kind of random Shaggy-Dog-Tale but true for all that and I have seen nothing like it since.

Shining Girl thought that it was a 'sign' that I should or would go West and move to Ireland. Oaf, in his wisdom offered his favourite Irish Joke instead when I asked his opinion. "Knock, knock", he said, "Who's there?" I replied, "Joe", "Joe who?" I continued, "Burt Lancaster", said Oaf. I know, don't ask.

All hopes now lay with the Film Developer, Mr Spielman, but several days later when the box of slides arrived in the post there was no joy there either, as the transparencies of the arrow-head in Kerry were all blank, and the shots at Hey Farm never happened, as the film had finished and come away from the spool. Every Man-Jack of them a dud, while the beautifully exposed shots of the Holy Well and it's finger-worn grooves still sit in a little plastic case somewhere.

Chapter Seven:
The Longdendale Lights.

Daniel Defoe, 1660-1731, should perhaps wash his mouth out as he once described Longdendale as, *'Perhaps the most desolate, wild and abandoned country in England'*, and although Dan undoubtedly had a fantastic imagination, most famous for his novel Robinson Crusoe, he was miles out with the Valley. The same was true of his latter-day compatriot, Alfred Wainwright, 1907-1991, renowned for his eulogies to the Lake District, when he claimed that, after he passed through Crowden on the Pennine Way, the best thing to do was get out of Longdendale as fast as you could, and be careful to look over your shoulder for 'Big Brother'. Wainwright was referencing the bailiffs and watermen of North West Water, who used to frog-march hikers from off the Reservoir Catchment Areas. I'd like to think that I changed all that 'get off my land' mentality, reasoning that if someone had made the effort to walk so far up the valley then generally they were okay, and the only thing I took exception to was swimming in the Reservoirs, not least because it was so dangerous. True or not, one story I was told illustrates the folly of Reservoir swimming. Five young men who had allegedly been drinking at one of the Valley's many public houses had decided to stop for a swim near the Woodhead Dam on their return to Glossop. Five jumped in and only two came out alive. At any time of the year once you get a few feet down the water is icy cold.

With regard to our two literary critics, I suppose if you only visit Crowden once in your life, and it was raining, blowing a gale and winter was sitting on every shivering branch it might sway your perception of the place somewhat, so in this instance and for once only, the pair can be forgiven their slanderous mutterings.

Defoe, to his credit had a wonderfully varied CV, as in no particular order he was a trader, writer, journalist, pamphleteer, spy and inmate of Newgate Prison. One week after his release from gaol Defoe witnessed the Great Storm of 1703, which raged through the night of 26/27th November. The storm caused severe damage to London and Bristol, uprooted millions of trees and killed more than 8,000 people, mostly at sea. The event became the subject of Defoe's 'The Storm' (1704), which includes a collection of witness accounts, often regarded as the world's first example of modern journalism.

In 1987, I was privy to another great storm which once again robbed the British landscape of millions of trees, and I described the aftermath a year later in the Sunday Times Newspaper, as leaving the countryside with just the..*'Shades of glades gone by'*. I was proud of that line, still am. Crowden, with hardly any trees, thanks to hundreds of years clearing for the incoming sheep, and virtually none at all compared to the time of the Domesday Book, when a squirrel could have jumped from branch to branch, from Sherwood to Woodhead without touching the ground got off lightly in '87.

The sessile oaks suffered no damage whatsoever, not least because they are a kind of dwarf oak and they snuggle up to the hillside in small plantations impervious to the most tormenting north easterlies. The valley was a very different place in days of old, packed with not only trees, including oak, ash and willow but all the attendant wildlife that goes with it. Wolves, wild boar, red deer, lynx and even brown bear up to 1,000 years ago. The very notion that so many wild animals were abroad around Crowden may have added to the bad reputation the valley had garnered over the years. Although having said that, the discovery of Neolithic arrowheads in the silt of the Longdendale Reservoirs demonstrates that early man knew where his bread was buttered.

Just a mention of Neolithic Man has me frustrated as a writer, as there is a book in that alone, and there is more than one book in historical overviews of Longdendale but, dipping in and out of ancient time-scales will have to satisfy me for now, and I am hoping it can help to fill in the gaps of valley generation and regeneration over the Millennia. Give readers a 'feel' for the place. I had better not mention the dinosaur footprints discovered near Valehouse Reservoir as they will complicate things even more.

Imagine yourself outside St James Church as this will afford you 360 degree views of Longdendale across the ages.

12000 to 8000 BC (late upper Palaeolithic)

Environment - Tundra, main trees were dwarf birch and there were beaver, fox, horse and badger present. Land bridge to Europe still viable.

8000 to 4000 BC (Mesolithic)

Environment - Warmer conditions, birch and pine giving way to deciduous forests. Wet, many small lakes, rivers and streams. Land bridge to Europe now cut off by rising sea levels. Peat formation initiated.

Archaeology - Microliths, a small flint tool, indicating a hunter-gatherer culture with possible seasonal migration. There is no flint in Longdendale so these were brought in.

4000 to 2000 BC (Neolithic)

Environment - warm conditions with oak woodland dominant.

2000 to 700 BC (Bronze Age)

Environment - weather deteriorated towards end of the Bronze Age, main trees were oak, ash, hazel and elm.

Archaeology - Tools or mainly stone and bone, stone circles with possible astronomical alignments, jewellery, weapons that appears to be more about status than fighting, barrows, and the arrival of the Beaker culture.

Local evidence of this period was hard to come by until, with a little bit of luck a beautiful bronze ingot fell into my hands thanks to Farmers Daughter

Berrie Broderick. These artefacts described by an Archeologist friend of mine as 'Rare as rocking horse shit' were not only used to make things but also as a form of currency. Ruby tells a lovely story about how her Father, the late Wright Cooper, of Townhead Farm, Tintwistle, chanced upon the small Bronze Age hoard from so long ago in the late 1940's. "My Dad was out gathering sheep when a storm got up so he took shelter out of the wind and rain on the side of a peat grough. He got to poking about on the ground with his Shepherds crook and opened up a small crevice, curious he pushed his crook into the hole and heard the sound of chinking metal and as he dug further with his hands, several ingots, a bowl, a ladle, arrowheads and spear tumbled out at this feet". Wright handed over the find to Manchester Museum and they have now vanished again as they are nowhere to be found in the bowels of the Museum. Fortunately for me, Wright had the foresight to hold on to a couple of examples and Berrie's prize possession, possesses a lustrous verdigris, and close up the imprint of the back of a human knuckle; engaging evidence to demonstrate how the Bronze Age smelter formed the clay-mould with the back of his or her hand. Known as 'bun' ingots because of their shape, most are found broken and in pieces, which makes Wright Cooper's example very rare indeed. More information about bun-ingots is being unearthed every year and each new find providing more interesting background to the way our forebears lived their lives but, where did the Bronze Age Smiths of Longdendale obtain their metals and indeed their understanding of how to work it. Firstly, Bronze is an alloy of 90% copper and 10% tin, both metals were readily available in the British Isles at this time, and secondly they will have learned the skills from an early European Free Trade arrangement, which just shows to go that, we can always benefit from sharing our skills and experience.

The beginning of the Bronze Age in Britain can be put to around 2,000 BC and it is generally thought that the innovative bronze tools and weapons identified with this age were brought over from continental Europe, and very likely by the Bell Beaker folk, so named because of the shape of vessels found in their graves. They probably came up through the south-west coast of Britain, which at the time had rich deposits of copper and tin, and undoubtedly set up shop there. The visitors had the technology, which helped the Brits put one and two together and get bronze but demand soon outstripped supply, and just as a people, we demanded more 'spuds' once they had arrived on these shores, our Longdendale ancestors would have been keen customers. Apart from the tools and weapons, bronze ingots were also imported, and it is very likely that 'tin' was exported. Some compelling evidence of this two-way trade-route was discovered in 2009 during a dive of a Bronze Age vessel, 300 metres off the coast of Salcombe in Devon.

Jim Tyson, of the South West Maritime Archaeological Group said, 'The ship was carrying hundreds of copper and tin ingots. We have already found 286 of them, including a 'bun' ingot, (*the same as Berrie's*), which would have been melted together to make bronze for weapons, tools, and household items. This is the first Bronze Age ship in the United Kingdom to be found with its cargo still on board. The especially large load is very exciting because it indicates that Britain's trade links with Europe at the time were extensive and that more metal was coming into the area from abroad than had previously been thought. Another surprise was that the ingots came from a wide variety of locations across Europe, indicating a more sophisticated network of sources than scholars have imagined'.

This information produces as many questions as answers for example, let's assume that, the Bronze Age Folk who lived above Town Head Farm traded goods for their ingots, so what did they trade, where did they trade and who did they trade with. This trade may seem a difficult prospect but, not as difficult as, for example, the trade, three million years earlier, of stone-age axes made of porcellanite, a hard, dense rock similar in appearance to unglazed porcelain, and only found on Rathlin Island off the North East Coast of Northern Ireland and in the Glens above Cushendall on mainland Antrim, which found their way to Cornwall.

I would love to jump in the Tardis and watch on as the bronze ingot made its 300 mile journey to the Long Dale. Perhaps like a latter-day trip to the corner shop for some errands, the Bronze Age Valley Folk, only recently on with farming livestock, having partially moved on from hunting game animals, would salt down their meat and set off to Mid-Cheshire to exchange their goods for more salt, or perhaps jewelry, or even an ingot to make their own. Where is the Doctor when you need him. Meanwhile, the actual Town Head Bronze Ingot sits on a desk in Padfield approximately half a mile from my desk. After realising that Berrie's family have lived in the valley for over 200 years I asked her if she would read the manuscript and check my 'local dialect' which I had written down after speaking it out loud to myself. Thankfully the dialect got the thumbs up but, by chance she gave me so much more and she became quite emotional in the telling. "Your Pawdy Blanche, the Irish soldier, I saw him fifty years ago and at last your book has vindicated me. Nobody believed me at the time and I've just kept it to myself ever since". Berrie and her first husband had gone to look at the Rifle Range house, as it was for sale, and while she was moving from to room to room she caught sight of Pawdy outside on the path which led to the billets. I had a feeling that I was not the only person to see the walkers.

700 BC to 50 AD (Iron Age)

Environment - even cooler and wetter than at end of Bronze Age.

Archaeology - some hill forts and crop marks of settlements, generally poorly represented.

50 - 350 AD (Roman)

Archaeology - Minor Roman forts e.g. Melandra, Roman roads.

400 - 900 AD (Saxon)

Archaeology - Carved crosses, barrows with grave goods and also place names. Saxon Trading route the 'Portweg' (Portway).

900 to 1600 AD (medieval)

Archaeology - Norman castles e.g. Peveril Castle and motte and bailey castles, Manorial centres. Ridge and furrow cultivation

At this point, I need to mention a tantalising link to the Valley of both Daniel Defoe, and one of my most interesting walkers, John Hadfield, who was born at Crowden Hall in 1757 and hanged at Carlisle Jail in 1803. Both men served time in Newgate, and Hadfield along with his muse, the Maid of Buttermere, will feature in a later chapter.

Another fortuitous link to the pair, had me rubbing my hands with glee; Defoe's, Robinson Crusoe was published by a Mr Taylor, whose publishing house was purchased (circa 1724) for £2,282 9s. 6d. by the fledgling Longman Publishers. Longman was based in Pater-Noster-Row, near to St Paul's Cathedral, London, and went on to publish the works of the Lake Poets, Wordsworth and Coleridge, who both were friends with, and wrote about, Mary Robinson, aka, The Maid of Buttermere. Serendipity at its finest.

For the benefit of readers and myself alike, it would be really useful if I could do as, Bill & Ted, in their most, 'Excellent Adventure', and go back in time to meet, and talk to historical figures to help with my final draft but, In my own way, I suppose this is exactly what is happening. Bodacious to be sure.

Just a little delving into the writing of Defoe, reveals that he would have been the perfect candidate to argue the toss about, walkers and the the infamous 'Longdendale Lights', although he does get too muddled up with religion for my liking in places.

One of the many subjects discussed in his writings is the existence of spirits or ghosts, and claims that the Bible itself speaks of them, so (he says) there is no reason to disbelieve in their existence. At the same time, in an age when belief in superstitions, folklore and the occult were common, Defoe cautions those who are inclined to see ghosts where none exist in one of his pamphlets but he also seems to set himself up as the judge of whether reports are to be believed or not. Defoe the arbiter.

True Relation of the Apparition of one Mrs. Veal, the next Day after her Death: to one Mrs. Bargrave at Canterbury. The 8th of September, 1705. London: Printed for B. Bragg, at the Black Raven in Pater-Noster-Row, 1706.

Defoe re-tells a story that was in circulation in Canterbury in late 1705. The text is presented as having been dictated to a Justice of the Peace in Maidstone by a neighbor of Mrs. Bargrave, who told her the story of how her long-time friend Mrs. Veal (whom she hadn't seen in years) appeared to her one day, only to discover that Mrs. Veal had in fact died the day before.

Defoe uses the story for two things: to argue for the existence of spirits and to urge people to consider that, there is a Life to come after this. (The great arbiter believed this story)

With perhaps the world record for the longest title, *An Essay on the History and Reality of Apparitions. Being an Account of what they are, and what they are not; whence they come, and whence they come not. As also how we may Distinguish between the Apparitions of Good and Evil Spirits, and how we ought to Behave to them. With a great Variety of Surprizing and Diverting Examples, never Publish'd before. London, 1727.*

Defoe is attempting here both to assert the reality of apparitions and of the devil as well as to play down the frequency at which these beings make themselves known in the world. He provides many anecdotes about those who have seen and interacted with an apparition, giving his judgment as to whether the ghosts in each account are likely real or imaginary, for he says, *'Our Hypochondriack People see more Devils at noon-day than Gallilaeus did Stars, and more by many than ever really appear'd'.*

Defoe could be talking about one of my walkers and he does it, like me, in a matter of fact way. I believe his use of religious beliefs and references to the Devil are more to do with the times he was writing in and how people interpreted such things, or more importantly, the need to label stuff, give it a meaning and make sense of it, or not, as the case may be. Once again like myself, Defoe plays Devil's advocate, by littering his writing with more prosaic descriptions of sightings which as first were thought to be supernatural of nature. My favourite, could have been written about a gentlemen riding along the Old Salt Road which meanders, high and low, through Longdendale.

'The darknefs and rain put him a little out of humour but, in the way was a small river but there was a good bridge over it, well walled on both fides; fo that there was no danger there. But the gentleman kept on his fpeed to go over the bridge, when being rather more than half over his horfe ftopped on a fudden and refuffed, as we call it, he faw nothing at firft and was not discompos'd at it, but fpurred his horfe to go forward. The horfe went two or three steps and then ftopped again, fnorted and ftared, then the Gentleman looked forward to fee what was the matter, and faw two broad ftaring eyes. Then he was heartily frighted indeed...

...Fpurring his Horfe again, got over the bridge, and paffed by the Creature with Broad Eyes, he affirm'd pofitiviely, when he was pafs'd, was a great black BEAR, and confequently muft be the Devil..'

This passage is written in 'Old English', where the 'S' that we know is written differently according to its position in the word. The f-like (S) (like an f without the crossbar) was a tall variant used at the start, or in the middle of a word, while the modern 'S' was used at the end, or after a tall 'S'. It was to distinguish between a hard 's' and a soft 's'. The 'f' represented the soft 's' which is why you will find it spelt 'houfe' and 'houses' in old English texts.

The gentleman in question had his servant, Gervais, with him and when the both arrived home, the stories quickly diverged, the Master - upstairs- sticking to his notion that he had indeed seen the Devil, while Gervais -downstairs - in the kitchen with the other servants, claimed that the frightening creature was nothing but an ass.

This is a good example of how stories of sightings, become exaggerated and distorted, and how one man's alien is another man's 'earth-light', or indeed, how a glow-worm or firefly, which are tiny bioluminescent beetles, can transform itself into a fairy after a pint of porter. The fairies can be ruled out from my account, as to the best of my knowledge they did not occur in Longdendale during my 28 year tenure.

From a natural history perspective Defoe's story of the Black Bear is technically array from the off, as there were no black bears in the UK, and the brown bear a native mammal was extinct long before Mr Defoe wandered along Pater Nosta Row, or indeed, Defoe's gentleman rode over the bridge, and also, not that I wish to be too picky but, as a species they have rather small eyes. Yes I know, as I have already illustrated, stories do grow in the telling.

Arthur Brocklehurst thought that wolves and bears were still alive and well in Scotland in the 20th Century, and I could not convince him otherwise, even though the last wolf in the UK was reportedly killed in 1680, and the last brown bear was lost sometime around one thousand years ago. I told him about a friend of mine who had a large parcel of land above Loch Ness who was keen to see the wolf reintroduced, and Arthur was not impressed, "Nae lad' nae", is all he could say on that score.

Having said that Arthur was much more commonsensical about the 'Lights', and after a few scoops with Daniel Defoe I have a feeling he would be with me, another pragmatist playing down the excitable interpretations.

If readers were to search online for the natural phenomenon known as the 'Longdendale Lights', a veritable boatload of references, photographs and film clips will emerge on your computer screen, it's a 'lights' overload. The 'Lights' in question are no big deal and I saw them many times and was regularly quoted and misquoted, on paranormal websites, in newspapers, numerous books, and on many TV Shows from here to Timbuktu. The 'spooking-up' of my stories really annoyed me so I stopped giving interviews, and if it is faux-drama and histrionics you want please look away now, because the 'lights' are just the 'lights', and there will be no exaggerated melodrama here. Fascinating maybe but, my version will contain none of following examples, which were found during a brief trawl of the Internet and all referring to the Longdendale Lights and their supposed effect on the person...'A terrifying night-time drive into the twilight zone'...'The family's nightmare'...'I was profoundly disturbed'...'I was convinced we were being invaded by extraterrestrials', or even, 'I've never been so scared in all my life'.

Dr David Clarke, was the first person to write about my experiences with the 'Lights', and to be fair his account is still the most accurate. Dr Clarke's pragmatism matches mine and there was always a mutual respect for each others views. During our meetings in the early 90's, I was very tempted to share some of my tales about the walkers but kept quiet, until now that is and I am very grateful to David for his comments and for allowing me to quote from his writings.

'Sean Wood won't take the mick. His window fronts directly onto the carriageway of the busy trans-Pennine Woodhead Pass. He told a local newspaper with blunt sincerity: "Quite simply, there are bright lights which appear at the top end of Longdendale; there's no doubt they exist, but what they are I have no idea". When I visited Sean's home he described the lights he had seen, pointing towards Shining Clough, a rugged and desolate mountain ridge which dominates the southern horizon from his home at the watershed of the valley. He first saw the lights there in the early 1980s shortly after his family

moved to live at Bleak House which stands directly below Woodhead's fourteenth century chapel-of-ease".

"It was about 9.30 p.m. on a November evening when I walked into one of the front rooms at Bleak House to chastise someone for shining a torch through our window", Sean explained. "Of course there was no torch, nor indeed any person outside. However, the light filled the room with a chilly, moonlike glow. The effect was heightened by the lack of street lighting at this altitude and when I went outside to investigate I saw a large pulsing ball of light directly above the house, and not too far from the aptly-named Shining Clough. With the hair on the back of my neck bristling I went to telephone my near neighbours at the Crowden Youth Hostel. Guess what. They were outside watching the light in the sky too. This was just the beginning.Two years after that I saw it again, beneath the skyline. In all I've seen them more than thirty times over the sixteen years I've been here", Sean explained. "One of the times it was very, very big, and between fifty and seventy feet from the ridge; it was pulsing again and then stopping, moving back and forth and up and down. I've also seen three lights together, much smaller in size, like in a string, moving in an arch. I've seen these a few times, and also the big ones a few times".

Reading my description after so long was like looking back on my youth, as I was only 26 years old when I first saw the 'Lights', and although I was tempted to change a few things and add the many updates with regard to subsequent sightings, David's version is spot on.

To bring the, 'Lights', back down to earth, because that is where they are from I will need to cover for the sake of being comprehensive a selection of the Scientific Theories. I am no expert in this area but, rather a witness to the 'Lights', a watcher, and a man who has never lost his sense of wonder.

Shining Girl and Arthur Brocklehurst, were cut from the same cloth on that score, and they both called the lights, 'Will-O'-The Wisp', and 'Jack-O'-Lantern', respectively. Arthur once told me, "Folk int' Valley, were ne'r worried about Thow'd Jack tha knows but, in thw'd days, summat lasses thought their beau would dee if they walked out we 'im when Jack wor about '.

Will-o'-the-wisp, or, 'ignis fatuus', meaning 'foolish fire', in the Latin, is the name given to small bright lights seen flickering over marshes and fens, recorded for thousands of years by different cultures across the world. They have a hundred different names and, as it is science we are talking about, nomenclature. The, 'Wisps', referred to in the British tradition, as far as I can gather, where lighted bundles of sticks or hay which were used as torches or beacons and the name Will, was attached to it, to personalise the lights, in similar fashion to Jack, and his 'Lantern'.

Arthur Brocklehurst, although less-travelled, was a well read man, and he quoted the following from John Milton's, 'Paradise Lost', as his preferred description of the 'Lights'. "Lad, tha canna beat 'Paradeece Lost' tha knows, it's reet onth'nail", said Arthur, before reverting back to his Sunday-best voice to recite the passage:

> *"Compact of unctuous vapour, which the night*
> *Condenses, and the cold environs round*
> *Kindled through agitation to a flame,*
> *Which oft, they say, some evil spirit attends,*
> *Hovering and blazing with delusive light,*
> *Misleads th'amaz'd night-wanderer from his way,*
> *To bogs and mires, and oft through pond or pool,*
> *There swallow'd up and lost, from succour far . . .ah',* he said,

"That's enough o' that".

Other names associated with the 'Lights' reveal how different cultures interpret them, because for sure we are not alone in sightings of mysterious lights, for example, 'treasure lights', of Danish origin, suggests that they are the marking places for treasure; 'corpse candles', regarded as souls of the dead in Somerset, while, 'fairy lights', from the Shetlands is self explanatory, as is, the Scottish, 'merry dancers'.

The 'lights' are often linked to the leading astray of weary travellers into a swamp or dark woods, by a mischievous spirit, and on one occasion, an hour before the, 'Lights', were on show I was lead astray myself but, not by the 'Lights', or any 'spirit' but, by a bird, in fact two birds, a nightjar and a long-eared owl.

Dusk was rapidly dropping in, like a graduated grey blind being pulled down across the landscape, and the call of a nightjar could still be heard from amongst the sessile oaks on the railway side of the valley. This crepuscular time of day was usually my signal to get back down to the house, or cross over to the far side of the reservoir, as in this particular evening, because as much as I might contest that my walkers were a non-frightening and commonplace experience, you wouldn't catch me on the Salt Road, near the Church, or outside Hey Farm in the dark, not in a million years. 'T'other side ot valley', was a different story, just one walker, Bill Edmunds, and there were no murders or suicides and many times I sat in those woods, fighting off midges and taking in the view back across the Woodhead Dam to Bleak House. I was, without a care in the world, even when it was as dark, as dark could be.

Nightjars are nocturnal birds and can be seen hawking for food while there is just enough light at dusk and dawn. With pointed wings and a long tails their shape is similar to a kestrel or cuckoo, and their cryptic, grey-brown, mottled, streaked and barred plumage provides ideal camouflage in the daytime, making it possible to walk up to a bird as they sit characteristically on a tree stump or fallen branch in the bracken, perhaps completely confident that their disguise is safe. The first indication that a nightjar is near is usually the male's churring song, rising and falling with a ventriloquial quality, making it very difficult to pinpoint where the sound is coming from.

The matter was further confused on this occasion when the single plaintive call of a young Long Eared Owl vied for airspace with the nightjar. These stunning little owls, often played tricks with my sensibilities and even though they were a quarter of a mile away on the starter slopes of Bleaklow, at times it sounded as though they were behind me, and then at the side of me, and then a mile away, and then on this night, I could have sworn the owl was in the same spot as the chuntering nightjar.

Having failed miserably to locate either bird I decided that our futile game of hide and seek could wait for another day, and as I made my way back down the hill, gingerly, as the bracken is very good at hiding leg-breaking gaps between the grit boulders, I had 'that' feeling, and just to reinforce it, Moira, my first wife was in the window gesticulating in the direction I had just come from.

There were three purple orbs beyond the tree line, and they hovered and pulsed thirty or forty feet in the night sky above a relatively flat expanse of the landscape. This was a quiet zone, still is, no road noise, very rarely people and a mixture of worked stone, boulders, fallen down shelters, heather, cotton grass and grouse. Boggy in places but, not your actual 7,000 year old peat bog giving up its secrets.

There are similar tales and descriptions of 'lights' from across the world which can in turn, be comforting because they validate my own sightings, while at the same time prove a little deflating because the many and varied reports only demonstrate that the 'Lights' in Longdendale are far from unique. This is also very true of the more fanciful explanations which need to be taken into consideration to a greater or lesser degree.

My favourite, 'Will O' The Wisp story perhaps unsurprisingly, is the Irish tale of 'Stingy Jack'.

'Stingy Jack was a miserable, old drunk who loved playing tricks on anyone and everyone. One dark, Halloween night, Jack ran into the Devil himself in a local public house. Jack tricked the Devil by offering his soul in exchange for one last drink. The Devil quickly turned himself into a sixpence to pay the bartender, but Jack immediately snatched the coin and deposited it into his pocket, next to a silver cross that he was carrying. Thus, the Devil could not change himself back and Jack refused to allow the Devil to go free until the Devil had promised not to claim Jack's soul for ten years.

The Devil agreed, and ten years later Jack again came across the Devil while out walking on a country road. The Devil tried collecting what he was due, but Jack thinking quickly, said, "I'll go, but before I do, will you get me an apple from that tree?"

The Devil, thinking he had nothing to lose, jumped up into the tree to retrieve an apple. As soon as he did, Jack placed crosses all around the trunk of the tree, thus trapping the Devil once again. This time, Jack made the Devil promise that he would not take his soul when he finally died. Seeing no way around his predicament, the Devil grudgingly agreed.

When Stingy Jack eventually passed away several years later, he went to the Gates of Heaven, but was refused entrance because of his life of drinking and because he had been so tight-fisted and deceitful. So, Jack then went down to Hell to see the Devil and find out whether it were possible to gain entrance into the depths of Hell, but the Devil kept the promise that had been made to Jack years earlier, and would not let him enter.

"But where can I go?" asked Jack.

"Back to where you came from!" replied the Devil.

The way back was windy and very dark. Stingy Jack pleaded with the Devil to at least provide him with a light to help find his way. The Devil, as a final gesture, tossed Jack an ember straight from the fires of Hell. Jack placed the ember in a hollowed-out turnip...one of Jack's favorite foods which he always *carried around with him whenever he could steal one. From that day forward, Stingy Jack has been doomed to roam the earth without a resting place and with only his lit turnip to light the way in the darkness.*

Theories of the 'actual' source of the lights are myriad, complex and confusing, for example, could they be ignited marsh gases, perhaps methane, combusted with phosphine. The latter is the compound with the chemical formula PH_3. It is a colourless, flammable, toxic gas and pnictogen hydride. Pure phosphine is odourless, but technical grade samples have a highly unpleasant odour like garlic or rotting fish, due to the presence of substituted phosphine and diphosphane. With traces of P_2H_4 present, PH_3 is spontaneously flammable in air, burning with a luminous flame. Never say never, and maybe, this is the answer.

Phosphine however, is not to be confused with 'phosphene' as this is a phenomenon characterized by the experience of seeing light without light actually entering the eye, however, some of the resultant experiences may link the two inextricably. The word phosphene comes from the Greek words phos (light) and phainein (to show).

Phosphenes can be directly induced by mechanical, electrical, or magnetic stimulation of the retina or visual cortex. Phosphenes have also been reported by people who go for long periods without visual stimulation, sometimes known as the 'Prisoners Cinema', including people confined to dark cells, and by others kept in darkness, voluntarily or not, for long periods of time, including truck drivers, pilots, and practitioners of intense meditation. Also astronauts and other individuals who have been exposed to certain types of radiation, have reported witnessing similar phenomena, as have those who used hallucinogenic drugs. Food for thought there, as truck drivers populate the Valley by the hundreds every day and night, and as for 'Pilots', they have a chapter all to themselves in Volume 2.

As for intense meditation, it is not my bag but, being confined to darkness at Bleak House was a fairly regular thing when I first saw the 'Lights' in the early 1980's. Imagine the scene: it's the middle of winter, night time, no street lights and the electricity goes off, followed by the phone line, and then calamity beyond compare you run out of Irish whiskey. We were off the grid. Throw in the road being closed because of snow and you get that rarely seen phenomenon, a white-out-black-out. In those days Crowden and Woodhead could have been twinned with Svalbard, the only thing missing were the polar bears and walrus and after three days, I was always happy to see the snow-plough and the postman. I used to get some stupid phone-calls from Bottom's office, so the line being down was a blessing but, believe me, it wasn't long before they were buzzing with idiocy again.."Morning Sean, we have had no reservoir Levels from you for two days, can you check as a matter of urgency please and call me back?"

It is just a pity there were no mobile phones in those days, as I could have sent them some images of the twenty feet high snow drifts preventing me from doing anything, or moving anywhere safely. 'Yes, I will give you a call as soon as I can', I probably said rather lamely.

You would have thought the North West Water officer-dwellers would have known some of the history of severe weather in the Valley so I did not bother to tell them that the drifts in the courtyard at Bleak House reached our bedroom window, or that there was ice on the inside of the windows. In 1894 just the tips of telegraph poles were visible at Woodhead, and retired Railwayman John Davies claimed that in 1940, another 'bad un', that you could have walked from his red-brick railway cottage above Crowden Station, straight across the frozen Woodhead Reservoir and out onto the A628 the snow was that deeply drifted.

Over the years several friends asked with regards to the 'Lights', 'What were you on?' I never tried drugs, save for a few puffs on a joint and most of my sighting were achieved with a clear head but, evidence has shown that the so-called 'psychedelic' substances can cause thought, visual and auditory changes and a heightened state of consciousness. Major psychedelic drugs include LSD, Magic mushrooms and Mescaline, an active ingredient of peyote. Lophophora williamsii, or peyote, is a spineless cactus containing psychoactive alkaloids, particularly Mescaline. The English common name peyote originates from the Aztec, peyōtl, said to be derived from a root meaning 'glisten' or 'glistening'. Other sources translate the word as 'Divine Messenger. Native North Americans used peyote, often for spiritual purposes, for at least 5,500 years.

Carl Sofus Lumholtz (23 April 1851 – 5 May 1922) a Norwegian Ethnographer, best known for his research on the indigenous populations of Mexico, also wrote, 'Lacking other intoxicants, Texas Rangers, captured by Union forces during the American Civil War, soaked peyote in water and became intoxicated with the liquid. This is probably, the first documented use of peyote by non-Native Americans. It would appear that people with a penchant for this type of 'high' have always managed somehow to acquire it, in one form or another, and the remains of several hallucinogenic plants have been discovered in Neolithic cave dwellings,

The aforementioned DMT, or N,N-Dimethyltryptamine is a tryptamine molecule which naturally occurs in many plants and animals. It can be consumed as a powerful psychedelic drug and has historically been prepared by various cultures for ritual and healing purposes. Dr Rick Strassman called DMT, the 'spirit molecule', and devoted several books to the subject, including, *'Inner Paths to Outer Space: Journeys to Alien Worlds Through Psychedelics and Other Spiritual Technologies'.*

When I first saw, 'Alien', in the title, I nearly didn't bother, bearing in mind my earlier comments about the 'Lights' being just 'Lights', and in my view absolutely nothing to do with ET but, the word, alien, does however fit in very well when used in the sense that my Crowden, was unfamiliar, and I suppose to other people, could be viewed as disturbing.

The book has been described thus.. *An investigation into experiences of other realms of existence and contact with otherworldly beings, and this struck a chord with me, as a similar expression, 'otherness', was used by well known author, David Clarke, when describing Longdendale and the Lights.*

David very kindly provided me with his definition of 'otherness': 'A temporary sense of dislocation from oneself and one's usual environment whilst in a familiar place'. David, like me, would claim that 'this' can happen to a person with no help or influence from any outside source or stimulus whereas, Strassman and his co-authors, combine science-fiction with psychedelic research and present a study of how human beings can reach these other dimensions of existence and in turn contact otherworldly beings. The authors claim that psychoactive substances such as DMT allow the brain to bypass our five basic senses to unlock a multidimensional realm of existence where the otherworldly communication can occur.

I was almost warming to Strassman with that notion but, at this juncture I feel the need to reiterate my assertion to my aversion to any of the above, not even magic mushrooms which grow in profusion around Longdendale, and certainly not the likes of 'peyote', which one of my musician buddies described as '..that crazy Native American hallucinogenic?' The most I will have taken before seeing the lights, will have been a few pints of Guinness, or a bottle of Italian Red, although generally nothing but coffee. After reading Strassman and bearing in mind my penchant for 'seeing things' without any help, it is probably fortunate that no Class A Drugs ever entered my bloodstream. The possibilities if they ever did gives me the retrospective 'willies'.

Suffice to say that, the jury is out on all theories pertaining to the 'Lights', both natural and unnatural. As a brief overview the postulations include, reference to the shape of Longdendale, with the climate and geology generating a massive electric charge, and that static electricity could be generated by strong winds.

Others believe the lights are powered by radioactivity and the decay of radon in the atmosphere and they advance the argument that. the 'Lights' are made from 'dusty plasma' containing ionised dust particles, which erupt from the ground and enter the air as a glowing orb.

Author, Paul Devereaux, *'Earth Lights Revelation'*, says:

'In Derbyshire there are numerous geological faults, mineral deposits, reservoirs and the weight of water on underground cracks like geological faults can cause movement of the Earth which could generate the sort of electrical magnetic forces that could produce the lights. This will sound unlikely to some, but people who have witnessed major earthquakes also report visions of lights in the sky'.

Dr Roger Musson, a Seismologist with the British Geological Survey, says scientists are trying to solve the puzzle of the Earth Lights through laboratory experiments. *"Some people have found that if you take rock samples and submit them to certain stresses and temperatures then you can get them to emit light"*.

It has further been muted that, some rocks can store energy like a battery, and that the energy is sometimes released into the atmosphere during times of geological movement. There are parallels here with a notion of mine, in which I suggest that, my walkers, are somehow recorded in the millstone grit and are played back as though on a 'tape' when the conditions or the person who witnesses them, are just 'right'. Unfortunately, this theory does not fit quite so well when the walkers interact with me.

As I have already said, I am no expert but, with regard to earthquakes and the subsequent upheaval both under and above ground, there is one particular series of seismic events where I can place a quake, or number of quakes, and sightings of the 'Lights' in the same timescale but, this evidence is offered as an observation and in no way presented as irrefutable evidence that the two go hand in hand.

A sequence of more than 100 earthquakes started in the Greater Manchester area of the United Kingdom on October 19, 2002, with the epicentre between Gorton and Ashton Under Lyne. The BGS received more than 3000 reports from people who felt the Manchester earthquakes. Most of the reports were from within 20 km from the Manchester city centre. Reports of minor damage, such as small cracks, falling tiles, shattered windows, falling rubble and plaster were also received. A maximum intensity of 5+ on the European Macroseismic Scale (EMS) was determined for the earthquake on October 21 at 11:42.

Three temporary seismograph stations were installed to supplement existing permanent stations and to better understand the relationship between the seismicity and local geology. Due to the urban location, the events were experienced by a large number of people. The first earthquake that was felt occurred on 21 October at 07:45:15 (UTC) with a magnitude 3.2 ML. A few hours later at 11:42:34, there was a magnitude 3.9 ML earthquake, the largest in the sequence, which was strongly felt throughout the Greater Manchester area. About 22 seconds later there was another earthquake with a magnitude 3.5 ML (Local Magnitudes) Numerous smaller earthquakes occurred until the last event on 30 November 2011.

Analysis of the events in the sequence showed that many of them were very similar. Such similarity only occurs if the earthquakes are closely located and have a similar fault mechanism. The coal measures in and around Ashton Under Lyne were worked extensively up to the 1970s. However, the earthquakes occurred at a depth of 6-7 km, which places them far below even the deepest mine workings.

Earthquake sequences can occur in two ways. Firstly, moderate to large size earthquakes are usually followed by aftershocks, which occur due to readjustment to a new state of stress. The duration of the aftershock sequence depends partly on the size of the event. Normally, the largest aftershock is about one magnitude unit smaller than the main shock. Secondly, earthquake swarms are sequences of earthquakes clustered in time and space without a clear distinction of main shock and aftershocks. Such earthquake sequences or swarms are relatively common in Great Britain, and have been recorded from the late 18th Century to the present day.

The first I knew of this seismic sequence was when the very large Victorian mahogany wardrobe began to shake in my Bleak House bedroom, and after sitting bolt upright in bed, and realising what was happening I felt for sure that the twelve feet high stone chimneys, were about to crash through the ceiling and join me on top of the duvet. Fortunately I am still here to tell the tale and the chimneys still stab skyward but, although there had been other such quakes since 1980, this particular quake, subsequent quakes and the multitude of aftershocks was the most memorable of my tenure in my rocky hillside home.

Calm was soon restored and others in the house slept through it all, so I got dressed and went downstairs, and put on the kettle before going outside to check the roof and chimneys, circling the house and training my flashlight skyward towards the roof. All was intact, and there was a discernible air of calm, when my attention was drawn to the front of the house as some mad driver, in the absence of others on the road, hurtled across the dam, before screeching around the bend on two wheels and heading towards Skew Bridge and onwards to Glossop. 'Dick', I thought to myself as I often did but then thanked him, or her, as once again, for the umpteenth time three floating orbs appeared directly above the railway cottages. On this occasion, they seemed to blink between deep purple and blue, didn't move about very much, and neither did they cast much light elsewhere. Three self-contained spheres.

The only factor which is one hundred percent certain about the 'Lights', is that Longdendale is certainly not on it's own with the experience, and as an addendum to my comment to David Clarke thirty years ago, I would say, 'The lights, are just the lights, and they are reported all over the world', including, the, Saratoga Light, which appears and disappears at random during the dark of night without explanation.

This light has been described as starting as a pinpoint among the swamp trees that grows to the brightness of a flashlight, then dims and fades away, changing from white to yellow. The colour has been described as similar to that of a pumpkin, and sometimes appearing red as it approaches the observer. Some witnesses have observed that the light will sway back and forth, as if someone were carrying a lantern and walking. Another common attribute given to the strange light is its unpredictable nature and some eyewitnesses have attempted to follow or approach the light with no success. However, there are some that claim that the light has actually followed or entered their vehicle while traveling the road at night.

The 'bung fai paya nak', or Naga fireballs, have displayed on the Mekong River in Thailand, for as long as anyone can remember. Each year, anywhere from 200 to 800 of the fiery orbs are sighted along a 60 mile stretch of the river. The October full moon is the most likely time for them to appear, and as a result up to 400,000 people visit the river to catch their appearance.

On the Econlockhatchee River of Florida, some claim there is a ghost light that chases cars. The 'Chuluota light', looks like a very faint glowing ball of fog rising up from the swamp. Usually there is only a single ball of light, but on rare occasions as many as five lights have been observed at the same time. Some witnesses have reported that the lights resemble the headlights of a car, while others say that they just stop and hang in midair.

The Martebo Light is reported to be a, so called, 'Ghost Light' and has been seen since the early 1900's on the Swedish Island of Gotland. The Islanders at one time believed that, the light represents the soul of an unbaptized soul, which attempts to lead travellers to water.

The need to explain things is a fundamental human requirement, and to use modern day parlance, we need, or desire some kind of closure on mysteries. As yet, with regard to the, 'Longdendale Lights', Defoe's 'Big Black Bear', and Arthur Brocklehurst's, 'Jack-O'-Lantern', there is no definitive conclusion forthcoming. Suffice to say, it is elemental dear reader.

Top Left : Hey Farm 2017

Top Right : Holy Well at Windy Gap, Co Kerry

Bottom Left : Bleak House and St James from Woodhead Dam

Bottom Right : Hey Farm Photo Chris Peate

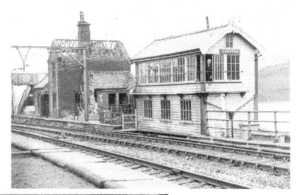

Top Left : Crowden Station
Top Right : Crowden Signal Box
Bottom : John Davies

Top Left : Staigue Fort, Derrynane towards Windy Gap
Top Right : The last freight train on the Woodhead Line from Bleak House 1981
Middle : George & Dragon, Woodhead 1930's
Bottom Left : Commercial, Crowden
Bottom Right : Woodhead Road after the downpour Circa 1981

Top Left : Maid of Buttermere
Top Right : John Crowden
Bottom Left : Crowden Hall
Bottom Right : Gareth Wilson and the Stone Trough, Crowden

Top : Flying Coach
Bottom right : 19th Century Hanging
Bottom left : Phaeton

Top : Bronze Age Bun Ingot

Bottom Right : Moira and Scarba by the Old Blacksmiths, Woodhead

Chapter Eight:
Of Lights And Men & A New 'Walker'

William 'Bill' Edmunds, was one of my walkers, hopefully still is, and I first saw him on a foggy night in 1982 after mistaking his lamp for a single Longdendale Light. It was one of those situations, when you spot something, and it either looks large and close in, or small and a long way off and it is difficult to determine which it is. On this occasion it was the latter but what threw me was that, the light appeared very close to the kitchen window of long time railway man, and Valley resident, John Davies. The light was close but not close enough, which is what made me look again. It just wasn't right. This light, on closer scrutiny appeared to be at the same level as John's back door but, to the right of where I would have expected it to be.

In the early 80's, John still had no electricity, even though his little red brick terrace was directly beneath the humming pylons which stride across the Valley, and he wasn't bothered one iota. He felt it was an affront when he was eventually more or less forced to hook up to the Grid and join the 20th Century and he in his early 80's at this stage. With his battery operated portable radio, the glowing Rayburn, a bottle of sterilised milk and yesterday's newspaper he was a contented man, and you know what, you will like him too.

I can still picture the long out of date Ovaltine Calendar on the wall and it's reference to the 'Ovaltineys'. The League of Ovaltineys was a children's club developed in the 1930s to promote the sale of Ovaltine brand drink in the United Kingdom. The club, founded in 1935, had its own radio show, 'Ovaltiney's

Concert Party', on Radio Luxembourg, sponsored by the manufacturer. It achieved five million members in 1939. This was a time when few people had televisions, and radio was all-important as a medium and had huge audiences. The show was broadcast on Sunday evenings between 5.30pm and 6pm on Long Wave and became well known throughout the UK for its theme song, 'We Are The Ovaltineys'. I couldn't help but sing the catchy song after every visit to John's house.

'We are the Ovaltiny's, little girls and boys…' Google helped me with the rest of the lyrics…

> *'We are the Ovaltineys, little girls and boys,*
> *Make your requests, we'll not refuse you*
> *We are here just to amuse you*
> *Would you like a song or story?*
> *Will you share our joys?*
> *At games and sports we're more than keen,*
> *No merrier children could be seen,*
> *Because we all drink Ovaltine,*
> *We're happy girls and boys'.*

Bill Edmunds and I laughed about our first meeting many times, and he took great delight in the fact that I looked petrified, which wasn't surprising as it soon became very obvious on that murky night that, it was a long time since Bill had actually 'worked' on the railways, and as it transpired, many years since he had died.

Bill and John knew each other well, worked together on the railway, and drank together in the Palatine Public House in Hadfield but, much more importantly in my mind John Davies knew about the 'Walkers', and so much more as you will discover.

On first spotting the red light on this dark night, bearing in mind that it seemed to come in and out of view as the fog was being blown about like net curtains on the breeze, I could have ignored it but I was a few years into my job by then, and knew full well from personal experience that hikers could and would get lost on the tricky and sometimes treacherous moors. The inexperienced and expert alike lose the paths and descend wherever and whenever they can, often to their cost. Like the father and son with their two dogs, who turned up at Bleak House early one evening, dishevelled, wet and exhausted. The dad asked, "Are we far from Greenfield?" "Ten miles", I replied. One wrong turn and that's your day spoiled but, things bucked up for the pair when I offered them a lift back.

So the decision was made for me really, the red light was not to be ignored, not least because someone in distress could be on the end of it. Cursing to myself, I climbed into my clothes, grabbed a flashlight and emerged into the Woodhead night. Don't ask me why but, I always looked up to the stone wall where the kids first shouted to me and inevitably got a chill up the back of my neck. It was par for the course and happened until I left Bleak House on June 10th, 2008. I only ever saw the children the once but, always felt their presence. There was one time when I saw six or seven smartly dressed children, wearing black and white uniforms, walking towards me on the old Salt Road, and my first thought was that they were walkers. They looked for all the world to be Victorian Sunday-School pupils on an outing from Crowden. Using a much used ruse of mine, I hid behind a stone wall, and waited for their arrival at a spot close to where I was concealed. In reality they were Orthodox Jewish school children from Manchester, who were indeed, on an outing with their teacher but, very much alive.

At 1am, the A628 was very quiet as it was three years yet before some bright spark opened the Stocksbridge Bypass, linking the M1 Motorway with the Woodhead Pass, and I was able to cross over without looking. The light on the hill was still visible and as I descended the stone steps on the other side of the road, as generations of watermen had done before me, I felt a certain sort of responsibility, and do you know what, a real satisfaction at being a part of the history of the Valley. The thought that pride might come before a fall as I advanced across the dam did not enter my head but, as I stopped to weigh up the light I soon realised that, firstly, it was not a lost hiker, and secondly, it was definitely not a light at John Davies window, and thirdly that, it was moving from side to side in some kind of purposeful action, or so it seemed. At this juncture the adrenalin kicked in because as the mist dissipated slightly, the nature of the light was revealed. It was a lantern with a red glow emitting from it, and it was being waved to and fro in the direction of Woodhead by a man in railway uniform. In

Universal-Train-Language, this signal means stop.

Nothing untoward in that you might think but, this particular less than thin Controller - he was well built - was around twenty feet above the level of the railway tracks which were gone at this stage, as the line had been closed in 1981, and he appeared to be standing in thin air.

No point hanging around at moments like this, at least not on the first sighting, and besides, now that it was clear there was no one in danger, my job was done and I shot back across the dam and sprinted up the stone steps like a rat up a drainpipe and you couldn't see me for dust.

There was no looking back that night and being accustomed to meeting the dead, as I had assumed Bill was, I waited until morning to ask John a few searching questions. John Davies enjoyed a chat but, he enjoyed a chat and bacon even more, and therefore armed with a chunk of heavily smoked Dutch Long Back, which I had been given for John by my dad, also John, a Butcher, I knocked on his back door which looked out onto the railway and part of the old platform, all that was left of Crowden Station.

"Morning Lad", he said, "I see you've got some of your dad's bacon for me, come on in and I'll stoke the Rayburn, the kettle's already on as I saw you walking over". "Thanks John", I replied, plonking myself down on the chair he had reserved for guests, and he entertained many, not least the postman. In those days the 'postie' had time for a brew and some good gossip, and sweetest of sweet, on a Saturday morning John would hitch a lift into Hadfield for some shopping and a pint, right up until some bastards broke into his house and roughed him up, which eventually led to him being confined to a care home, where he died. He was in his early 90's but he definitely went before his time, and I reckon John would have gone on to get his telegram from the Queen.

I told John that, for a moment I thought the lantern light may have been one of the 'Longdendale Lights', as discussed in the last chapter and although I soon discarded this notion, especially as it was red, and there are many anecdotal reports from different parts of the world, of railway lines being hot-spots for men with lanterns. The desire for an explanation, and then to 'flower-it-up' somewhat is obviously a global affectation.

For example, in living memory many residents of Le Seur, Minnesota, have told the story of a red light, that looks like a lantern floating down the Omaha railroad tracks.

An area south of the town, known as Old Brewery Hill, after a 19th Century brewery seems to be the epicentre for these sightings. Whether the sightings had a more obvious connection to the local brew is another matter. Two deep caves had been dug into the hill to keep the beer cool while it was being aged, and, although the brewery was destroyed by fire, if you are ever passing, it is still possible to see the remains of the cellars on the Eastern side of the Ottawa Road.

The stories began when a retired railwayman claimed he had to stop the train he was driving, because someone was carrying a red lantern along the tracks. When the driver got down from the train to remove the man from the track there was no one there, and many others on the train that night corroborated the driver's story.

It turns out, as is usually the case, that there is more than one possible explanation for these sightings, and after a recent so-called, 'paranormal investigation' in that area of Le Seur no red lanterns were seen but, a bright red orb hovering above the railroad tracks was recorded. My 'red light' on this occasion was not hovering and John soon began to wax lyrical about 'who' I had actually seen, and why he was in the air.

"That were Bill, he were a signalman at Crowden Station and the reason you saw him up there", he said pointing towards his door and in the general direction of where Bill had been, '..was that, he was up the metal gantry which used to cross the tracks, and he was probably stood just the other side of the middle and above the line in from Hadfield".

John continued, "I remember that night well. There had been a flash flood as we sometimes get, and Bill was having trouble getting hold of the signalman at Torside, so rushed, as best he could, to wave the red-lantern to warn the driver to stop. There was an obstruction on the tracks near the gamekeeper's cottage, right opposite the George & Dragon and what had happened was that, some giant boulders had come down the clough in the storm, and one, must have been six foot round, had virtually sealed off the tunnel which went under the embankment, causing the water to build up and eventually it or'topped the rails, carrying lots of smaller boulders with it and washed away the ballast. Stones were hanging int, th'air on't branches, like baubles on a skinny Christmas tree, we'a few dead sheep, one dead dog and a couple of old tractors among the tangle for good measure. The track were a right mess and very dangerous. Aye, he saved the day did Bill that night, and the driver pulled up as though nowt were going on and shouted to Bill to get a brew on. There were no passengers, just a few men and twenty wagons o' stone heading for Sheffield".

I was able to picture and understand the destruction that John described as there had been a similar, and very localised 'flash flood' earlier that year, quite remarkable in fact as from my vantage point outside the Valve House at the end of the Bleak House garden, I was able to watch the whole thing unfold. It began with a sudden darkening of the skies above Shining Clough, as though someone had thrown a bucket of black paint into the white clouds, causing them to billow angrily in a hundred different shades of grey, spinning in and out of each other like the very bad - but good - animation in the original 'Jason And The Argonauts film', it was unreal, and almost in slow motion.

There was no thunder or lightening initially but the rain began, not with the usual tiny drops before building up to a steady flow, because these 'drops' were like an egg-cup full of water and drenched you on first strike.

Boom, then came the first thunder and the ground shaking, followed by Zeus firing down his electric thunderbolts from on high, zigzagging, darting and crackling out of the heavens and one, a direct hit on the reservoir sending up an anti-plume of steam and iridescent rainbows as the late sun pushed through from Mottram and beyond.

On the hill movement was afoot, dry became wet, and oxbow lakes were formed in seconds, streams and gullies transformed into tormented rapids, of mud, rock and vegetation, which moved down the hill as a menacing lava taking anything in its wake, including, I found out later, the blanket and picnic items of two American ladies who had decamped on the edge of the clough; the Yanks were fine but, the clough was instantly re-shaped and twenty feet deeper in places as the moraine-like debris descended towards the back road and Skew Bridge.

One more enormous boulder did it and there was an audible 'pock' as the mighty rock jammed into the mill-race of the Paper Mill, and over she went, a tsunami of soupy brown detritus, cutting off and washing away the single track road to the Lodge, before laying a two feet thick carpet of mud and guts across the Woodhead Road. Rain stopped, job done, road blocked for three weeks. Well done Zeus - Gods 1 Valley 0.

The whole affair was over in fifteen minutes. With a month's rain in one go I thought that there was more than just the roads that needed looking at but I was wrong. The storm in relative terms, was literally in one place, at one moment in time, and although some of the stone walls on the reservoir side had succumbed, and the steady flow re-routed streams which had been shaped over one hundred years earlier, it was business as usual everywhere else.

I asked Bill whether he had seen the 1982 deluge but, he didn't confirm either way, and it transpires, or at least I think it is the case that, the walkers can only see things in the moment, for example, when talking or interacting with me or John Davies, and obviously they know things about the past and their own life experiences. This would suggest I fear that, as much as they were part of my own particular present, they were very much a fragment of the past who came in and out of our time, or rather my time as it pleased them, or when the 'conditions' were just right, a factor which Shining Girl had alluded to on several occasions. Most memorably when she turned up out of nowhere in Nerja, my favourite little town in Andalucia. It's a long story but has a bonus chapter all to itself later on in this adventure.

Bill Edmunds, for example, could remember that he had been successful in stopping the train approaching from Hadfield, and he liked to tell me on numerous occasions about the Commendation he received for his efforts but he had no knowledge of the more recent flash flood.

John Davies sometimes referred to Bill as 'Beds', as in, "I wonder if Beds is about today?" When I questioned him about this, thinking it was a nickname, John put me straight. "It's morse-code lad, them Signal lads used to communicate using morse-code as it was easier than using the phone." He then proceeded to write it down to demonstrate what he meant. If I recall correctly -... . -.. ... instead of -... .. .-.. .-. . /. -.. .-- .- .-. -.. ...

Bill's wandering loop, was the signal box, the platform, the waiting room and the gantry, and his best-loved, the little red-brick 'brew cabin'. Which brings me to the first time I met him.

When the railway closed in 1981, and the last diesel unit vanished into that Black Hole, which is the Woodhead Tunnel, there were some good pickings to be had, and Bill's 'brew cabin' was the only building of the old station still standing, and I had had my eye on the coal fired iron stove, with it's handy hot-plate, for some time. Crowden and Woodhead were deserted back in the day, and it was an easy job for me to jump into the Land Rover and drive up the tracks to the cabin. I press-ganged a friend into giving me a lift, and the two of us soon had the thing in the back and were ready for the short trip back across the dam booty safely stowed. My friend David, opted to drive, as I threw in a few chunks of coal which were still lingering, waste not, want not and all that, and a nice poker with the head of a bull on the top. I would have taken the 1952 Bovril calendar but it was all but perished, and fell apart as soon as I moved it.

"What did you do that for?", said a disembodied voice from inside the cabin, "Sorry?" I replied, "It's being knocked down next week, so I thought I'd rescue a few items", I replied, with the floundering voice of a tea-leaf caught in the act, without considering the provenance of a voice from the empty building I had just been in. "Bloody blow-ins", came back the retort, followed by a loud belly laugh, a cross between Tommy Cooper and the Laughing Policeman. I now know, it was Bill Edmunds.

Although these sort of encounters were becoming commonplace for me at Crowden, Bill was unique in two ways, firstly, as time passed by he proved to be the only walker on the railway side of the valley, don't ask me why, and secondly, it was Bill, and I suppose Shining Girl, to a large extent, who seemed to be able to show some empathy with the living, rather than the likes of Pawdy Blanche, who not only walked in a figure of eight but, went round in circles with his conversations about his own woes. Bill was also able to crack a joke and when he asked me why I had removed the calendar he quipped, "I won't able to tell what day it is now".

I looked into the brick cabin and he was sitting down on a wooden form with the air of a happy man about him, and although his railway uniform was a little frayed in places, and as thin as the hair on top of his head, he looked the part and was certainly not frightening.

Here's the intriguing thing, he asked if I wanted a brew and gesticulated towards the stove, which of course was stone cold, as was the kettle on top of it. John Davies came up behind me and made me jump when he said, "I've just made him a brew in the house Bill, so we'll see you in a bit, okay?" "Aye, that'll be fine", Bill replied, "I've only got one mug anyway and he's not having mine, I don't know where he's been". One more quip and another loud chuckle.

"I think he gets confused sometimes," said John, as we walked up the slope of what was left of Crowden Station towards his house, "Because he always asks me when I see him if I want a cup of tea, and when I have pointed out the kettle is not on, he says, 'Don't be daft lad and sit down', and there's no chair either'. It was me that was laughing now, not at Bill but rather at the way John Davies was describing the situation in such a level-headed manner, we were kith and kin with regard to walkers. John also told me that Bill sometimes preferred 'Camp Coffee' and subsequently I was able to chat to Bill about this, as this brand of bottled coffee with added chicory was all the rage when I was a lad. At the time I thought it was very exotic and extremely sophisticated, whereas these days with a love of real coffee I wouldn't dream of drinking it, it is vile. Originally on the bottle's label there was a Sikh Soldier dutifully serving a be-kilted and sitting British Officer his cup of 'Camp Coffee', these days in deference to the PC Brigade, both men drink from a tea cup. I am all for being PC but, come on, drinking coffee from a teacup, that will never do.

I enjoyed John's company more than his taste in coffee but, some of his tales were a little too far-fetched even for me. Says me, who writes about a long dead beautiful girl, and an Irish Soldier called Pawdy Blanche, also deceased. Bill Edmunds and I, and sometimes John, often discussed the A628, probably because both from John's kitchen and Bill's brew cabin you could not miss it, and you could often hear it. Not the actual road obviously but rather the vehicles using it, and the sirens of fire engines, ambulances and police cars, were a daily sound pollution to the countryside, with the attendant screeching of wagons brakes as they negotiated the treacherous Bleak House corner. Add to this the blaring of horns by impatient drivers and the smog on a Friday afternoon when the traffic was backed up from the Gun Inn at Hollingworth to the Glossop turn-off and beyond, the record during my tenure was Saltersbrook, a further three miles and just into Yorkshire.

John Davies had watched the traffic for many years, and had a collection of press-cutting relating to the A628, and some of them he had inherited from his Father. One in particular he liked to produced when someone observed how dangerous the road was. "It's always been the same", said John before producing the following from the dawn of the 20th Century:

A Sunday at Woodhead 1901

Police Court Sequel
James BORSEY, of Duke-street, Ashton-under-Lyne, was brought before the County magistrates at Hyde on Monday, charged with furiously driving a horse and trap on the Woodhead-road, Crowden, on Sunday, the 12th May.

Constable DUDLEY said he was standing near his home in Woodhead-road about five o'clock p.m. on the date named, when he saw defendant driving a horse and trap at a furious pace, and shouting at the horse and thrashing it with a whip. A short distance in front of defendant was a wagonette and defendant was evidently trying to pass it. He was driving in a most reckless fashion and several times nearly collided with the wagonette. He continued to drive in that fashion and thrashed the horses unmercifully up hill and down.

There were two or three other people in the trap beside the defendant, and they were holding on to the side of the conveyance. A short time afterwards, the witness received information of an accident having occurred, in consequence of which, he proceeded to the Angel Inn, Woodhead. Defendant was pointed out to witness as the man who had caused the accident, the nature of which was a collision between defendant's and another man's conveyance. Witness at once told defendant he should report him for furious driving. In answer to Superintendent COOPER, witness stated that when defendant passed him, the horse was travelling at a rate of 15 or 16 miles an hour.

Defendant: The horses cannot do six miles an hour; it simply shied, and I hit it with the whip.

Joseph WHITTAKER, a steam crane driver of Crowden, deposed that when defendant passed him he was flogging the horses unmercifully. He was going at the least 12 miles an hour up the hill.

Ernest BOARDMAN, saddler's apprentice, of George-street, Glossop, said he remembered Sunday, the 12th May. He had been driving to Woodhead with his mother and two sisters and on returning, he saw defendant coming along at a furious pace, driving on the wrong side of the road. He seemed to be coming at about 16 miles an hour. Witness tried to drive out of his way but was unable to do so and a collision took place. Which resulted in witness's conveyance bring much damaged.

The magistrates considered their verdict and fined defendant 20 shillings.

Some things never change it would seem. Early on in my tenure, there was a head-on collision on the Bleak House bend when a saloon car had somehow drifted under the front of an articulated lorry coming the other way and Bill said, "That's another one for the morgue". He wasn't far wrong, and in the few years I had lived on that bend we had motorists and their passengers dead, dying and indifferent on the floor of the Bleak House kitchen, it came with the territory.

Bill, and John were both matter of fact when it came to the various fatalities in the Valley, Bill having witnessed a woman throw herself in the path of a locomotive passing through Crowden Station, and John with a string of 'death tales' as long as your arm. Of the suicide he witnessed Bill said, "She just sort of fell in't path o'thengine (engine), and although she was alive when I got to her, poor lass only had time to look into my eyes before she slipped away". Bill had kind eyes and you could only hope that, the woman felt some momentary comfort before she passed away.

By this time I had already found a few dead bodies myself, and in fact by the time I left Crowden in 2008 I used to say to people, "We need to leave soon, I have found nine and only need one more for the set". Macabre maybe but death was a fact of life at Crowden. One of my bodies was discovered within a hundred metres of Bill's brew cabin. Both men hunkered down when I first told them the story, Bill and John loved a good story.

It was late November back in '84, early evening, snow falling and as I crossed the courtyard to fetch logs there was a loud crash over the road from Bleak House. Here we go again I thought, so wearily I donned my boots, jacket and rabbit skin hat to investigate. For once the road was quiet and I could hear an engine running down on the back road into Glossop, and as I walked down the stone steps I saw the car. It had been driven straight into the stone buttress at some speed, the bonnet and front end were smashed in, the engine just about to give up the ghost and the driver's door was hanging open but there was no sign of the driver or any passengers. I turned off the engine and put the car keys in my pocket, and climbed back up the steps to Bleak House, firstly to call the police and then to return with a torch.

As there was snow on the ground I could see that there were no skid marks, no evidence of last second avoidance tactics and to all intents and purposes, the car looked to have been driven directly into the wall. I immediately thought it was a suicide attempt gone wrong and looked for footprints, and although there were some near the car, they petered out when they reached the road, as there were clear patches of tarmac where other vehicles had driven. The size of the footprints suggested that it was a man, and I reasoned that if he was trying to kill himself, and either he didn't drive fast enough before impact or chickened out, then he may try and drown himself in the reservoir. After checking the walls for disturbed snow, and finding none I walked slowly over the embankment checking for footprints but it looked like he may have walked on the iced-over tyre tracks. The police arrived and took a statement and that was that until a week later when the ex-wife of the guy, who was still missing, no name, no pack drill and all that, walked into the kitchen with an odd looking chap. "He's a dowser", she said, "and he can find dead bodies with his rods". "Oh really", I replied. The man proceeded to spread out a map on the kitchen table and suspended his divining rods over the topography of Crowden. He was very, very serious and when the rods, they looked like coat hangers to be honest, began to dip close to an area below the embankment where I had recently released several hundred rainbow trout, I said. "He might be sleeping with the fishes", both the ex-wife and the diviner were not amused at the time but, Bill and John both chuckled away at that bit and Bill said, "And then what?"

"Well", I said, "I took them down there and there was no body, and they left, and that was that".

Christmas came and went, frogmen came and went, and New Year came and departed with no sign of the missing man. Rumours circulated that he had scarpered with a woman and money from his business, while counter rumours claimed his business was struggling and that after he failed in his suicide bid he had fled the country. All wrong as it turns out.

Woodhead Reservoir was frozen over for a couple of months either side of Hogmanay, and with ice, as mentioned earlier, the temptation to throw big stones to try and break the ice is ever-present. Pretty soon, and with regular flurries of snow, the frozen water takes on the appearance of a boulder strewn Moonscape. After a week or so, with the water partially melting before icing over again, I was very impressed to see what looked like a large coping stone the size of football about 100 feet away from the embankment wall. Even though I assumed it had been ripped from the top of one the nearby walls and had probably slid some way like a curling stone, it was still one heck of a chuck.

All was explained a few days later when the temperature rose and the ice began to break up and the snow melted from on top the large stone. It wasn't stone at all, it was the head of the missing man, half submerged with rest of his body like an iceberg hanging below the surface.

With the police duly informed I awaited their arrival with a flask of coffee and a hip flask full of Jameson's Irish Whiskey, it was cold after all. The duty officer was a Sergeant nearing retirement age and he had brought with him a wet behind the ears constable who looked about twelve years old. (Apologies if you recognise yourself now)

By this time the dead guy was around ten yards from the measuring platform above the overflow, too far to reach without getting wet, even if you climbed down the cast iron ladder which was secured to the side. "Sod that Woody", said the sergeant, "Have you got a tow rope and a house brick?" "Yes", I replied, and five minutes later with the brick tied to the end of the rope an unsightly hoopla game ensued as the Sergeant attempted to cast the brick behind the body and drag it in.

I will forego the full and gory details of what happened when the house-brick struck flesh, suffice to say that when the corpse was within reach, the sergeant turned to hand over the recovery to his young charge. Unfortunately he had fainted and was crumpled in a heap upon the floor. The sergeant asked for my hip flask to bring him round and took a glug himself before sighing, "Bless his cotton socks, he'll see much worse than that before he gets to my age".

Bill, while obviously feeling sorry for the deceased, was particularly keen to hear the full unexpurgated version of events, and always went on during conversations such as these to provide of few graphic stories of his own in similar vein, and perhaps surprisingly his involved the A628 as well, and not the railway, likewise with John Davies. In their working lives they were both called over the embankment, or went of their own volition on a semi-regular basis to help out at the scene of one tragedy or another.

To be fair, both men enjoyed a bit of straightforward humour as well as the dark stuff, Bill with the funny aside, for example, he had chickens at home and used to sell his eggs on the platform of Crowden Station. Generally people would leave the money in a wooden honesty-box, as Bill was busy signalling but, on occasion when on a break and if he was asked for eggs by a lady, he would ask back with a twinkle in his eye, "Which do you want, cocks or hens?" before roaring with laughter at the uncomfortable look on his victim's face, especially when some said, "Sorry, I didn't know there was any difference". He was Ronnie Barker's 'Arkwright' at Crowden Station I reckon.

John on the other hand was Bill's counterpart, the straight guy, and he loved facts and was often able to produce old newspaper cuttings to back up his stories, his 'search-engine' was an old bureau in the small living room which was never used.

Some of these cuttings detailed the many and varied aircraft crashes in the Dark Peak, and I am talking an extensive collection as there have been fifty or so since the last war and many more before that. Those with a penchant for the hyperbole have dubbed the area, 'The Bermuda Triangle' of England. The BBC posted on their webpage, 'In the 30s 40s and 50s, the area was the scene of over 130 deaths from plane crashes, many of which remain largely unexplained'. I can buy that to a certain extent but 'largely unexplained' is poor journalism. Most of the aircraft were flying too low for whatever reason and they hit the hills, so nothing like the Bermuda Triangle then. Except though in regard to insurance, because Longdendale is used countless times every day as a run-in to Manchester Airport by many airlines without any expensive premiums. Likewise with that area on three points in the North Atlantic Ocean between Bermuda, Florida and Puerto Rico. The Marine Insurance Leader, Lloyds of London does not recognise the Bermuda Triangle as an especially hazardous place. Neither does the U.S. Coast Guard, which says: 'In a review of many aircraft and vessel losses in the area over the years, there has been nothing discovered that would indicate that casualties were the result of anything other than physical causes. No extraordinary factors have ever been identified'.

John Davies told me that, he had seen and heard what he thought was a ghost-aircraft many times above Bleaklow, and here I find myself analysing his tales with much more scrutiny than I would expect readers to question mine, and although this might seem a tad unfair I think there is a touch of the, 'precious', centred around my own stuff, perhaps even a hint of jealousy from my perspective that someone else had an inexplicable Valley story to tell.

John and a friend retrieved pieces of an old plane from a nearby crash site, and stored them in a garage close to their Longdendale homes. John's story holds that, they were in the garage late one night, when they were terrorised by the sound of a large beast sniffing and patrolling around the outside of the building. They said the sounds resembled some kind of big cat, possibly a lion. Years later, John said of the incident: "My father didn't believe in ghosts but he said to me, 'I'd get rid of those bits of Perspex if I were you', good advice I thought, so I took it right up t'moors and buried it", said John.

The subject of the aircraft crashes in Longdendale has been covered extensively, and although I have no 'Airmen Walkers' to talk about, I thought it prudent to read up a bit and give them a mention. In one of the reports it is recorded how a local man, Phil Shaw, acted as guide for a couple of relatives of crewmen who had perished on the moors. By coincidence I have a friend of the same name, and I asked him if he was the person mentioned. He was not but he told me, "When my dad started work, he was employed by a company in Dukinfield that was sent out by the Government to salvage the many crashed aircraft, so they could recycle all the materials for the War Effort. He knew every site, and believe it or not he was called George Bernard Shaw!"

John Davies was never very happy when negotiating Devil's Elbow or so he told me but, I could never tell whether he was hamming up the legends of this hairpin bend, because as soon as someone starts talking about the Devil and evil spirits, my old Catholic antipathy begins to ooze from every pore and takes me back to my youth when certain priests and some Teachers used to ram the mumbo jumbo down our young throats. A classic example would be, we were told that if you did not go to confession before taking Holy Communion your tongue would turn black at the altar. Yeah right. So I owned up one time on the Monday after Sunday's Mass, and said, "Father, I didn't go to Confession on Saturday because Father John told me to go away as there were too many people waiting and he wanted his lunch but my tongue didn't turn black when I received Holy Communion". I was eight years old, and this was probably my first schoolboy-error as the priest hauled me out in front of the class, and gave me a dressing down and a clip round the back of the head before explaining to my peers that, I had the, "Devil in me", and, "Woe betide", anyone else who told such a tale. As I write, July 2017, the Pope's Chief Adviser is in an Australian Court facing historical sexual abuse charges. Fortunately, I didn't have to suffer in that fashion, possibly because I was too 'gobby', and not as malleable as some others and therefore too high risk for grooming. My sister, Laraine, went to a Convent School in Loughborough, and the nuns seemed to go from the ridiculous, which I suffered, to the sublime, with their hammering home of the Doctrine. A couple of belters from her time, were, 'Don't wear patent leather black shoes, because men will be able to see your knickers', and, they were warned if someone turned the lights off at a party when both sexes were present that, they should stand up and announce, 'Please turn on the lights I am a good Catholic Girl, and a Temple of God'.

John Davies was amazed by the story of the priest's blind dogma, "And you, nowt but a strip of a lad, what was he thinking?" he asked, flabbergasted. Both John and Bill only had fond memories of Crowden School, and Sunday School, with thankfully nothing to match the cruelty I described to mar their time there. It is my recollection, aside from my Communion-story that John and I never talked about religion, and I couldn't really tell you who he batted for on the ecclesiastical wicket. Nevertheless, John stuck to his guns about Devil's Elbow and he was even more resolute in his sighting of the Roman Legions.

With the former, John often walked or cycled the road but, laughing he told me that he always went a little faster round the bend and whistled loudly, and said to me one time, "For some daft reason, I always walked in the middle of the road, I think I thought the Old Bugger won't be able to reach over the wall and grab me if I'm in the middle".

Writers and visitors to the Valley have often upped the ante with their descriptions of, the 'Devil's Elbow', for example, the first time I drove around the bend as a passenger in 1975, my friend said, 'Hold on tight, there's been loads of accidents on this hairpin and if we get round okay we'll then be on the Woodhead', as he flung his Renault 4 around the, admittedly curvaceous crook. I played along with the drama at the time but, in hindsight, Steve Coult, had no idea how right he was to stoke up the hype with regard Woodhead.

The following from, 'The Legends of Longdendale' is the first written description of the 'Elbow' I read, and one of the stories attached to it. Make of it what you will but, for my money and in modern day parlance, here comes a 'spoiler': the route it follows around the hillside was the easiest to walk around, simples, and like many an ancient track in Longdendale it is still in use and has nothing to do with Old Nick.

'It frowns high over the course of the stream. The situation of the rock is certainly romantic: the wild moorlands of bog and heather stretch away on either side, in fact the rock stands on the verge of some of the wildest mountain scenery of Great Britain. The very name of the place is suggestive of legend, and one is not surprised to learn that there are some queer stories related concerning the neighbourhood; one of these explains how the rock came to receive its name'.

A local baron, De Morland, had a daughter named Geraldine, who was born on May day, and was as sweet as the month in which she was born. Her teeth were like pearls, her hair gleamed like gold, her skin was the fairest, and her figure the most beautiful ever known in Longdendale. Altogether she was a maid to set the hearts of men aflame with love'.

I read this passage once to Shining Girl and said it could be her, and also asked what she thought about the stories of Devil's Elbow. With regard to my compliment she was delighted but, like me, was dismissive of the links with the Devil and said, 'It's just a road with a bad bend but I do hate it so'. It transpired that her uncle, used the more elaborate tales of the 'Elbow' when he first began to give Shining Girl, her 'lifts' to his own ends, and although as usual she would not go into too much detail she did let slip that he would try and frighten her, and then encourage her to move closer to him as they negotiated the bend.

'Now it should be stated at the outset that the maiden had been wooed by more than one noble suitor, but she had an eye to none save a brave young knight who came from Mottram. His name was Sir Mottram de Mossland, and he was lord of a castle—something similar in appearance to that of the Baron de Morland, but not quite so grand—which stood on a bold ridge near Mottram town. This knight had long been in love with the lady Geraldine, and on several occasions had managed to get interviews with his lady-love. We may be sure he lost no time in making known to her the state of his heart, and in ascertaining the

exact condition of her own. They kissed, and swore fidelity to each other, and generally behaved like all young lovers do. But bye and bye the Baron de Morland got to hear of this lover's business, and he swore a terrible oath concerning it. Now, the Lady Geraldine was bold enough, as became a daughter born of a race of fighting men, and, having pledged her word to her lover, she had no intention of going from it. So, on the day appointed, she proceeded to a certain spot, where her lover met her, all prepared for flight. The lovers kissed, and then the knight began:

"Dear Geraldine," said he.—But before he could proceed further, an awful thing happened. A dark form rose up between them, and, on looking at it they knew it was the Devil. He was in his own shape, with horns, hoofs, and tail complete. With a mocking laugh he bent his elbow, and made as though to seize the maid, but Sir Mottram, throwing his arms about her, turned and fled, hoping to be able to cross a running stream before the devil could touch them, and then, by the laws of sorcery, they would be free from satanic molestation.

The devil, however, gained on them rapidly, and it appeared certain that he would catch them, when, just as he put out his hand to touch the maid, a strange light appeared in the sky, and a voice called out the one word—"Hold."

The Devil staggered as though he had been shot, and when he recovered the light had vanished, and with it the maiden and her lover.

They were never seen again, but the legends say that they were made perfectly happy by the fairies, and that they still haunt the banks of the Etherow at certain seasons of the year in the forms of two white swans.

As for the devil, he received a shock. At the moment the light appeared, his right arm had been bent at the elbow for the purpose of seizing hold of his prey, but lo! when his victims had disappeared, he found that the powers which had delivered them from him had turned his right arm into stone. Not a muscle of it could he move, it would not bend, it was worse than useless, it was an encumbrance.

So Satan, being a philosopher in his way, determined to make the best of a bad job. He tore the arm out by the roots, and left it there—the elbow showing prominently over Longdendale. And that is how the great rock known as the Devil's Elbow came to be perched high up above the Etherow valley'.

As for John's Legions, and I know this might sound like the kettle calling the pot black but, I could never get my head around the ghostly Romans. Not least because I cannot imagine a group of soldiers all being walkers at the same time and in the same place. My walkers, were mostly loners and each one had some reason however tenuous, to be there, to be part of the landscape where they lived or worked, and with myriad experiences in their personal history which were never quite resolved, which left them in some way, searching. And I guess they always will be, as I can confirm that not one of my walkers ever said that they were leaving or bid me goodbye. Shining Girl threatened a few times when I annoyed her but she never did leave while I lived at Bleak House.

Chapter Nine:
John Hadfield, The Maid and the Gallows.

There's an old stone trough by the single track crossroads at Crowden, grown over and weed clogged these days, and even sometimes with no water in at all, while at others, full of frogs and tadpoles, or worse, ice-cream wrappers. This would never have done in the days of Crowden Hall, which was built in 1692, and any of the Hadfield's Servants would have been up for a right old rollicking, if it wasn't sweetly overflowing and clear as a whistle. This trough was for the horses, both those belonging to the Hall, and also to the many travellers who would have passed through, and there is also a small trough at its foot, and this was for the dogs who accompanied riders and horse drawn vehicles. A nice touch.

Perish the thought that word got back to Sheffield, or Chester about the Hadfield's manky trough. I'm talking late 17th Century here, with the Bubonic Plague which had decimated the Village of Eyam in 1665 still a living memory and palpable fear, Cholera was all the rage, and clean water was treasured, so much so that people drank ale instead, and had done for a long while. Not all bad then.

These days the spring which feeds the trough, is often blocked further up the hill, whereas, even in my day I would ensure that there was a steady flow and no weeds. I'd let the occasional water-boatman away with it, and would often just sit and watch as they dived into the water buoyed by the use of an air bubble, or even more impressive were the pond skaters, defying the laws of nature and walking on the 'surface tension' of the water. Although relatively young, I was probably one of the last of the 'old timers', in that, I cared about the day to day running of the Valley. Many a hiker, filling their bottles, thanked me for keeping that trough clean, including, John Noakes, of Blue Peter fame, and he also let 'Shep' his famous sidekick have a drink. Noakes was being filmed walking the Pennine Way, the long distance footpath which opened in 1965, and depending which way you walk it, is either the last stop before Edale, or the first stop after Edale, which was Blue Peter's preferred route. Being the Water Man and general Warden type-go-to-guy at the top end of the Valley, I was asked to supervise the filming, or in other words make sure they made no mess and kept out of the reservoir enclosures. Noakes was filmed stroking the dog, before setting off over the little wooden bridge traversing Crowden Little Brook, and then for about thirty metres of walking onto the flat expanse beyond Crowden Weir, before someone shouted 'cut', and the director said, 'Thanks John', before they all packed up, and drove off into Yorkshire to the next section. I thought, you little fibber John, walking the Pennine Way my-foot, as the saying goes. The latter expression being a derivative of 'My ass', first used in the 18th Century. Several years later, the ill-fated sitcom 'Bootle Saddles' was filmed in the same location, complete with fake cowboy-town and horses, and the latter were billeted in the outbuildings at Bleak House. This was much to the delight of my late father-in-law, John Crean of Dinting, late of Athleague, County Roscommon, and a long-time employee of Glossop's Lancashire Chemicals; all that manure for his garden, he literally was that happy chap in the proverbial.

The idea of a footpath from Derbyshire to the Scottish Border area was first mooted by the late Tom Stephenson, Secretary of the Ramblers Association, in 1935. It took 30 years for this idea to come to fruition, and the route was officially opened in April 1965 after years of negotiation with the landowners along the route. Since then many thousands of people have walked the route, which goes from Edale to Kirk Yetholm. On the way it passes or crosses many of the landmarks of central northern England - Kinder, Bleaklow, Malham Cove, High Force, Cross Fell, Hadrian's Wall, and others. At about 270 miles (430 km) it's a long walk, which takes most people who attempt it between two and three weeks, though it has been run in just a few days. One of the marathon-men who have run the 'Way' was Mike Cudahy, who often stopped at Bleak House for a brew The Peak District section of the walk takes in all the major gritstone peaks of the area. Mike was the first person to run the 'Way' in under three days, and on his seventh attempt, he also completed the 'Coast to Coast' long distance footpath in under two days. His description of how he felt after finishing the latter basically sums up in an amazing way, what it is, what it means, to pit yourself against the hills.

"Never have I felt such sheer joy at the end of a run. Moments such as these not only provide the answer to why one does things like this but why we are alive at all. One moment of such joy is worth far more than countless years of steady rational living. To have encountered hardship, discomfort, to have experienced one's physical, mental and spiritual limitations and weaknesses, to have found a path beyond them, not conquering them but accepting and yet transcending them, to have been supported, guarded and guided lovingly by friends represents, for me, a joy both sublime and supreme. I ask for no more."

The Pennine Way starts at the Nags Head in Edale. The current route reaches Kinder Downfall by skirting the southern edge of Kinder to ascend Jacob's Ladder at the head of the Edale Valley, then up to Kinder Low and along the western edge of the Kinder plateau to reach the Downfall. This is maybe less interesting than the original route which headed up Grindsbrook and over the top of Kinder Scout, crossing to Crowden Brook and upstream to Crowden Head, the highest point of the Kinder plateau, before dropping down into Kinder River, which was followed to the Downfall, but the passage of lots of walkers across the top of the plateau caused a lot of erosion.After Kinder Downfall the route heads north-west along the edge of the plateau before descending to Ashop Head and climbing up to Mill Hill to follow the long ridge which connects Kinder to Bleaklow.

The path crosses the Snake road and the old track known as Doctor's Gate and then follows a feature known as Devil's Dyke to reach Hern Clough, the upper section of the Alport river. This is followed upstream to the Wain Stones and Bleaklow Head, the high point of this hill. From here the path swings west for short distance to drop into the stream system of Torside Clough, which is descended to Crowden. Birdwatchers might be interested to discover that Hern, is a derivative of Erne, the old name for an eagle, and it is almost certain that eagles, either golden, or even white-tails were present in the area. Other similar Derbyshire place names which would evidence this, include Hern Stones and Hernside, and literally four miles and a mere flap of an eagles wing from Crowden, Arnfield beyond Tintwistle.

From Crowden the path follows the west bank of Great Crowden Brook upstream to Black Hill, detouring at Oaken Clough to climb over the top of Laddow Rocks. Obviously John Noakes did not get that far. At the head of the clough, it heads straight up Dun Hill to reach the summit of Black Hill, an extremely boggy area known as Soldier's Lump. Here the path divides, with the modern advised route heading almost north to drop down to Wessenden Head and follow the chain of Wessenden Reservoirs down to Marsden. However, the original route continued north-west along the watershed to cross White Moss, Black Moss and take an almost direct line to Standedge, where the path leaves the Peak.

In any century the choice of a good walk, usually out of necessity depended on which direction you turned your head, and whichever route was selected, you would be in for a long slog for sure. Tintwistle was the nearest village, four miles away, Saltersbrook and a pint at Ladysmith about six miles, over the hill to

Greenfield via Laddow Rocks and Chew, or even into Yorkshire along a well worn track skirting the often damp heights of the aforementioned Black Hill. The way South was blocked by the big lump called Bleaklow, although once on top, and if you knew your way, it was relatively straight forward, until of course, the mist dropped low. Every single person down the ages, including the many thousands who have walked the Pennine Way, even John Noakes and Shep, will have passed by this stone trough at the little cross-roads at Crowden.

The trough also had a special relevance for me, due to the occasional sound of a man crying within the vicinity, and believe it or not, I once mistook his weeping for the voice of a stoat. This is a bit of a chicken and an egg story because, quite unlike me, I did not jot down at the time when these things happened, and therefore, I am unsure which came first, the man, or the musteloid.

For argument sake, I will plump for the stoat, as I knew a family often took up residence in the rocks just behind the trough, and on a regular basis I attracted them out into to the open, by pursing my lips on the back of my hand and making the sound of a squealing rabbit. Although this old country method works a treat with the inquisitive little blighters and they just could not resist the chance of furry treat. First the nose, soon followed by the eyes and ears, and then he shoots out, looks around and stands on his back legs to scan the surroundings, and spies me instead. Not one for anthropomorphism but he always looked pretty pissed off to me. This trick also works with weasels, however, a word of caution if you try it yourself, make sure no one is coming, because it can take some explaining to a stranger what exactly you are doing.

The crying man, takes even more explaining and the following is my first attempt ever, raw and as it was. As usual I had been at the Outdoor Pursuits Centre filling my face and chatting to the girls, and yes I was getting paid for this, however, while retracing my steps to check the water supply at the Youth Hostel I was stopped in my tracks by the sound of someone crying, a man I thought. The sound was carried towards me on the wind initially but, as I neared the stone trough, there was no mistaking the full blown sobs of a bloke, and he sounded very close to me. There was no one there, at least visible any roads, and I sped off towards the hostel to escape the dilemma but not before the crying briefly stopped, and a disembodied voice of a man said, "Evvy, the only one I really loved".

I'm guessing this was 1984, because as I said earlier, I have no notes to back this up but, let's face it, it's not the sort of thing you can make up unless you're Stephen King, and besides after a tip off from the Shining Girl the story which unfolded was largely historical fact, and links Crowden with the Lakes and The Maid, or Beauty of Buttermere, Melvyn Bragg, Wordsworth, Coleridge, and the gallows at Carlisle Jail but not necessarily in that order.

A few days later, and I'm sitting above Hey Farm watching the Shining Girl walk the path below me. She was on the original route to the farm which now marks the top end of a small utility planting of pines, and appeared as though she was about to pass by and say nothing. The plantation was a bedraggled mess in 1980, and is not much better as I write. When I worked in the Valley, I asked if I could sort it out for them; thin out the pines, free up some of the struggling native oak and lime which were all but suffocated but, the haughty response of, 'We have a Forestry Section to carry out that kind of work, you're a Reservoir Keeper', was all I got. Obviously I did it anyway and the little plantation, at least while I was there, became much more attractive to wildlife, and from an aesthetic point of view it was a pleasure to walk in.

Shining Girl was in one of her playful moods, and just as I thought she had gone for the day she sat down beside me beautiful as ever. As I was halfway through telling her the story of the crying man she said, "That's John Hadfield', and he'll be crying for ever after what he did.

"You see, Crowden and his father's linen trade were not good enough for John, and he chose to ignore the prophecy he was given before he left for

London to seek his fortune, or as it happens, other people's fortunes", she said, laughing at her own little joke. Cotton was soon to become King in the Region and it is no surprise that the Hadfield's would be involved in some way. Valehouse Mill was built further down the Valley, a huge building which housed hundreds of workers. The Mill, plus a small village around it, was built in 1795 by the Thornley brothers, and the local Methodists used a room in the mill until in 1804 when a certain John Thornley loaned them £200 to build their first chapel, in Hadfield. The Mill was sold to Manchester Corporation in 1867 and demolished to make way for the reservoir, although you can still see a bit of it when the water's very low.

Shining Girl went on to explain that if I wanted to, the next time I heard Hadfield crying that I could make him appear, and maybe even talk to him. I was to 'challenge' him to show his face, by focusing on the spot where the sound was coming from however difficult it was to actually pin-it down, and encourage him to put in an appearance. My modus operandi in later encounters was to say out loud a very simple, "Go on then lad", and subsequently, it worked almost every time.

Years later, in 2000, after my dad, John, had died in the January, my daughter Niamh was born two months later. One out, one in, such is life with it holds and thrusts but, my dad knew we were expecting a baby and when I went to his house there was a crocheted baby blanket all ready to give to us. Very sad and I know he would have adored Niamh, and vice versa. While in the house I found a camera in one of his drawers with half the film used. When I had the film developed there were photographs of his lurchers, Shamrock, Seamus and Paddy, a couple of his little boat on the River Soar at Zouch, and then there was one image which stood out of my Dad's favourite rose bush. You couldn't see him in the picture but his distinctive shadow filled the lawn in the foreground.

Later that night on returning to Bleak House I wrote these words, immediately sent them to my co-writer at the time, Sean De Burca, and a moving tear-jerker was penned in less than an hour all in.

There's a shadow on the photograph, it's me Dad alive and well,
You can't see him in the picture but it's him you sure can tell
He's a big man with wavy hair and shoulder broad and strong,
I shook his hand on Monday but by Friday he was gone.

His outline and dark reflection were moments caught in time,
It's a pity he's not here now to see me daughter shine,
He would have loved her smiling face just like he loved her brothers,
And although he didn't know it, in a way he was like no other.

He wasn't one for compliments and his tone was often stern
But it never seemed to bother him, he never seemed to learn,
I can't recall I love you but he often said well done,
And although I rarely saw him, I'm glad I was his Son.

Ironically the 'Shadow On The Photograph' was first performed in The King's Arms in Hawkshead village, not so far from the scene of Hadfield's undoing at Buttermere, and there were few dry eyes in the house for sure.

I sang the song to Shining Girl and she too became emotional, and she said like so many since that the song reminded her of her own father. A few months after Niamh was born, I had her in my arms at the front of Bleak House and was mimicking the black-headed gulls which wheel above and about the house in the summer and nest in their hundreds on the banks of Woodhead Reservoir. Niamh was smiling and I was undoubtedly talking Daddy-Buffoon language, we all do it, and as I walked towards the gate I got one of those unmistakable feelings and was certain that my dad was standing there, just like he used to when he drove up from Leicestershire and stepped out of his Mercedes G-Wagon and looked around at the view. Once again after the initial, and most natural hair up on neck moment, I settled to the notion that he was there and was able to see his Niamh, not only that but she was wrapped in the woollen blanket he had got someone to make for our baby. In modern day parlance I felt a kind of closure in that moment but with a touch of bravado I had to take it one step further and utilised one of my John Hadfield summoning tricks only pulling out at the last moment just as I felt for certain my dad was about to appear. I chickened out basically.

Back in 1984, Shining Girl continued with, "The prophecy was given to Hadfield on New Year's Eve when he had just turned 21 years old, by a soothsayer at Brushes over the hill and close to Greenfield, I think his name was Robinson. According to what I was told it went something like this, 'Fate's resistless hand, will seal your fate in Cumberland'.

In those days, travelling to either London or Cumberland, would have been a fair old trek, not least because the roads were not the best and, as is still true today, the transport and access from Glossop to the rest of the world was difficult. My advice to Hadfield would have been to stay put, and enjoy the Valley, and although my Bleak House proved to be a wonderful place to live, his Crowden Hall, was a building second to none. Thomas Hadfield, his great grandfather, who built the Hall had been a Yeoman, as were his descendants but Thomas died in 1697.

A Yeoman held a mid-ranking position in society, and may have a fine freehold or leasehold property, land, livestock and servants, and the Hall was a Yeoman's House. The Concise Oxford Dictionary, 1972, describes a Yeoman as, 'A person qualified by possessing free land of 40/- (shillings) annual [feudal] value, and who can serve on juries and vote for a Knight of the Shire. He is sometimes described as a small landowner, a farmer of the middle classes'.

A Yeoman's wealth and the size of landholding varied. Sir Anthony Richard Wagner, Garter Principal King of Arms, wrote that, 'A Yeoman would not normally have less than 100 acres (40 hectares) and in social status is one step down from the Landed Gentry but, above, say, a husbandman'.

It would appear that, it was hard to distinguish minor landed gentry from the wealthier Yeomen, and wealthier Husbandmen from the poorer Yeomen. My guess is that the Hadfield's were of the wealthier variety.

The stone trough is a grand piece of rock, hewn to good use but, the Hall, now that was what you call a piece of class, demolished in the 1930's by Manchester Corporation simply to avoid the upkeep as they had no tenants. A very unhappy day in the history of Crowden.

The stone trough aside every time I visit Crowden, when I look at the place where the Hall stood, I can still see it in my mind's eye, sometimes so clearly that, I wonder if it's my imagination or that, it is actually still there. What I have would have given, for a mooch through that house. Standing one hundred yards back from the turnpike, now the A628 road, the Hall faced Bleaklow, and my room would have been the one which was just above the imposing studded oak front door, with cut sandstone surrounds, two perfectly symmetrical mullion windows sitting half way up, and either side of the door. Handsome and substantial quoins, nine masonry blocks suring up each elevated corner of the wall. In some houses they were used to provide actual strength for a wall made with inferior stone or rubble, where as at Crowden Hall they made a feature of a corner, a display, creating an impression of permanence and strength, and reinforcing the onlookers sense of a structure's presence, and then just to finish off with an architectural flourish, six beautifully carved stone finials, which are basically ornamental terminal features at the top of a gable, sometimes referred to as hip-knobs.

Above the door, one more piece of stone, a datestone, inscribed 1692, and the initials THED. You would have to have some sympathy with the original

Thomas Hadfield who died in 1697 as he only had five years to enjoy the building. The Jury is out on what the ED stand for on the carving, although his Will says he married Helen, and as local writer and historian Glynis Greenman told me, in the later 17th Century the H was often replaced with an E, and vice versa. The D may have been her surname which was not recorded.

If I had chance to live there, the room which would have been my eyrie, my lookout on the Valley boasted a triple mullion and although the vista would have been impeded slightly by the leaded lights, this was the place to watch, just to watch.

In the lee of the hill, the slopes were clothed in a close knit and crouching forest of native sessile oak, a hill-hugger species designed especially to survive the Woodhead winds, tight together, safety in numbers, by staying almost prone, and Hobbit-like, close to the ground. Even their acorns have adapted to windy environments, emerging directly from a twig, unlike their cousins the pedunculate which flap about on the end of an even smaller extension which, come the autumn, makes them easier to fall as the life slips out of the tree. Closer to the fast running River Etherow, now disguised by the Victorian's with the Reservoirs for Manchester, grew reeds and willow, and the sallows and island eddies, in the margins splashed with life. Water voles, in abundance, and although this creature, an essence of England, was named 'Ratty' in the book, 'The Wind In The Willows', he's a vole, and that's that. A rat indeed, perish the thought but, he did have his predators, the red fox and grey heron, to name but two, but no invasive American mink though, which was a blessing, and both 'Ratty' and his most beautiful of neighbours, the brown trout, also a victim of this furry-yank, survived in relative peace and harmony. The pesky mink began the invasion of Britain in the early 20th Century when, some of their number were either freed, escaped or released, due to slack husbandry, the vagaries of fashion, or over-zealous do-gooders. The resultant decimation of such native species, in particular the water vole, is now well documented. The mink, a mustelid, already well represented at Crowden by the stoat and weasel, is not fussy with its diet, and on occasion their scats will show remains of fish, birds, mammals, reptiles, amphibians and insects. If I could press a button, and every single mink would vanish from the U.K, consider it pressed; they have even been spotted swimming from island to island in the Outer Hebrides, and at Bleak House, they killed my chickens and dragged them away in broad daylight. The bastards.

In the early eighties, I never saw a mink at Crowden; the glory days when I could catch the little brown trout with my bare hands, before releasing them gently back into the watercress beds, their luminous target-like markings flashing back at me in red, bronze and gold, and in spite of the reptilian heron, who timed his visits from Old Glossop each year to harvest my little-darlings as they appeared, as if by magic, life in the Etherow and on the edges was a, kind of, natural status quo. You won, or you lost, it was nature, and as they say it was red in tooth and claw.

All of this was John Hadfield's but, with the mercury rising in his veins, he was off, for what you might call his gap-years to oblivion. He should have stayed where he was, and certainly listened to both his father's and the soothsayer's advice.

Hadfield was born in 1757 at Crowden Hall, and although his birthplace is recorded as Mottram, as this was his Parish Church, Crowden fell under Mottram's jurisdiction, and was also a part of the 'The Hundred of Macclesfield', an ancient division of Cheshire which was known to have been in existence at least as early as 1242. In 1361 Edward the Black Prince was lord of the Hundred, Manor and Borough of Macclesfield. This information, and so much more can be found in manuscripts of the day lodged at the British Library. These records were all hand-written in Latin, on rolls of vellum, painstakingly translated by, John Harrop, in his, 'Extent of the Lordship of Longdendale 1360', and were produced basically to show who owned what in the Valley in the mid 14th Century.

One record in particular caught my eye, where it was written down how much a farm-hand could expect to earn for a day's labour at the time. For example, if you were haymaking at Crowden in 1360, and the hours were probably a little more than 9 to 5, you would receive, a handful of oatcakes, a local staple at the time, six herring and a barrel of ale. Seems fair enough to me. The ale, was drunk as a matter of course, because the brewing process purified the water which was used, another fail-safe against disease and seems an altogether much better idea than chlorinated water to quench your thirst.

Jumping on a few years, as my research bears some rich fruit, J Aikin, in his book of 1795, 'Forty Miles around Manchester', provides us with a tantalising description of Mottram; the village where Hadfield would have, by all accounts, strutted around like a peacock, in a full-skirted knee-length coat, knee breeches, a long waistcoat, linen shirt with frills and linen underdrawers. His lower legs were set-off by silk stockings, the outfit of the day completed with leather shoes, which were stacked heels of a medium height. His whole ensemble as topped by a shoulder-length full-bottomed wig, which was tied back and known as the 'tye' or 'bag-wig', and a tricorne (three-cornered) hat with an upturned brim.

'Mottram is situated twelve miles from Manchester and seven for Stockport, on a high eminence one mile to the west of the Mersey, from which the river ground begins to rise; half the way being so steep as to make it difficult to access. It forms a long street well paved both in the town and some distance on the roads. It contains 127 houses, which are for the most part built of a thick flagstone, and covered with a thick, heavy slate, of nearly the same quality, no other covering being able to endure the strong blasts of wind which occasionally occur. Of late, many of the houses in the skirts of the town are built of brick. About fifty years ago, the houses were few in number, and principally situated on top of the hill, adjoining the churchyard, where is an ancient cross, and at a small distance the parsonage house, now gone much to decay and occupied by

working people. It is only of late years that the town has had any considerable increase, which has been chiefly at the bottom of the hill, but some latterly on the top.'

Unfortunately for myself, and indeed any other local historian who attempts to plot the course of Hadfield's life there is no comfortable ride, as his story has been changed, adapted, and in the case of Melvyn Bragg in his 'Maid of Buttermere' (1987) by his own admittance, completely doctored to suit his historical novel. The really difficult task is cutting through all the extraneous and erroneous detail to find the truth, or as close as possible to the facts. I wrote to Bragg and asked him, firstly, why he had not mentioned the Crowden connection, and secondly, why did he miss out Robinson's fabled prophecy. To both questions he claimed he did not know about them as his research had stopped with the Newgate Calendar but, he did say with good grace, "I wish I had known, as I would have used the information in my book".

The Newgate Calendar was a general title given to a number of popular publications of the late 18th and early 19th century. The books began as compilations of the broadsheets sold by peddlers at fairs and public executions. These broadsheets fed public interest in the crimes, trials and punishments of notorious criminals. This was one 'Who's Who', you would not want a mention in.

The original issue was published in 1773 and reported on crimes from 1700 to the date of publication. Originally, as the name suggests, the information concerned prisoners who had been incarcerated in Newgate Prison but, was soon expanded to cover the whole of England to satisfy the morbid curiosity of the public in these matters. Newgate Prison was sited at the corner of Newgate Street and Old Bailey just inside the City of London. It was originally located at the site of Newgate, a gate in the Roman London Wall. The gate/prison was rebuilt in the 12th century, and demolished in 1904.

The full title of this edition of the Calendar is:

The Newgate Calendar; comprising interesting memoirs of the most notorious characters who have been convicted of outrages on the laws of England since the commencement of the eighteenth century; with anecdotes and last exclamations of sufferers .

As the Newgate Calendar recorded Hadfield's birthplace as Mottram, Melvyn Bragg looked no further.

To this end I am indebted to Graham Hadfield, of Teesside, who saw my plea for information on the Hadfield family on the 'Tintwistle Then And Now' Facebook Page. Graham researched his family history in the late 1990's and very generously handed them over to me. It was like winning the Lottery.

For a start the John, I refer to, of Crowden Hall, was John Hadfield, not Hatfield, which has been assumed by many writers along the way, including Melvyn Bragg, and he was born, as mentioned earlier in 1757, not 1759, as recorded elsewhere. Graham nails it for me with: 'To an extent the "D" and "T" spellings were interchangeable given the lack of standards of the day but "D" was dominant west of the Pennines.

I have copies of three Crowdenbrook (Craddenbroke) wills, including that of Thomas the father of the fraudster, and all use the "D" spelling'.

The following account, I believe, is as close to the truth as you are going to get, and not that I wish to claim superior knowledge to past writers and researchers but, John Hadfield, the Crying Man by the Stone Trough, related some of his story to me. He was one of my walkers, and although I never saw him walk anywhere at all he was certainly a talker on the occasions we met.

Soon after Shining Girl had given me advice about making Hadfield appear when I heard him crying, I got the chance to put it into practice. I had been called to sort a sewage problem with one of the houses at Crowden, as this type of work was in my remit, mostly easy jobs, if a little unpleasant, although on occasion it took hours to sort, as they were all septic tanks of one kind or another, and mostly installed in the 19th Century with all the pipes having their own little idiosyncrasies, some went left, others right, up, down, round the bend, back on themselves. A nightmare initially but once you knew their foibles you were fine.

It should be mentioned at this point that, although most people, and there were only a few, who lived in the family were all lovely folk, at times they were at least thoughtless, at worst wankers, and some had kept the notion from times past that, watermen, were at their beck and call. On this morning the drains were blocked because, with someone very sick in the house with what could have been a contagious condition but definitely involved loose bowels and regular clean-ups. It was 'thoughtless' to flush a ton of tissue down the pan, not least because septic tanks are not designed for this and the residents should, and did, know better. After clearing this drain with a couple of rods, and with no one opening the door to allow me to wash my hands, I meandered up the lane towards the stone trough to, at least, give them a swill before I got home. It would be difficult to forget this walk, not least because my hands had a nasty aroma but, also for the twenty ring ouzels feeding on the manicured grass of the the Campsite, it was a worm-fest but, more importantly an ouzel-fest as you normally only ever see this 'mountain blackbird' in ones and twos, a rare treat. Unfortunately, my sighting was over thirty years ago, and the ouzel is now classified as being on the Red Data List as, 'Globally threatened with a historical population decline in the UK during 1880 – 1995 with at least a 50% decline in the UK breeding population over the past 25 years'.

It was around 7.30am when I reached the trough and the crying began almost as soon as I stuck my hands in the freezing cold water. There was no one about and the air was still. In spite of the usual moment of disquiet at times like these I quickly resumed my calm persona and focussed on where the weeping was coming from. As I did this it stopped, something which Shining Girl had said would happen, but I carried on with my focussing and for the first time tried an encouraging, 'Go on then Lad, show yourself, I know you are there'. I could actually feel a presence, and redoubled my efforts, momentarily stopped in mid-flow by the Land Rover of the North West Water Gamekeeper, Gordon Woodhead, passing by.

'Go on lad', I repeated in some kind of incantation, half hoping, and half dreading what might happen but, with little time to consider what I would do if he appeared, he bloody well did and without further ado said, 'I see you were admiring the Michaelmas Thrushes just now'. This was a name given to the bird because of their habit of leaving the U.K. for the sunnier climes, of Southern Europe and North Africa, on or around the 29th September.

"Yes I was, I've never seen as many in one place at one time, I love 'em", I replied, "But I've never heard them called that before", I said. This is a classic example of the semi-normality of many of my walkers and most times our introduction happened in a similar fashion with some disarming comment or greeting.

"I myself had not heard tell of that name, as we call them Mountain Blackbirds at Craddenbroke", said Hadfield, "Until I was given a book by my father, 'The Natural History and Antiquities of Selbourne', by the English parson, Gilbert White, who enjoyed writing about the birds of the air, and beasts of the land in the environs of his Parsonage in the County of Hampshire and that good fellow refers to them as being with us at that time".

Reading some of White's words out loud, is like listening to Hadfield speak, for example this taken from a letter dated 8th December 1769:

'The ring ousel, you find, stays in Scotland the whole year round; so that we have reasons to conclude that those migrators that visit us for a short space every autumn do not come from thence. And here, I think, will be the proper place to mention that those birds were most punctual again in their migration

this autumn, appearing, as before, about the 30th of September; but their flocks were larger than common, and their stay protracted beyond the usual time. If they came to spend the whole winter with us, as some of their congeners do, and then left us, as they do, in spring, I should not be so much struck with the occurrence, since it would be similar to that of the other birds of passage; but when I see them for a fortnight at Michaelmas, and again for about a week in the middle of April, I am seized with wonder, and long to be informed whence these travellers come, and whither they go, since they seem to use our hills merely as an inn or baiting place'.

Gilbert White was my kind of naturalist, a generalist interested in everything, curious, unassuming and sometimes wrong but, we only know that with over 300 years more experience than him. He was always troubled by the puzzle of migration, and one theory of the time was that birds, perhaps even ring ouzels, hid under water in pairs, mouth to mouth, and revived each spring to appear again. White did not believe this but, without concrete evidence, he never completely dispensed with it either. I would love to be able to phone him up, or write to him, and let him know the answer, and also share some little snippets about the natural history of 'our' patch, as he enjoyed corresponding with like-minded people in other parts of the U.K. White would surely have enjoyed learning that Ring Ouzels were found in Derbyshire as far back as 12,000 years before his birth. Excavations at Robin Hood's Cave, Creswell Crags, in 1969 unearthed the bones of not only ring ouzels but, Goshawk, Ptarmigan, Black Grouse, Short Eared Owl and many more.

White, I'm guessing, would have been staggered by the full history of the caves and what was found there. A wide range of stone tools were recovered during the 19th and 20th century excavations. Tools left by Neanderthal people between 60,000 and 40,000 years ago included some hand axes and scrapers made from flint, quartzite and clay-ironstone. Excavation also uncovered leaf point arrowheads deposited between 40,000 and 30,000 years ago.

Toward the top of the deposits evidence was found for Late Upper Palaeolithic hunters from 12,500 years ago. The finds include some of the most notable discoveries of flint and bone objects including the only engraving of an animal found in Britain. Recent research on cut marked bone from this cave has shown that people were trapping and butchering arctic hare during the late stage of the Ice Age between 12,600 and 12,300 years ago.

Many of the animal bones from the cave show a characteristic pattern of gnaw marks indicating that spotted hyaenas used Robin Hood Cave as a den during the Ice Age. Bones, which must have littered the cave floor, indicate a wide range of animals including wolf, bear, lion, horse, giant deer, reindeer and bison as well as smaller mammals like arctic hare and arctic lemming.

Early deposits in the central chamber were building up even before the Last Ice Age. Buried within these layers were remains of hippopotamus and a narrow-nosed rhinoceros, animals which lived at Creswell when the climate was as warm as today. One of the biggest mysteries of the cave is the find of a tooth from a lesser scimitar cat. These animals are known to have become extinct long before the last Ice Age.

That's the type of mystery White would have liked to get his teeth into, no pun intended, however, he may not have been quite so pleased to learn that the ring ouzels were most likely part of early man's diet.

The book was first published in 1789 by the author's brother, Benjamin, and it has been continuously in print since then, with over 300 editions up to 2017. Thou shalt not covet thy neighbour's tome but, a copy of a First Edition fine calf-bound rarity would sit very well on my shelves.

It is fairly safe to assume that most if not all of these species were found in Longdendale as it is only forty five miles to Creswell, and although there are not many caves in Millstone Grit, finds in Longdendale include flint arrowheads and tools, and dinosaur footprints were discovered embedded in the shale at Valehouse Reservoir.

Hadfield enjoyed our discussions about Gilbert White and on one occasion said,

"My father was not happy with the course I had taken and said that I should stay at home and write about the animals and birds around the Hall, in the same vein as the Reverend Gilbert White, I can now vouchsafe that indeed I wish I had adhered to his request".

To late, came the cry for Hadfield, because by this time and him only 32 years old, he had already married Ann Sutton, on 12th 1777, at Mottram Church when he was 20, and had two children with her. Evelyn Georgina Hadfield, birth date unknown, and Harriet Manners Hadfield, baptized 9th July 1782 in Whitchurch, Shropshire. The trail almost goes dead here as there is no evidence to fill in the blanks on his time in Shropshire, and no accounts of what happened to his wife Ann, or his two daughters, and Hadfield was loathe to talk about this period of his young life, and when I asked him outright he said, "Dear Boy", as he always referred to me, "Suffice to say, I am sorry for their lot". Quite why Hadfield felt the need to convey this apologetic comment to me I never quite fathomed, as he seemed, if not proud, unrepentant for his actions.

I didn't have children at the time of my first meetings with the man but, I do recall asking him whether he regretted, missing Evelyn and Harriet growing up. However, with questions like this, Hadfield, either said nothing or chose to leave the scene. In my opinion for what it is worth, he was a psychopathic liar with little regard for anyone but himself. Having said that I still liked the man, so his charm may have worked a little on me as well as many of the unfortunates he came into contact with and duped.

The trail of Crowden's infamous son, John Hadfield, is as circuitous as a maze but, furnished with the priceless information from Graham

Hadfield on the family lineage, conversations with the man himself, and the deconstruction of several accounts of his life and times I would like to think we are very close to the full story.

There were a number of ways Hadfield could have set off for his further and ill-fated ventures into the outside world. Perhaps he would have stabled his horse in Mottram or Glossop, to be ridden back to the Hall, and jumped aboard the Stage Coach bound for Sheffield or Manchester, and thence to London.

Originating in England in the 13th century, the stagecoach as we know it first appeared on England's roads in the early 16th century. A stagecoach was so called because it travelled in segments or 'stages' of 10 to 15 miles. At a stage stop, usually a coaching inn, horses would be changed and travellers would have a meal or a drink, or stay overnight.

The first coaches were fairly crude and little better than covered wagons, generally drawn by four horses. Without suspension, these coaches could only travel at around 5 miles an hour on the rutted tracks and unmade roads of the time. In a conversation about the transport system of old with John Davies, he observed, "Not good for your piles them coaches".

During cold or wet weather, travel was often impossible. A writer of 1617 describes them as follow,'...*covered waggons in which passengers are carried to and fro; but this kind of journeying is very tedious, so that only women and people of inferior condition travel in this sort.'*

In 1673, it took eight days to travel by coach from London to Exeter, however the formation of a stage company in 1706 established a regular coach route between York and London and soon there were regular coach services on many other routes.

Coaching Inns sprang up along these routes to service the coaches and their passengers. Many of these Inns are still trading today: they can be recognised by the archways which allowed the coaches to pass through into the stable yard behind the inn. The Norfolk Arms in Glossop, formerly the Tontine, is an example of this but was built in 1823 after Hadfield's time.

In the 17th and 18th centuries stagecoaches were often targeted by Highwaymen such as Dick Turpin and Claude Duval. Today we have rather a romanticised notion of highwaymen with their cries of 'Stand and Deliver!' but in reality these masked men terrorised the roads of England. The punishment for highway robbery was hanging and many highwaymen met their maker at the gallows. Anyone caught robbing a coach in this neck of the woods may well have ended up at Gallowsclough, Mottram's favoured dispatching location. To be fair, or indeed unfair as the case may be, in those days a person could get hanged for much less, and local records show that two young men, boys really, were hanged for causing affray and stealing from a shop.

In 1754, a company in Manchester began a new service called the 'Flying Coach', which it claimed would, all things being equal, and with no hold-ups, travel from Manchester to London in just four and a half days. As I wrote 'hold-ups', it came to me that, the expression may have come from the activity of the Highwaymen, and that it has come to mean in the vernacular, the day to day 'hold-ups' we experience on our roads.

A similar service began from Liverpool three years later, using coaches with a new steel spring suspension. 'I'm sure they were much better for those troubled with hemorrhoids,' said John Davies. And I'm sure he was right, and on top of this, these coaches reached the great speed of 8 miles an hour and completed the journey to London in just three days.

John Hadfield, could have benefited from the new-improved 'Flying Coach', and the better roads, however, in amongst the various reports of his life there are several mentions of him using a 'phaeton' as his preferred means of transport and this is where I put my money. He was a 'fancy-pants' and would not have wanted to mix with the riff-raff on a rickety stagecoach.

A phaeton was a light four-wheeled carriage with open sides in front of the seat, generally drawn by one horse. The term was first applied to classify a carriage during the late 18th and early 19th century period in France when it was so fashionable to use classical pseudonyms. Usage of the term spread quickly to England and America. The word comes from the Greek phaethon-to shine, and also a character in mythology. Phaethon was a boy who tried to drive the sun chariot, who was destroyed by Jupiter with a thunderbolt to prevent him from setting the world on fire. Hadfield is my 'Phaethon' but, as you may imagine he was not keen on the analogy for obvious reasons.

Once he hit the metropolis, wife and daughters left behind, it was reported that he was perpetually at the coffee-houses in Covent Garden, describing himself to whatever company he chanced to meet as a near relation of the well to do Rutland family, and *'Much vaunted of his parks and hounds, and soon became known as, 'lying Hadfield'.* Not a good start then, and he was committed to the King's Bench Prison, for a debt amounting to the sum of one hundred and sixty pounds.

There is enough intrigue, more twists and turns than a slalom and downright skulduggery from Hadfield over the next few years for a book in its own right, involving, more women, numerous children, lots more lying and fraud, and there were sordid sojourns in Dublin, Tiverton, Scarborough and London, which invariably included, arrests, visits to the assizes and spells in prison. A pattern formed with landed gentry, usually besotted women, paying off his debts and having him released, probably in the the hope that his protestations of innocence and romantic overtures had some substance. Slim chance it turns out, and the Walter Mitty in Hadfield, his obvious arrogance and Cavalier attitude had the Devil's coachmen speeding towards him at great pace in July 1802 when he arrived at the Queen's Head in Keswick, in the heart of the English Lake District.

In his, 'Vagabonds All', published in 1926, His Honour Judge Edward Abbot Parry, gathered together, in a latter-day Newgate Calendar, eleven Vagabonds of note, including Madame Rachel, The Go-Between, Robin Hood, The Brigand, Mary Anne Clarke, The Courtesan, James Alan, The Wandering Minstrel and John Hadfield The Imposter.

Before we travel over the hill to the gallows with Hadfield, I think it prudent to give you Parry's definition of a vagabond, which he himself lifted from 'The Compleat Constable' by Thomas Bever from 1708.

'Such are all seafaring men that beg, wandering persons using unlawful games, subtle crafts, or plays, or telling fortunes. All jugglers or slight of hands artists pretending to do wonders by hocus pocus, the Powder of Pimp le Pimp, all Tinkers, Pedlars, Chapmen, Glassmen. All collectors for Jails or Hospitals, Fencers, Bearwards, common players of interludes, and Fiddlers or Minstrels wandering abroad'.

Basically, most of my friends and acquaintances are in there somewhere on the Constable's List, me as well. Funnily enough the first band I ever played in was called 'Vagabond', and our first paid performance was at Crowden Youth Hostel in 1980.

Hadfield started life 223 years earlier, and only a throw of a stone from where I sang, and as you will see he was very keen from the following account on getting paid himself and the Devil may care how. I have Judge Parry to thank for the following account in the language of the day because in his *'Vagabonds All'*, there was a single engraved plate of John Hadfield and beneath the handsome picture was a reference with regard to the source of image:

From a contemporary engraving in Kirby's.
'The Wonderful And Scientific Museum'.
A Magazine of Remarkable Characters Including all the curiosities of nature and art, from the remotest period to the present time.

Kirby's was a 'Strange But True' publication, and similar to the 'Newgate Calendar', full of stories about unusual and far-fetched phenomenon like a French woman with a mans head and beard, and botched executions. A six-volume voyeuristic compilation of extraordinary animals, ballooning, bizarre punishments, boiling fountains, child prodigies, crossdressers, dwarfs, extraordinary burials, conjuring, eccentrics,foxes, ghosts, giants, gypsies, hermits, long-livers, mermaids, misers, odd crimes, pygmies, self-crucifixion, strange murders, ventriloquism, visions, witches, etc. etc. The work was produced by R. S. Kirby, a London bookseller, who had had worked for one Alexander Hogg, publisher of a similar cabinet of curiosities, the "Wonderful Magazine and Marvellous Chronicle" which appeared in parts in the late eighteenth century. The two worked together in the early years of the nineteenth century on another so-called 'Wonderful Magazine, until Kirby allegedly purloined not only Hogg's ideas, but much of his work and produced his own publications. A lawsuit followed but Kirby continued to publish and completely went his own way when he produced his 'Kirby's Wonderful and Scientific Museum' between 1803 and 1820. Kirby was not simply a plagiarist but keenly sought out material himself, as a Chronicler of the time wrote,

"Kirby himself appears to have been present at the remarkable 1804 trial of Francis Smith for the murder of the 'Hammersmith Ghost'

Ironic that Kirby, a crook himself, should include an account of the life and times of John Hadfield in Volume 1, published in 1803 under the headline, 'An uncommon Impostor, Swindler, Seducer, Bigamist, Hypocrite?' but, oh so sweet for myself after months of painstaking research to find an authentic voice from the very year in which Hadfield was executed, complete with records from the trial and first hand accounts of the actual execution.

One of the highlights for me in this account is the use of 'Craddenbroke' (Crowden Brook) also recorded in the Family Tree supplied by Graham Hadfield.

The only caveat on the following is for the reader to understand that this account was written for the titillation of the early 19th Century pallette but also that I use sections of it untouched by my 21st century editorial tourettes. The two first hand accounts of his trial and execution are very, very similar and I use one of those in this chapter as my benchmark.

Particulars of the life of John Hadfield, Kirby's 1803.

Among the list of those names that swell the numerous instances of human depravity, we believe not one will scarcely be found with so many claims to the notice of our readers, as the present.

John Hadfield has not become a victim to the offended laws by any sudden gust of human frailty or passion, any deep-laid scheme, or dangerous situation, prepared for him by others. Neither are his crimes the effects of youthful inexperience, any of which might have claimed his behalf the sigh of sympathy, or the tears of pity.

On the contrary, for twenty years past, John Hadfield has been the calm, the studious, and the deliberate over-reacher of the industrious, the innocent, and the unwary. This disposition, so destructive to the peace and good of society, it will be found, has by him been carried to such a degree, that as far as his propensities were to be gratified, either by swindling or intrigue, he may be compared to our Henry VIII. Of whom it has been said, that he neither spared man in his anger, nor woman in his lust.

I thought this initial condemnation was worth including, as I could just imagine some agitated reader from 1803 becoming more and more disgusted with Hadfield's crimes.

John Hadfield is about 45 years of age: was born in 1757 at a place called Craddenbroke, at the extremity of the country of Chester, adjoining to Yorkshire and Derbyshire. His father being a clothier, he followed that business under his father, then removed near Chester, and afterwards to Liverpool, where he passed for a gentleman, and where we find nothing of his character, but pleasure and extravagance.

His amours, it is said, he commenced near his own native place, with ensnaring the natural daughter of a noble parent, it is said of the late Lord Robert Sutton, brother to the late Marquis of Granby, with a handsome independent fortune, who ran away with and married him.

Kirby's researchers were getting carried away here and perhaps just a little lax with the facts because, at this juncture Hadfield had already left his first wife Ann Sutton. We know from Parish Records that he was with Ann from 1777 when they married, until 1782 when their second daughter, Harriet, was born in Whitchurch, therefore and by all accounts his errant ways began when he returned *'near to his own native place'* sometime after Harriet was born.

Hadfield was not impressed when presented with this early summation of his character and said with regard to the author, *"I would have run the man through"*. This expression comes from 'running' someone through with a sword but, perhaps in a duel. Although bravado seemed high on Hadfield's list, it is very likely that he had taken part in a duel, or duels as there was enough cause against him for many a gauntlet to be 'thrown down' by a disgruntled Father, Suitor, Brother, Debtor, Banker or Soldier.

Dueling with swords was on the wane when Hadfield was up to his tricks but matched pistols were still very popular. A pair of pistols was later found in his personal belongings.

The tradition of dueling goes back centuries, and it is believed the word duel, derived from a Latin term (duellum) meaning war between two. By the mid-1700s dueling had become common enough that fairly formal codes began to dictate how duels were to be conducted

In 1777, delegates from the West of Ireland met at Clonmel and came up with the Code Duello, a dueling code which became standard in Ireland and in Britain. Many duels were avoided by the men involved either apologizing or somehow smoothing over their differences, and I have a hunch that this is how Hadfield avoided the steely stare of a many a challenger. Hadfield also had a habit of upping-sticks very quickly when the finger of suspicion pointed in his direction. However, to be fair to the man, I'm surmising that if there was no expedient way of escaping the challenge, he would take part, and further if this is true, he was either a good swordsman and a fine shot as he had obviously lived to tell the tale.

Whilst checking a few details about the history of dueling, I searched for, 'Famous duels in the 18th Century', and by chance discovered why Pawdy Blanche would occasionally proclaim on the dangers of another boxer taking him on in the ring: *'If I ever kilt' a man I'd wear a glove like Dan!'.*

The duel in question involved Ireland's 'Liberator', Daniel O'Connell and a man called D'Esterre. O'Connell was mentioned in the earlier chapters concerning Pawdy Blanche and 'Windy Gap'.

D'Esterre shot first, but miscalculated and fired too low but when O'Connell returned fire he wounded D'Esterre in the groin, the bullet lodging in the base of his spine. A newspaper of the time proclaimed, *'D'Esterre fell, and the crowd roared'.*

O'Connell was shaken to find that the man had bled to death two days later. Saddened by the outcome he paid an allowance for D'Esterre's daughter until his death over thirty years later. O'Connell would never duel again and from then on always wore a glove on the hand that fired the fatal shot while attending church or passing the door of D'Esterre's widow. Hence Pawdy's proclamation.

Kirby's:

Hadfield soon squandered his wife's money, (That of his second wife) and left her a beggar. For some time she existed on a stipend provided by her friends, and then died of a broken heart. By her he had three daughters, whom he deserted, and one of them is now living in the lowest state of servitude. In the course of his career he visited America, and travelled over many parts of Europe, representing himself as a major in the army, and was much in Ireland, where he was engaged in many duels. The next scene of his exhibition, we hear, was Scarborough and the particulars of his transactions at that place, are thus detailed in the following letter:

Scarborough, 17th Nov 1802
Hadfield came to Scarborough in March 1792, without any attendants. Possessed of a good address and insinuating manners, he soon introduced himself to persons of the first respectability in the place. He stiled himself Major Hadfield in a regiment of foot, which had served in America during the late war between that Country and England. He further added, that he was connected with the Duke of Rutland by marriage, and that he expected in a few weeks to be proposed to represent this borough in parliament.

He apologised to his new acquaintance for his humble appearance, intimating that he had left his carriages, servants, and horses at York, as the object of this visit (he said) *was merely to see the place which he should soon represent in parliament. He acquitted himself at the head of his table with a gentlemanly ease: and the conversation on that day chiefly turned on his services in America, and when in Ireland, as aid-de-camp to the late Duke of Rutland, the Lord Lieutenant of that kingdom.*

A fortnight or three weeks having elapsed, Hadfield's worthy host ventured to ask for some £20 to settle his account which was never paid. In consequence of this, and some other suspicious circumstances, his pretensions began to be generally disputed, and at length it was thought prudent to arrest him for the tavern debt. On the 25th of April 1792, not being able to procure bail he went to the gaol, and in June 1793 a detainer was lodged against him by Mr. Hamilton of London for 80 guineas.

During his confinement he experienced many vicissitudes, receiving from some quarter unknown to any person at Scarborough except himself, several remittances, which many times exceeded his debts, but which he hastily spent in idle extravagances.

Every half year during his imprisonment, he had the impudence to request the attendance of a magistrate to swear him to an affidavit, in order to obtain half-pay as Major or Lieutenant-Colonel Hadfield.

It was impossible for me to take Hadfield to task on these matters during our conversations, because at the time all I had to go on was a small pamphlet, *'The History of Tintwistle',* where Hadfield was given a few pages. He was basically described as a bit of a lad, and the account also contained the one and only mention that I have seen, then and since, of the soothsayer Robinson's prophecy which Shining Girl had mentioned: *'Fate's resistless hand will seal your fate in Cumberland'.*

Kirby's:

Hadfield obtained his discharge, and also the hand of Miss Nation, a young lady who had a window opposite the prison to him.

It seems that Hadfield had been visited by Miss Nation's mother while incarcerated, promised her some estates in Derbyshire, which obviously were not his to give away and in return she secured his release. We should perhaps not be surprised by the seemingly witless attraction to Hadfield, and there are many parallels today, with women who visit, become attracted to and even marry hardened criminals while they reside in prison. There are also many examples of women from the U.K. who start out as pen-pals to men on Death Row in America, before eventually marrying them. In this case the Mother believed that Hadfield intended to take up with her daughter but, there was little chance of that happening and as Kirby's reported: *So soon as he (Hadfield) was liberated, the next morning he returned to Heal-Bridge in the parish of Dulverton and while there his extravagance continued in so much that, in one instance, though he lived only two miles from the church, he sent to Tiverton, the nearest place being twelve miles from his home, for a post chaise to carry himself and his wife to church.*

In some ways by interjecting here and there during this account from Kirby's I feel that I should apologise to the Chronicler from 1803 but, on occasion the language of the day and the repetition of the same information every few sentences can be very confusing, as can the sudden inclusion of earlier incidents in Hadfield's life which is why I have tried to unpick the details and make the account more coherent.

Kirby's:

Soon after his arrival in Devon, by the most artful means and insidious misrepresentations, he prevailed on a worthy clergyman, Mr Nucella, to accept his drafts to a large amount on the persuasion of his remitting property to provide for them when due. On the strength of this property, and other insinuations, he became a partner in the firm of Dennis and Company, in that County. He now visited town, and with his carriage and establishment made a splendid figure. Suspected however, by some of his creditors, and threatened with being arrested, he gave up the parliamentary scheme, and having procured a few hundreds he decamped, leaving his second wife (now his third wife, and by my maths six children and one on the way) *in Devonshire with a young infant, and pregnant with another, dependent on the charity of the world.*

Hadfield's avarice combined with his 'eye' for the female form, especially one with money and land, was soon to combine in his downfall, as he, like many others had heard about Mary of Buttermere, who became known as the 'Beauty' and latterly the 'Maid of Buttermere', and probably that her parents owned a public house and land.

As with all good stories, the life of John Hadfield, has a beginning, a middle and an end, and although the middle in Hadfield's case has been mired with two hundred years of contradictory accounts, we can be fairly sure that Kirby's, is close to the mark, and further that his 'end' came very quickly once he crossed from Lancashire into Cumberland in pursuit of the 'Maid'.

Mary Robinson, described in the Oxford Dictionary of National Biography as a 'shepherdess and social celebrity', first gained some measure of fame in 1792 when Joseph Budworth (writing as Joseph Palmer) made mention of her, and *her abundance of physical charms'*, in his guidebook, *'A Fortnight's Ramble To The Lakes of 'Westmoreland, Lancashire and Cumberland'.*

Palmer described Mary somewhat breathlessly as an *'angel'* possessing *'a ,fine oval face with full eyes and lips as sweet as vermillion and her cheeks had more of the lily than the rose.'*

Mary Robinson became the late 18th-century equivalent to an overnight sensation and soon became known as the Beauty of Buttermere. If she was around now, she would surely have been a guest on 'Big Brother', or 'I'm A Celebrity, Get Me Out Of Here'. Her family's establishment, the Fish Inn, at the time, 'The Char', so named after the Char one of the rarest fish species in Britain, found mainly in deep, cold, glacial lakes, was soon bursting at the seams with a new phenomenon, 'tourists'. Travellers were keen to witness this Cumbrian Beauty in the flesh, not least the Lake Poets, Coleridge and Wordsworth. The pair encountered Mary Robinson together on a month-long tour of the Lakes in 1799 and her natural appearance and gentle character appealed to their romantic notion of natural beauty, as did her wide-eyed demeanor and innocence. Wordsworth would later write his own ode to Mary in Book VII of The Prelude. He referred to Mary as an *'artless daughter of the hills'* of *'modest mien / And carriage marked by unexampled grace.'* He goes on to extol, *'Her just opinions, delicate reserve / Her patience and humility of mind.'* Coleridge, in a later newspaper article, is somewhat more frank in his assessment: *'To beauty, however, in the strict sense of the word, she has small pretensions, for she is rather gap-toothed, and somewhat pock-fretten. But her face is very expressive, and the expression extremely interesting, and her figure and movements are graceful to a miracle. She ought indeed to have been called the Grace of Buttermere, rather than Beauty.'*

Despite the unexpected and unsought attention lavished on her as a result of being thrust into the limelight, Mary it seems, was unaffected. Wordsworth, again in The Prelude, claimed that she remained, *'Unspoiled by the excess of public notice'.* If Wordsworth had been blessed with foresight, he may have advised Mary to, *'Beware false suitors',* as our man from Craddenbrooke was heading over the Pass in her direction.

Kirby's:

But the event which gave the greatest éclat to John Hadfield was in consequence of his visiting Keswick in Cumberland, on a fishing party, in August 1802. This he undertook in his own carriage, but without any servants; and then took up his abode at the ale house of Mary's Father, old Mr. Robinson, at the foot of the small lake. Here he called himself Hon. A. A Hope, Member for Dumfries, and first paid his addresses to Miss D, a young lady of fortune, from Ireland, who was there at the same time. He even obtained her consent, and gone so far as to buy the wedding clothes. However, a friend that was in the interest of the lady, as it will appear in the sequel, happily prevented this union. Fortunately for her, the marriage day was not fixed.

It would appear that Hadfield could not help himself as even in pursuit of the 'Maid', he took up with the anonymous and mysterious 'Miss D' who according to Kirby's was from Ireland. In modern day parlance, maybe she was able to obtain a 'gagging order' to keep her name out of the newspapers. The embarrassment of falling for Hadfield's advances too much to bear.

As for Mary and her parents, Hadfield worked his magic and the union came very quickly. In the way of things, one can only imagine how much Hadfield upset other men who already had their eye on Mary, maybe even the Lakes Poets. From a local's point of view, here's this 'posh-guy' riding into town and stealing 'their' Beauty from under their noses. I did have the opportunity to talk to Hadfield about this part of his life thanks to the short chapter about him in the aforementioned, *'History of Tintwistle'*. I worked on the premise that in many ways Hadfield's story, and his infamy were mostly due to his relationship with Mary, the handsome Lass of Buttermere. I thought he may rail at this suggestion, full of himself as he was but, he agreed and with regard to his behaviour he said that most people were just too gullible, and that it was not his fault that his victims were so stupid to fall for his pretence. No regret there then, or more bravado.

With reference to his early success in duping the Cumbrian folk, he took great delight in saying that he couldn't understand a word they said, and that the closer he got to Buttermere, the more difficult it was to make any *'sense whatsoever'* of conversations and that he sometimes resorted to sign-language.

Hadfield took great delight in impersonating the local accents, which he said that the deeper one ventured into the hidden valleys became stronger and more impenetrable by the mile, and although initially I believed he was 'hamming' it up by the stone trough for effect, the following is a fairly close rendition of a conversation Hadfield said he had had with a young Shepherd of Borrowdale with regard to obtaining a passage to Ireland. This was possibly Hadfield's Plan B, or even Plan C. Always thinking ahead it would seem.

'I tell the amackily what dreedfull fine things I saw ith rwod tyu, an at yon Dublin; an t'harships I've bidden. I set forrat o' Midsummer-day, an gat to Whitehebben a girt sea-side town, whore Sea-Nags eat cowls out o' rack-hurries, like as barrels dus yale drink: I think Sea-Nags is nut varra wild, for tha winter them ca girt foalds wi'out yates; an as I was lyukin about to gang to Ierland, I so twea duzzen o' fellows myakin a Sea-Nag tedder-styack ov iran; I ast yan othum if I cud git ridin tu Dublin? an a man in a three-nyuk'd hat, at knact like rottin sticks, telt me I mud gang wid him; for a thing tha caw tide, like t' post oth land, was gangin, an wadent stay o' nea boddee nivir. Than four men in a lile Sea-Nag, a fwot I think, at tha caw'd a bwot, helter'd our nag, and led it out oth'

foald; than our nag slipt t' helter an ran away; but tha hang up a deal of wind-clyaths, like blinder-bridles, we' hundreds o' ryaps for rines. Land ran away an left us'.

In fairness to Hadfield his micky-taking also included a fair bit of ribbing for some of his neighbours at Crowden, who he claimed were, 'Nonsensical'. I have to say that during my time at Crowden, I understood every word that born and bred Valley folk said, although there were a few individual words I did not understand until explained but, I can imagine that two centuries ago there was some tricky dialect going on. The term 'dialect' generally refers to regional speech patterns, but can also be defined by other factors, such as social class, a sociolect, an ethnic group an ethnolect, and a regional dialect, a regiolect. I'm not so sure about the farming community and for the following example of early 'sheep counting' in Derbyshire, as explained to me by Hadfield I have invented 'farmiolect'.

Yain, Tain, Eddero, Peddero, (1, 2, 3 and 4) simple enough but jump to 18, 19 and 20, and you had, Eddero-o-bumfitt, Peddero-o-bumfitt and Jiggit. There were no numbers after twenty and when checking his flock the shepherd would throw a stone on the ground, or transfer a small pebble from one hand to the other, like a cricket-umpire, as a mark of 20 and then repeat the operation. The origins of this type of language could well have been, 'Cumbric', a variety of the Common Brittonic language spoken during the Early Middle Ages in the Hen Ogledd or 'Old North'. In those days Cumbria was much larger than the current County.

It is easy to see where the Derbyshire counting method came from but not so simple to pinpoint exactly where, as even the different Lakeland Dales used, similar, but 'different' words for numbers. For example in Coniston the number 7 was Slatta, in Borrowdale Lethera, and in Eskdale Seckera, whereas they all agree that number 10 was Dick.

I suggested to John Hadfield that he could have used this method to count the women in his life. He was not amused.

Kirby's:

The pretended Colonel Hope, in company with the clergyman, procured a licence on the 1st of October, and they (Hadfield & The Maid) *were publicly married in the church of Lorton, on Saturday October 2nd 1802. Is there on earth that prude or bigot, who can blame poor Mary? She had given her lover the best reasons to esteem her.*

A Mr Hardinge, a Welsh Judge, passing through Keswick heard of this adventurer, and sent his servant over to Buttermere, with a note to the supposed Colonel Hope, who observed that it was a mistake, and that the note was for a brother of his. Our adventurer made a blank denial that he, had ever assumed the name but Sir Fred Vane, a magistrate near Keswick granted a warrant for Hadfield's apprehension, on the ground of his having forged several franks, as the Member of Llinlithgow. Hadfield, however, made so light of the matter, that ordering a dinner to be got ready at the inn at three o'clock, after his repast he said that he would go and amuse himself on the Lake.

Judge Hardinge had read the reports concerning Hadfield in the London newspapers and very quickly put one and two together.

One publication advertised a £50 reward for information about Hadfield, describing him as a notorious impostor, swindler, and felon, who lately married a young woman, commonly called the Beauty of Buttermere, under an assumed name.

The London Sun:

His height is about five feet 10 inches, age about 44, full face, bright eyes, thick eyebrows, strong but light beard, good complexion, some colour, thick but not very prominent nose, smiling countenance, fine teeth, a scar on one of his cheeks near the chin, very long thick light hair, with a great deal of it grey, done up in a club. Stout, square shouldered, full breast and chest, rather corpulent and, stout limbed, but very active, and has rather a spring in his gait, with apparently a little hitch in bringing up one leg; the two middle fingers of his left hand are stiff from an old wound, and he frequently has a custom of putting them straight with his right.

Surely this could be the evidence to perhaps prove but, definitely suggest that Hadfield had been a duelist, an injured hand *'from an old wound'*. Cuts to the hands and arms were very common injuries for during a duel with swords. Couple this with the pistols found in his possession in the Lakes. Where's Sherlock when you need him.

Another report was written by Samuel Taylor Coleridge of 'The Ancient Mariner' fame and it appeared in the London papers on October 11th 1802. By November 6th, 1802, the London 'Sun' was informed by Colonel Hope's Brother after reading Coleridge's article that, the real Colonel Hope was actually abroad at the time. If I can inject a little personal supposition here, I believe that Coleridge had a soft spot for the 'Maid' himself and was very jealous of Hadfield, riding-into-town, and stealing her from under his nose.

Kirby's:

Hadfield, (By now fully aware that he was being actively sought) went out in a boat, accompanied by the fishing-tackier, and a little before three o'clock, a considerable number of inhabitants assembled at the foot of the Lake, waiting anxiously for his return, and by far the greater part were disposed to lead him back in triumph. The truth is, the good people of the Vales had as little heard, and possessed as little a notion, of the existence of the sort of wickedness practised by Hadfield, as of the abominations of Tiberius at Caprie.

Kirby's were going for the jugular by comparing Hadfield to Tiberious, just the sort of lurid details the readers loved. The Emperor had left Rome and decamped to the Isle of Capri, where it is said he was able to, *'finally give in to all the vices he had struggled so long to conceal'*. Hadfield on the other hand made no real attempt to hide his vices, he just moved on as fast as he could.

Kirby's:

But our adventurer, in his flight from Keswick, leaving behind him in his carriage a handsome dressing-box, containing a pair of very elegant pistols, and a complete assortment of toilet trinkets, all silver. The whole value of the box could not be less than eighty pounds. There were discovered only some letters, a cash-book, and the list of several cities in Italy, with a couple of names attached to each.

Italy could have been Hadfield's intended destination of flight as the net grew tighter around him, he would undoubtedly have realised the consequences of his actions if apprehended. If only we were privy to the names and the places he had written down.

From the cash-book nothing could be learned, but that he had vested considerable sums in the house of Baron Dimsdale and Co. Baron Thomas Dimsdale FRS was an English physician, banker and MP and was created Baron Dimsdale of the Russian Empire by Catherine the Great. He was born in Theydon Garnon, Essex, the son of John Dimsdale, a surgeon, and his wife Susan.

This brief description of Baron Dimsdale and his circumstances provides an accurate 'blueprint' for the type of person Hadfield actively sought out. He was the consummate con-man.

From another letter, aided by a list of towns, a marvellous story was extracted. The letter was said to be from an Irish banditti, urging this Colonel Hope to escape with all possible speed, informing him that a price had been set upon his head, and stating the writer's eagerness to assist him, but that his wounds confined him to his bed. It was concluded, therefore, by the people, that this pretended Colonel Hope was a great leader in the Irish rebellion.

We know Hadfield spent a short period in Dublin, where as you may imagine, his usual modus operandi was employed, before once again he was exposed as a fraud and he was off again. The third letter was reported to be from a Exciseman in Northern Ireland and illustrates where Hadfield travelled to from Dublin, and more importantly, why he went in that direction.

A grateful epistle from a poor exciseman at-Glenarm, who had escaped with his life from an overset boat, and to whom our adventurer had performed some acts of kindness.

'*Marvellous story*' indeed. Glenarm on the Antrim Coast, was a small coastal village renowned for smuggling in the 17th and 18th centuries, drink and tobacco mostly, so no surprise again that John Hadfield was interested in visiting. The only surprise, nay bombshell, in this account is that Hadfield appears to have helped someone rather than helping himself. Too late now to discover Hadfield's so-called '*acts of kindness*' but, my 'Crying Man' helped a drowning '*Excise Man*' in some way or other. This is just one more snippet I would have enjoyed running by John Hadfield if I had known the information at the times we had met. It strikes me if nothing else, Hadfield was certainly resourceful not averse to travel and more importantly always looking to the main chance.

And this much I already knew from the accounts I had read, which is why I dug deep with regard to his, 'Evvy', the Evvy he lamented near the stone trough at Crowden, and I can tell you that with regard to this Evelyn, his first born daughter by Ann Sutton he really did have a heart. "Once again I beseech you to refrain from such interrogation on the subject of my daughter Evvy, and I vouchsafe in the presence of the Almighty that she is under my skin like a gadfly".

A gad or warble fly which looks like a harmless bumble bee, burrows a hole into the skin of cattle, deer and sometimes humans and lays eggs beneath the hide. As the grubs develop they cause the host species an enormous amount of discomfort, irritation and sometimes infection.

By using the analogy of gadfly Hadfield demonstrates that he was ahead of the game in his knowledge of natural history, and he went on to explain that some Valley folk blamed the 'goatsucker' or nightjar, the harmless beauty of dawn and dusk whose creaking-gate call was heard up and down Longdendale before a national decline. Funny how when looking for explanations people associated animals they did not really understand as the culprit. The nightjar had both barrels of misguided folk lore, not only blamed for the work of the warble fly, but named 'goatsucker' because it was thought that they drank goats milk in the night, and then to cap it all, Gabble Ratchet in Yorkshire, where it was believed the bird was a repository for the souls of unbaptised children.

Gilbert White, Hadfield's 'David Attenborough', and obvious reference, referred to the nightjar as a 'fern owl', and John Hadfield had once reminded me of this by reading a passage from the Reverend's, Natural History of Selborne which he always kept with him.

'The country people have a notion that the fern owl ... is very injurious to to weanling calves ... [but] the least observation and attention would convince men that these birds neither injure the goatherd nor the grazier, but are perfectly harmless and subsist alone on night insects. 'It is the hardest thing in the world to shake off superstitious prejudices: they are sucked in as it were with our mother's milk ... and make the most lasting impressions, become so interwoven into our very constitutions, that the strongest good sense is required to disengage ourselves from them.'

From my perspective as a writer, what a delicious irony that, to 'gad' or 'gadabout' is defined as go from place to place in the pursuit of pleasure', that will be John 'Gadabout' Hadfield then.

Kirby's:

The supposition of so great a man as Colonel Hope, Member for Llinlithgow in Scotland, and brother to the Earl of Hopetoun, having married a poor young woman at a village in Cumberland, as it could not fail being descanted on in the newspapers, was also very soon contradicted upon the best authorities, by the Lord Advocate of Scotland.

The gadding was over for Hadfield and although there is no actual account of his apprehension, the enormity of his crimes saw him in front of the Judge at Carlisle Assizes.

Kirby's

There were three indictments preferred against him. In the first of these he stood charged with assuming the name, of the Hon. Alexander Augustus Hope, and under that name drawing a Bill of Exchange on one John Crump, Esq. payable to George Wood, a publican, in Keswick. In the second he was charged with forging, under the same name, another Bill for thirty pounds, with intent to defraud the same persons. The third indictment charged him with, counterfeiting Colonel Hope's hand-writing, in superscribing various letters, with a view of defrauding government of the postage. The prisoner pleaded Not Guilty.

Mr. Scarlet, Counsel for the Crown, opened the case by declaring that Hadfield had committed many crimes, under cover of the name of a most respectable gentleman, who belonged to a noble and an ancient family.

Mr. Nicholson also swore to his being the person who married the prisoner to Mary Robinson, commonly called Mary of Buttermere, on the 2nd of October 1802—that after his marriage, he was on terms of intimacy with the prisoner. After a variety of evidence, Col. Parker was sworn. Said he was well acquainted with Col. Hope, brother to the Earl of Hopetoun, a General in the Army, and Col. of the 17th Regiment of Dragoons.—He had been in Ireland about three years.—He said the prisoner at the bar is not Col. Hope. Here the evidence for the prosecution closed.

The prisoner then addressed himself to the Jury.—" He said he felt some degree of satisfaction in being able to have his sufferings terminated, as they must of course be by their verdict. Hadfield declared he had been dragged from prison to prison, and torn from place to place, subject to all the misrepresentations of calumny. "Whatever will be my fate, (said he) I am content; it is the award of justice, impartially and virtuously administered.—But I will solemnly declare, that in all my transactions, I never intended to defraud or injure the persons whose names have appeared in the prosecution. This I will maintain to the last of my life."

The Court were also given a letter from Mary Robinson which was read out to a hushed Courtroom, this would be called a 'Witness Statement' these days, and it almost certainly provided the proverbial final nail.

Kirby's:

Universal silence prevailed and the auditors were full of expectation, whilst Mr. Reeves read the following letter, which had on it the postmark of Keswick:
    Sir, The man whom I had the misfortune to marry, and who has ruined
    me and my aged and-unhappy parents, always told me that he was the Hon. Colonel Hope, the next brother to the Earl of Hopetoun. Your grateful and unfortunate servant, Mary Robinson.

At eight o'clock the next morning (Tuesday), the Court met, when the prisoner appeared at the Bar, to receive his sentence.

After proceeding in the usual form, the Judge addressed him in the following terms:—"John Hadfield! after a long and serious investigation of the charges which have been preferred against you, you have been found guilty by a Jury of your country.—You have been distinguished for crimes of such magnitude as have seldom, if ever, received any mitigation of capital punishment, and in your case it is impossible it can be remitted. Assuming the person, name, and character of a worthy and respectable officer, of a noble family in this country, you have perpetrated and committed the most enormous crimes. The imprisonment which you have undergone, has afforded time for your serious reflection, and an opportunity of your being deeply impressed with a sense of the enormity of your guilt, and the justice of that sentence which must be inflicted upon you; I wish you to be seriously impressed with the awfulness of your situation, and to reflect with anxious care and deep concern on your approaching end, concerning which, much remains to be done lay aside now your delusion and imposition, and employ properly the short space of time you have to live. I beseech you to employ the remaining part of your time for eternity, that you may find mercy at the hour of death, and in the day of judgment. Hear now the sentence of the law."

His Lordship then pronounced sentence of death Upon the prisoner, in the usual form; who heard it with firmness, bowed respectfully, and was taken away from the Dock. A post chaise conveyed him from the hall to the prison; he was cool and collected during the time he was in the chaise; and as soon as he got back to his room, he fell upon his knees, and prayed in a fervent and serious manner for about half an hour; after which he desired some refreshment. .

Another letter of the day says, *" Since I wrote to you last, Hadfield continues to pass his time in writing to his friends, and in reading. His appetite has failed him, and he lives chiefly upon coffee. I had an opportunity of seeing and conversing with him to-day for some time. He applied this morning to one of the clergymen who attends him, Mr. Pattison, to recommend him a tradesman to make his coffin. Mr. Joseph Bushby, of this town, took measure of him about half an hour ago. He did not appear to be at all agitated while Mr. Bushby was so employed. He told the latter that he desired the coffin to be a strong oak one, plain and neat. 'I request, Sir,' he added, 'that after I am taken down, I may be put into the coffin immediately, with the apparel I may have on, and afterwards closely screwed down, put into the hearse which will be in waiting, carried to the church-yard of Burgh on Sands, and there be interred in the evening.'*

From the hour when the Jury found him guilty, he has behaved with the utmost serenity and cheerfulness. He received the visits of all those who wished to see him, and talked upon the topics of the day with the greatest interest or indifference.

It was common practice for visitors, some genuine and most, probably voyeuristic, to 'buy' their way in to see a prisoner before execution, especially with someone with a reputation like Hadfield. It is known that on the morning of his departure, Wordsworth and his sister Dorothy were allowed to visit Hadfield but that he refused point-blank to see Coleridge, which was not surprising as Hadfield obviously knew that Coleridge's article in the London newspapers was instrumental in his capture and ultimate conviction.

The Letter continued:

He could scarcely ever be brought to speak of his own case. He neither blamed the verdict, nor made any confession of his guilt. He said that he had no intention to defraud those whose names he forged; but was never heard to say that he was to die unjustly."

Another account says,—*" A notion very generally prevailed that he would not be brought to justice, and the arrival of the mail was daily expected with the greatest impatience. No pardon arriving, Saturday the 3rd was at last fixed upon as the day of execution. Accordingly the post coming in a little before three o'clock, and bringing neither pardon nor reprieve, the Under-sheriff and a detachment of the Cumberland Yeomanry immediately repaired to the prison near the English gate. A prodigious crowd had previously assembled. This was* the market day, and people had come from the distance of many mile out of mere curiosity. A post-chaise was brought for him from the Bush Inn. Having taken farewell of the Clergyman, who attended him to the door, he mounted the step with much steadiness and composure.—The Gaoler and the Executioner went in along with him.—The latter had been brought from Dumfries upon a retaining fee of ten guineas.

"It was exactly four o'clock when the procession moved from the gaol. Passing through the Scotch gate, in about twelve minutes it arrived at the Sands. Half the Yeomanry went before the carriage, and the oilier behind.—Upon arriving on the ground, they formed a ring round the scaffold.—It is said that Hadfield wished to have had the blinds drawn up, but that such an indulgence was held inconsistent with the interests of public justice.

"As soon as the carriage door had been opened by the Under-Sheriff, Hadfield alighted with his two companions. A small dung-cart boarded over, had been placed under the gibbet. A ladder was placed to this stage, which he instantly ascended. He was dressed in a black jacket, black silk waistcoat, fustian pantaloons, white cotton stockings, and ordinary shoes. He wore no powder in his hair. He seemed at least fifty, and there was something grave and reverend in his aspect, which for a moment made one forget all the crimes laid to his charge. He was perfectly cool and collected; at the same time he showed no disposition to die game. His conduct displayed nothing of levity, of insensibility, or of hardihood. He was more anxious to give proof of resignation than of heroism: His countenance was extremely pale, but his hand never trembled:

He immediately untied his handkerchief, and placed the bandage over his eyes. The Executioner was extremely awkward, and Hadfield found it necessary to give various directions as to the placing of the rope, and the proper method of driving away the cart. He several times put on a languid and piteous smile. He at last seemed rather exhausted and faint. Having been near three weeks under *sentence of death, he must have suffered much, and a reflection of the misery be had occasioned must have given him many an agonizing throe.*

"Having taken leave of the Gaoler and the Sheriff, he prepared himself for his fate. He was at this time heard to exclaim, 'My spirit is strong, though my body is weak.'

"Great apprehensions were entertained that it would be necessary to tie him up a second time. The noose clipped twice, and he fell down above eighteen inches. His feet at last were almost touching the ground. But his excessive weight, which occasioned this accident, speedily relieved him from pain. He expired in a moment, and without any struggle.

"He was cut down after he had hung about an hour. On Wednesday last he had made a carpenter take his measure for a coffin. He gave particular directions that it should be large, as he meant to be laid in it with all his clothes on. It was made of oak, adorned with plates, and extremely handsome every way. A hearse followed with it to the ground, and afterwards bore him away. He was then buried in a corner of the Churchyard of St. Mary's, Carlisle, at a distance from the tombs, without any ceremony; and in less than two hours, the whole of the crowd had dispersed."

One thing still we ought not to omit is a report that Mary of Buttermere opened and carried on a correspondence with him by letters, while he was in confinement, and was scarcely dissuaded by her friends from paying him a personal visit'.

The following poem was found in Hadfield's belongings after his death and it is assumed that he wrote it himself while awaiting his fate, he was kidding himself right up until the end.

> *'Lo! where the ancient marbles weep,*
> *And all the worthy Hadfields' sleep,*

Amongst them soon may I recline,
Oh! may their hallow'd tombs be mine.
When in that sacred vault I'm laid,
Heaven grant it may with truth be said,
His heart was warm'd with faith sincere,
And soft humanity dwelt there.
My children oft' will mourn their father's woe,
Heart easing tears from their sweet eyes will flow'.

As for the stone troughs at Crowden, they are running clear again and both horses and dogs and indeed humans can readily quench their thirst as the Hadfield's intended. The Water-Boatmen will soon be back spinning their magic, and who knows, another family of stoats may appear over the wall and if you hear someone making the sound of a squealing rabbit, it will likely be me.

Chapter Ten:
An Irish Wedding In Nerja & A Surprise Guest...Shining Girl.

As the Crowden Years creep into 1985, and as I pen my way into a tenth 'Bonus Chapter' it is slowly dawning on me that, this story of mine is much more than one book but, without wanting to put a number on it at this stage, I would like to use a well known line from Irish comedian Jimmy Cricket, with whom we shared the bill at St George's Hall at Belle Vue in the same year.. 'And there's more', said Jimmy, "There will be if you drop my microphone again", said I.

There was much more to come as it turned out, and one amazing surprise in Spain as I skip to the early 90's.

Nerja in Southern Andalucia, a mill pond sea and North Africa a mere hop across the heat haze. I had landed for a week off with no gigs, no rain gauges, no articles to write and seven days away from the Valley. I was chasing birds and warm blooded mammals for my sins but first, there was the relaxing, beers to be drunk, tapas to be eaten and gushing admiration of the view from a beach-side restaurant. A dozen waiters were setting up for a large party, as it turns out a wedding. I was actually following up on a story idea for the Sunday Times Newspaper about Alpine Swifts and Iberian Lynx and was accompanied as usual by my long-time companion, Peter 'Oaf' Bromhall, Oaf of the 'Warburton Toastie Record' as if you needed reminding.

Sadly my dear friend Oaf passed away in December 2017, and he will be much missed by family and friends. I had the honour of giving his eulogy to a packed St Mary's Catholic Church in Glossop, a thousand in they reckon, a great testament to his popularity. I soon forgot my nerves because, this was no normal funeral, sad yes, but so much love and happy memories under one roof. It was like the best wedding you have ever been to and my eulogy felt like the best man's speech. Ironically Oaf and I had discussed this matter a number of years earlier after another funeral where I did the eulogy, and he had said prophetically, "You'll be doing mine Woody...make sure you make 'em laugh and then make 'em cry." I told him that was the wrong way round and he agreed but, as it happens I did a bit of both all the way through.

Oaf was funny without knowing he's funny, a rare talent. The example I often use to demonstrate his great skill revolves around a time when we were on the west coast of Ireland. I had woken Oaf early for breakfast, the full Irish obviously, even though we were both a little worse for the Guinness from the night before. Oaf wasn't happy but, I had asked the landlady for an early call so we could get out the shore before anyone else. I really wanted to photograph a sanderling, a Lilliputian wading bird of great beauty, named Canutus, after the king who tried to stay the tide. Sanderlings do a better job of it and very rarely get their feet wet.

They proved devils to photograph, as I trained, or attempted to train my lenses on their erratic meanderings, back and forth, to and fro, as they avoided the incoming tide. Oaf had wandered off grumpily, and I forgot he was with me until came the familiar call, everything prefaced with, "Woody", "What?" I replied, indignant at being distracted from my quest. "There's a dog down there chewing a fish". This I had to see, so caught him up and looked in the direction he was pointing. I might of known... "It's an otter, you daft bugger", I laughed.

Oaf had an inkling of my Crowden stories but, was never really interested in the lives of deceased valley residents and if the truth were known, probably thought I was bonkers. Our lives, apart from our immediate family, revolved, as they still do today, around Glossop Rugby Club, beer and food. The other constants in my own life have been writing and Irish music, and there's a whole book somewhere in the depths of my bonce about the days when Oaf was the band's Roadie. I loved Oaf dearly.

In 1992 we were still in our 30's, and in hindsight we probably could have knuckled down a bit more, maybe even, been a bit more responsible, although to a large extent we were governed in our outlook on life by Oaf's mantra, "Woody, we're not here for a long time, we're here for good time'.

"Woody", said Oaf, "Snap out of it". I had drifted off to Dog's Bay in Connemara, far away from the wedding scene, before Oaf brought me right round by clicking his fingers saying, "Where you been, somewhere nice? now wake up and have a listen to them pair, they're having a right old ding dong they are", nodding in the direction of a couple of bickering women.

They were not getting on, to say the least, and after a quick glance I could tell that, they were obviously sisters and obviously Irish, dressed to the nines and close to spilling blood. There is no inference here that, I sussed they were Irish because they were arguing at a wedding, although that would not be a surprise at all, it was rather because of their accent. Either of them could have been my own mother, and their tone became increasingly agitated the more heated the quarrel became.

The older of the pair, a cross between the Italian actress Sophia Loren and the mummified body of Queen Nefertiti, said, "You think yer so fecking high and mighty, in yer big fecking house, with yer big fat fecking husband, driving ye around in yer big fat fecking car, don't ye?"

It was a more of a statement than a question, but the younger sister, possibly ten years between them, on the face of it, had everything her big sister did not, especially if one was to believe the rant about personal possessions, because she was beautiful. Naturally beautiful, in a Kate Winslet kind of way and unlike her sibling, she was devoid of make-up, wearing a one-piece low cut black dress, with her long dark hair breaking like a wave across her face as she moved her head. By now, the younger sister was fully aware that there was an audience, and it was not just us two, there were also half a dozen passers-by, and five members of the restaurant staff taking a keen interest in the explosive discussion.

At that point she turned away crying, and did not respond to her sisters barrage but, instead walked towards us and sat down. I handed her my serviette, and she did not seem to mind that the tomato sauce from my meatballs was staining the cloth. She said nothing for a few minutes, just watched on as the wedding guests began to arrive. Her sister; now involved in the meeting and greeting was the bride's mother.

"You okay?" I asked. "It's not true you know, what she was saying, we worked hard to get what we have, she's just jealous and on top of that, she doesn't know that, my 'big fat fecking husband', as she so eloquently put it has paid for most of this 'big fat fecking wedding', and look, see the big guy with her now, that's her 'big fat fecking husband' and he does know!" At this point, Dolores, we had asked her name, bent over to pick up the serviette she had dropped, and revealed rather more of her cleavage than I suspect she intended, Oaf, nearly choked on his seafood salad, and said, "You don't get many of them in a pound". Dolores either didn't hear him, or ignored his comment but, stayed with us for half an hour, the time it took for the restaurant to fill up. Two hundred and twenty she said.

Her husband, Paddy had joined us and he was not fat at all, just well built, and a real nice man. Turns out he had played rugby for the Dublin club, Lansdowne Road, against our own club, Glossop, when we had toured Ireland. There was even an outside chance that myself or Oaf had punched him, and Paddy, good man that he is, had the decency to join in with our reminiscences, holding his jaw saying, "I remember it well!" as he walked off with Dolores in the direction of the food.

At this point one of the waiters came over and handed me some more bread as requested, and the bread was on a blue majolica plate, which stopped me in my tracks for a second and catapulted me back to Crowden and thoughts of Shining Girl. Oaf saw the look on my face and asked, "What's up lad?", "It's a long story mate", I replied, "I'll maybe tell you later over a beer". "It's not to do with the 'Shining One' is it?" he asked, "The Shining One...what are you talking about?" I asked. I knew who he meant and it showed Oaf had been listening all along. Oaf put me straight, "Don't you remember you tried to tell me once when we were both scuttered and I just laughed but the story stayed with me. "Go on tell me now, we're in no rush and there's a wedding to watch, spill the beans. I'll go to the bar and get some more beer".

As Oaf wandered off I knew that from experience he could be away some time, as every visit to the bar involved a trip to the toilet, and vice versa for that matter. It was then that a barely discernible but unmistakable voice in my left ear, said, "Go on, why don't you tell him?"

It was the voice of my Shining Girl but, surely that was impossible I thought, as she couldn't travel beyond her Crowden loop, or so I believed.

"Ha", she continued with a smile, "If something happens that sets off a powerful feeling in a person, in this case you, after your friend's mention of me just now, some of us walkers can pick it up and then use the energy to transport ourselves to wherever the other person is".

"Yes, but I can't see you," I replied, "You can touch me though", said the Shining Girl. I reached out and she was right there beside me which was instantly comforting. Unfortunately I had been spotted by another guest moving my arm out to grab at what appeared to be nothing, so I smiled inanely and pretended to be doing exercises, repeating the operation several times.

"Why can't I see you", I asked, "There is a chance you could but, it would involve a mountain of will and concentration on your part but, let's talk about it later, here comes Oaf", she said giggling at the name", signing off by gently kissing my ear.

Oaf came and joined me and we carried on with the carousing, as the wedding party began to swing, the bride and groom had arrived, and it was easy to discern which guests were aware that a full scale family row had already taken place; some knew, and the others indignant because they did not. The youngsters thankfully oblivious, were getting stuck into the wine and beer, and the even younger ones playing hide and seek under the trestle tables and flying across the floor on their knees. That's what kids do at weddings the world over. The cooks were barbecuing the day's catch, the biggest pile of fish I'd seen for a long time. Metal spikes pierced the shiny darlings and they were placed on racks above the coals after being splashed with olive oil and massaged with herbs and garlic. The aroma was to die for.

Eight hundred years of Moorish rule of southern Spain left a culinary legacy in Andalucia of refined, almost oriental flavors, with opulent use of spices and herbs.

As the smell wafted tantalisingly in our direction and the wedding feast about to start, we made our farewells, Oaf, lingering just a fraction too long with the hug he gave Dolores as we headed off in search of some grilled fish of our own.

Shining Girl in Spain was a surprise all ends up, and I vowed to myself that I would try to make her appear the next day but then the drink took over, and there were no more encounters until that night. Inexplicably I found myself wondering if she would need sunscreen, her being so fair skinned.

As Oaf and I wondered off, the kiss still resting gently on my ear we found ourselves in the midst of another wedding party of sorts, a group of lads on a stag-weekend, and it occurred to me that Nerja made a pleasant change from the normal bachelor and hen party destinations, such as Riga, in Latvia, where Oaf nearly drowned in a steam bath, Poznan in Poland where he nearly got arrested, or Dublin's Temple Bar, where he got lost. Temple Bar was bad in 1992, and it is even worse these days, with hundreds of drunks of both sexes, standing outside the bars dressed as Leprechauns, trying to pronounce the name of one of the most famous Dublin pubs, the 'Oliver St Gogarty', after ten pints of Bulmers, before proceeding to ruin a good session of traditional Irish music by requesting the hackneyed, 'Wild Rover', and then to cap it all, both sexes, slobbering over any dark-eyed Dublin lassie, or indeed handsome lad like wet-jowled St Bernards. For anyone interested the pronunciation goes like this...Oliver singe n Go-garty.

Nerja was going to be different and as we waved goodbye to the stag party, like long lost friends, we hoped the lads would be sophisticated, that they would behave like gentlemen, and although they and us had seen better days, we all stayed happy in our work and upset no one, especially the locals. And so it came to pass, and all quiet in Nerja Old Town, with the Stag Group singing in the distance, when Oaf and I decided to check on the beach-side wedding party as it was still only 8pm.

By complete accident, honestly, Oaf and I took a wrong turn and ended back up briefly with the stag party on the Balcon de Europa, a regular promenading location for locals and visitors alike, and perhaps surprisingly the lads still standing, good effort I thought, and they were still well behaved but, it was a short stay of execution. Next up came the obligatory selection of vile shots and then it was goodnight Vienna, as they say. Having telegraphed the arrival of these insane concoctions I had ensured my seat was by an open window, and as a backup within easy reach of an exotic potted plant, thus enabling the surreptitious dumping of the drinks. As all heads went back in the traditional shot-glass action, my drinks vanished into the soil of the plant pot, or directly out of the open window, one a direct hit on the back of mangy beach dog, that scuttled off across the Balcon trying to lick its back.

Oaf and I thought it best to part company at this stage with the groom last seen with his head out of a window, scoring another hit on one more beach dog.

Oaf and I waved goodbye once again and marched confidently down the stone steps which lead to the beach to check on events at the wedding, and maybe speak again to Dolores and Paddy.

It soon became obvious that all was not well, it was nearly 10pm, and there was no noise, no music, no craic, it was dead, with that there 'wild west mobile grass' rolling between every row of tables, and a thick pall of cigarette smoke hanging over the proceedings.

"Come on," I said to Oaf, "Let's sort this out".

Even my hirsute friend got worried now, Woody was on one, and 'Woody being on one', roughly translated meant there were no barriers, no barricades and certainly no impediment for what I might do to liven things up, as Woody didn't give a flying fig. As a performer already experienced in the art of dealing with tricky situations, one needs a certain something and more to the point, a solution or a one-liner to 'come up in the lift' when most needed.

The 'solution' on this occasion would have to be a very good one, a ruse capable of bringing this Lazerus of a wedding party back to life. There were still around two hundred guests in the canopied outdoor restaurant, the food was cleared and the waiters and waitresses were smoking in a disinterested huddle. Even the kids were quiet, and apart from what appeared to be polite conversation between disengaged groups of flotsam washed up on the shore of this expensive charade, it was as good as over.

As my 'lift' sparked into life, the bellboy that is my brain, said, 'Go on then Sean, do your worst', so I stepped out and made my way to the 'top table', while Oaf lurked in the undergrowth and half-light but still semi-confident that his buddy would work something out. I introduced myself to the bride's father, who was sitting like a Captain about to go down with his ship. At this stage, I gauged that calling him 'Fatty', as Dolores had done several hours earlier, and announcing that Paddy and Dolores had actually paid for the wedding did not seem like a good idea, so I stuck out my hand to shake his.

Fatty had undoubtedly been a builder, or a farmer, or even both in a previous life, and I soon discovered that a handshake with him, should have been entered into with great care. As Freddie Laker once said, I should have 'booked early' and got in first, because he began to pulverise my best bodhran playing hand with no mercy, and when I asked, "Shall I sing you a song?" he said, "You may as well, it couldn't get any fecking worse"..

With a resigned expression on his face, as though the events begun earlier between Dolores and his wife had deteriorated to the extent that, jumping head first from the Balcone de Europe was a better option he shouted "Shusssh", and I stood on a chair, picked up a champagne glass, tapping the side with a knife to command some attention and my preamble went something like this…"Hello, you don't know me but, I'm Sean, me mother's a Dub, and I'm going to sing you a song and ye can all join in".

Risky strategy I know, especially as I had not thought of which song to sing by the time I had finished my introduction but then, my fairy godmother waved her magic wand, and in some extraordinary coming together of fear and confidence I began…

It was Christmas Eve Babe…

And the closest tables copped on.

In the drunk tank…

Further tables stopped talking.

An old man said to me, won't see another one…

Now, all two hundred guests were locked on to what I was trying to do.

Even Fatty and the top table began smiling, as Oaf stepped up to the plate and we became a duo.

And then he sang a song, the rare ould mountain dew,
I turned my face away and dreamed about you;
got on a lucky one, came in eighteen to one,
I've got a feeling, this year's for me and you babe,
so happy Christmas, oh I love you baby and I can see better times,
when all our dreams come true.

The latter extended into a few seconds of acapella harmonies, and the crowd knew they were in the presence of beauty. Oaf began the clapping with his hands in the air, as I tore into the fast-moving middle eight section. Two words in, and the whole place was joining in, the cooks came out from the kitchens, soon joined by the manager and his assistant, and all of the staff were clapping and waving as well. Of course, they knew the song, it had been a worldwide hit for Shane MacGowan and the Pogues in 1987.

They've got cars big as bars, they've got rivers of gold,
but the wind blows right through you, it's no place for the old.
When he first took my hand on a cold Christmas Eve,
you promised me Broadway was waiting for me…

Waving my arms like a conductor it was wonderful to hear the guests response, those furthest away had moved closer. Dolores and Paddy reserved their biggest smile of the day for us, and Oaf went all puppy eyed again.

You were handsome, You were pretty, Queen of New York City,
when the band finished playing they howled out for more.
Sinatra was swinging, all the drunks they were singing,
we kissed on the corner and danced through the night…

On the original recording Kirsty MacColl sings the female parts of the duet, but when I performed the song on stage with my band the Curragh Sons, I sang the lot, and as the first refrain kicks in you know whether the audience are with you or not.

And the boys of the NYPD Choir are singing Galway bay,
and the bells were ringing out for Christmas Day.

The sound was triumphal, a glorious communal singing of a wonderful song, a song that does it for people on so many levels; personally, I always think when I hear it, 'I wish I'd written that song', but in Nerja there was something unique taking place, and from the corner of my eye, I could see that at least another fifty promenaders were taking advantage of the impromptu free concert, smiling, clapping their hands and joining in with gusto; we suddenly had a massive audience. Best of all half way through the performance, Shining Girl, appeared two tables away looking up at me smiling, she had never seen me perform before, and her coming into view was the work of two wills working together, hers and mine, a meeting of minds and yes, I was thinking about her pretty much all the time to be honest.

Notwithstanding the arrival of my muse from Crowden, the whole affair was improbable, an Irish wedding going down the pan by the sea in Southern Spain, and me walking by, a singer from an Irish band on a week off.

The only probable that day was that, like many weddings, there was bound to be a fight but, I could see the two sisters belting out the words, arm in arm. The elder had literally let her hair down, and the make-up for the most part was gone as well, and when I caught Paddy's eye, he was grinning from ear to ear and telling everyone around him, "I was talking to them fella's before", and even Fatty, sorry I never asked his name, was jumping up and down like a pig on a stick.

Next up in the song comes a short musical interlude, which we have developed slightly in our often requested version, in that I quickly interject with, "And this is your bit," before singing,

Da, da, da, dada, dada.....da, da, da, da, dadaa, dadadadadadaaa,
dada dadadada, dadadadadaaa, dadadada, dada, dadadadaaaa.

I think I have put in place the correct number of 'da's', but feel free to try it yourself, either to accompany the song, or if you already have the air in your mind, go for it, I count forty.

You're a bum, You're a punk, You're an old whore on junk,
Lying there almost dead on a drip in that bed.
You scumbag, You maggot, You cheap lousy faggot,
Happy Christmas your arse, And thank God it's our
last...

It was the word 'faggot' that caused the upset with some TV and radio stations, not politically correct and all that, with it's homophobic connotations. Personally, I always thought a faggot was a cheap meatball cooked over bundles of wood on a campfire but, I did have an interesting upbringing.

The Nerja wedding party had got it, and even if there is no such thing as a New York Police Department Choir, the roof nearly lifted off the restaurant when they came in as one with:

And the boys of the NYPD choir were singing Galway Bay,
and the bells were ringing out for Christmas Day...

As a matter of interest for all trivia fans, there is a NYPD Pipe Band, but the words would not have scanned.."And the boys from the NYPD pipe band, were singing…" see, it just doesn't work.

The singing of...

I could have been someone,

Never fails to receive a heartfelt response whenever it is sung, and whether fueled by a deep personal resonance or just alcohol...

Well so could anyone…

Is then belted out with real feeling. Nerja was no exception, and was fast turning into a melee by the side of Burriana Beach with dozens of guests linking arms on the table tops as we carried on, lifted by the moment.

You took my dreams from me, when I first found you,
I kept them with me babe, I put them with my own,
Can't make it all alone, I've built my dreams around you...

At this point in the song, I make to turn around and carry out an exaggerated counting of the beat, before swinging back to face the crowd with,

And the boys of NYPD choir, still singing Galway bay,
And the bells are ringing out for Christmas day...

And here, just when they think it's all over, I throw in another,

Oh I love................ extending this note by at least five seconds, encouraging people to cheer with a strong-man pose whilst still singing....... *you baby, and I can see better times, when all our dreams come true.*

As I finished the song on one long lingering note, I could hear the crescendo of applause that was coming our way, deafening it was; clapping, chinking, cheering, whistling; never, and I mean, never, with brass knobs on, bearing in mind the context, have I, or should I say we, been so warmly received by an audience. Fatty jumped to his feet and clasped both of my hands in his. "Jasus, fair play to ye, you've the throat of a horse," he said, "And ye have hands of steel, let go ya big

palooka," I replied, both of us laughing our heads off at this stage. Friends for life I reckon, and all in the space of a few minutes.

Ironically I said to Oaf sometime later in the evening that, after singing Fairytale that night would have been a good time to retire from performing, as we could surely, never top it. In reality, we sang one more song, Pete St John's, 'The Fields of Athenry', to similar acclaim, said thank you, and left as mysteriously as we had arrived with the crowd cheering for more.

Applause and drink provide a heady brew, and with the morning's mountain walk in mind we made our way back to our hotel as a barn owl, like a giant white butterfly floated over our heads. That's the kind of nightcap I like.

Oaf said, "Nice one Woody, that's a beauty." It was indeed, and then Shining Girl joined in briefly by whispering in my ear, "I've seen a barn owl at the back of the Church in Tintwistle," she said, "I think they breed nearby". Her voice was as soothing as the day is long.

Once back to our room and Oaf asleep in a second, Shining Girl was immediately visible on the side of my bed. "Are you there all the time? I mean like, when I'm in the bathroom and stuff, it's a bit much if you are?" "If you think about me, I'm there, but not out of choice would I ever accompany you to the toilet". That last remark was a Shining Girl joke, and she was right about the barn owls, as I checked them out on my return from Spain, and as recently as 2016, a pair of barn owls bred in the same place.

The Carabeo, is expensive, but my favourite hotel ever; it is small and old worldly, with some fine oil paintings of Matadors and flamenco dancers on the walls, and even a tiny Toreador outfit in a glass case. Oaf, in typical rugby club fashion said, "I'm having that Woody". "No you are not, how do you think you'll get that on the plane?" I replied. My friend and I were well versed in the art of 'nicking stuff', to take back to Glossop RUFC but, a five foot glass case, or even the outfit inside it would be a tall order. Silly me, Oaf quickly reminded me of the time, Graham Morgan, our rugby playing archaeologist friend managed to steal a full size copper and brass diving helmet from Bermuda Rugby Club. With great guile he visited a local jeweller the day before we were to leave the Island, and had him inscribe a small self-adhesive brass plaque with, 'PRESENTED TO GLOSSOP RUGBY CLUB by BERMUDA RFC'. Graham proceeded to enter the Club House late at night, remove the helmet, stick on the plaque and blagged the helmet into the hold of the plane next morning. A stroke of genius.

We would not attempt the same trick with the Toreador outfit in Hotel Carabeo.

Unlike Ernest Hemingway, I am not a fan of bullfighting, but the exciting vignettes hanging across the hotels walls are particularly compelling. The marbled ground floor telescopes towards the sea, as if you were looking the wrong way down the glass, beginning with a pillared entrance lounge and bar, before slimming down to a dining area and outdoor swimming pool,culminating in a railed veranda sixty feet above the beach looking onto a mass of sculptured conglomerate rock, which has been caressed into shape by a thousand years of wave and wind. Most days the blue rock thrushes, spin from crag to crag in search of insects, while out to sea, anything can turn up, including a marauding goshawk, taking a shortcut across the sea to the woods, and the whiplash terns performing incredible acrobatics, and dives for prey, with never a splash, scything into the Persian-green wavelets before bursting skyward with another meal.

From a wildlife perspective, the Mediterranean Sea is a reliable provider of birds, but if you turnabout and look inland, there is even more promise for the birder. Nerja is protected by a ring of mountains, the Sierra de Almijara, which reach 1,832m, steep and unforgiving, which eventually give way to the Alpujarras and Sierra Nevada Mountains on route to Granada and this was where I intended to take Oaf the next day to photograph Alpine Swifts. The peaks are visible from the Balcon de europa and turned out to be anything but chilled, unlike the Rio Chillar which I knew meandered through watered and well worn gullies nearly 2,000 metres below.

Next morning, a small party of Oaf, myself and a couple of the Spanish lads, climbers as it happens, who we had convinced to come with us after a brief conversation the night before, set off a little later than I would have liked, because, by the time we reached the tortuous mountain trails, or should I say 'trials', a few miles outside of Nerja, the sun was already unforgiving and burning up the mist which hung like drapes around the jagged mountain backdrop. Three miles up a narrow dusty road, with the lofty peaks looming, my alarm bells rang. Roger Hargreaves, the creator of the, 'Mr Men', would have had a field day with Oaf and me. We were, in no particular order, Mr Wrong Trousers, Mr Wrong Shoes, Mr

Wrong Complexion, and if truth be told, Mr Wrong Body. Oaf is ginger, fair skinned and has freckles, and his party piece expression for describing his condition is, "Freckles made a vow, never to grow on anything fau'" 'Fau' meaning foul.

The two Spaniards however were about to show the 'Anglaise' how it was done and set of like mountain goats, and to make matters worse for the first hour, wherever they could, avoided every gentle slope, preferring to slice vertically through the roughest scrub and rockiest scree that they could find. My size 12 trainers, proved completely inadequate, while Oaf's bare legs were ripped to piece mercilessly by thorns and our ample calf muscles and ankles became an unexpected dining experience for all manner of flies and insects well practiced in the dark-art of bloodletting. Most annoyingly, our companions carried on an animated conversation as they marched, and one, I like to think of him as the Devil, even sang an Irish song to me, whereas I was soon beyond talking never mind singing.

I kept fairly calm but Oaf was becoming worried, and only had thoughts for discarding cameras, rucksack, and water, which, after only half an hour could have poached an egg. "Woody, I know I'm the 'roadie, meaning I understood that he had accompanied me on the trip to help me but, can you carry your own stuff now?" he gasped.

I feigned deafness but knew we had to stop soon, my throat was dry and my chest pounding as I checked my racing pulse, and I began to think playing rugby had done me no good at all, but then I thought, 'hang on a second, these guys are used to it, buy yourself some time Woody. Which is exactly what I did and in a scene reminiscent of all good action movies, when a wounded soldier encourages his comrades to save themselves, I sat down, pulled Oaf down with me, and shouted, "You go on boys, we'll be okay."

And off they went, vanishing into the depths of a bottomless canyon, still chatting away as though there was no tomorrow. 'The bastards, I thought, before wistfully thinking of the verdant Crowden hillsides, with their attendant bog cotton, cloudberry and merlin loudly 'kecking' on the wing, and yes, the rain, the glorious wet rain.

After ten minutes recovery, and finishing off what was left of our hot water, Oaf and I were able to take stock and look around us. The place was stunning. An untouched splendour of a rare kind, with huge shrubs of gorgeous red flowers, and a forest of wild rosemary we were suddenly able to appreciate, while in the air, three griffon vultures. I suppose the big birds could have seen us struggling, but I prefer to think they were looking for some other carrion.

When the vultures had passed by, we set off back for the small car park to wait for the Spaniards return, and it was here that the wildlife came to us which made me think we should have just stayed there in the first place. It has always been the best ploy, find your spot and wait, just like I always did in the Valley. Don't break the skyline, don't make any noise and in future, 'Sean', I said to myself, don't climb steep mountains unprepared when you could be in a tapas bar.

We could hear partridge chunnering, and the Alpine swifts screaming as they wheeled above the gorge, while in the distance, the melodious song of a warbler, which I could not give a name. There was no such trouble with the red kite, wheatear and linnet which followed. Our decision to wait and watch, rather than walk and die, had been a wise one, even though it was the first time the pair of us had ever dropped out of anything. Perhaps at last, in our late 30's we were becoming sensible. "Yea, right!" said Oaf, to that stupid notion.

Not quite as foolish was our decision to sit on the edge of a steep gully, as not only did it we get a relieving breeze up the legs of our shorts, it also put us right in the firing line of the very rapid Alpine Swifts, so, with the camera on sports-mode, and firing off five or six shots a second, I was fairly sure after getting through ten rolls of film that, there was a good chance one of the photographs would do. So there we were, fully recovered in the National Park, walking friends at least two hours away, probably still singing their bloody Spanish heads off, and the nearest bar half an hour by car. Walking was not an option, but before being faced with the choice of more leg action, a vehicle arrived out of nowhere in a cloud of dust. I asked where they were going, 'Nerja,' they replied, I could have kissed them. Thirty minutes later, mopped and stoned, we were back out in the centre of the town with a terrible thirst.

Two years later I was back in Nerja on another assignment. Deja vu began kicking in, when I overheard a couple of Irish accents in the gardens of Hotel Carabeo. There was also an English couple by the pool, and their young daughter was splashing away. Her mother chided, "Be careful now, there are people sunbathing," "Sorry Mum," said the little girl before carrying on where she left off.

"She's not a bother, the little dote", Claimed the Irish girl, backed up by her partners more robust, "Don't mind your ma, you splash away girl".

The father, another Dubliner it turns out, seemed familiar somehow, and when that happens, I always think 'rugby' and sure enough he had played for Blackrock RFC, from outside Dublin, one of the oldest rugby clubs in the Ireland, and five minutes later we were best of friends but, then it got ridiculous, as I began to tell my Nerja Irish Wedding story… "You won't believe this but a few years ago, I sang…"

The guy cut me dead.

"Were you dat fella that sang Fairytale at the Flanagan's wedding? Jasus, I taut I knew ye?" He had been there that night, who'd a thought it.

Lightning Source UK Ltd.
Milton Keynes UK
UKHW032232041218
333454UK00007B/451/P